*JAPAN, SOUTH KOREA,
AND THE UNITED STATES
NUCLEAR UMBRELLA*

Contemporary Asia in the World

CONTEMPORARY ASIA IN THE WORLD

David C. Kang and Victor D. Cha, Editors

This series aims to address a gap in the public policy and scholarly discussion of Asia. It seeks to promote books and studies that are on the cutting edge of their disciplines or promote multidisciplinary or interdisciplinary research but are also accessible to a wider readership. The editors seek to showcase the best scholarly and public-policy arguments on Asia from any field, including politics, history, economics, and cultural studies.

Beyond the Final Score: The Politics of Sport in Asia, Victor D. Cha, 2008
The Power of the Internet in China: Citizen Activism Online, Guobin Yang, 2009
China and India: Prospects for Peace, Jonathan Holslag, 2010
India, Pakistan, and the Bomb: Debating Nuclear Stability in South Asia, Šumit Ganguly and S. Paul Kapur, 2010
Living with the Dragon: How the American Public Views the Rise of China, Benjamin I. Page and Tao Xie, 2010
East Asia Before the West: Five Centuries of Trade and Tribute, David C. Kang, 2010
Harmony and War: Confucian Culture and Chinese Power Politics, Yuan-kang Wang, 2011
Strong Society, Smart State: The Rise of Public Opinion in China's Japan Policy, James Reilly, 2012
Asia's Space Race: National Motivations, Regional Rivalries, and International Risks, James Clay Moltz, 2012
Never Forget National Humiliation: Historical Memory in Chinese Politics and Foreign Relations, Zheng Wang, 2012
Green Innovation in China: China's Wind Power Industry and the Global Transition to a Low-Carbon Economy, Joanna I. Lewis, 2013
The Great Kantō Earthquake and the Chimera of National Reconstruction in Japan, J. Charles Schencking, 2013
Security and Profit in China's Energy Policy: Hedging Against Risk, Øystein Tunsjø, 2013
Return of the Dragon: Rising China and Regional Security, Denny Roy, 2013
Contemporary Japanese Politics: Institutional Changes and Power Shifts, Tomohito Shinoda, 2013
Contentious Activism and Inter-Korean Relations, Danielle L. Chubb, 2014
Dams and Development in China: The Moral Economy of Water and Power, Bryan Tilt, 2014
Marching Through Suffering: Loss and Survival in North Korea, Sandra Fahy, 2015
The Japan–South Korea Identity Clash: East Asian Security and the United States, Brad Glosserman and Scott A. Snyder, 2015
Nation at Play: A History of Sport in India, Ronojoy Sen, 2015
The China Boom: Why China Will Not Rule the World, Ho-fung Hung, 2015
Japan's Security Renaissance: New Policies and Politics for the Twenty-First Century, Andrew L. Oros, 2017

Japan, South Korea, and the United States Nuclear Umbrella

Deterrence After the Cold War

Terence Roehrig

Columbia University Press   New York

Columbia University Press
Publishers Since 1893
New York Chichester, West Sussex
cup.columbia.edu

Copyright © 2017 Columbia University Press
All rights reserved

Library of Congress Cataloging-in-Publication Data
Names: Roehrig, Terence, 1955– author.
Title: Japan, South Korea, and the United States nuclear umbrella :
  deterrence after the cold war / Terence Roehrig.
Description: New York : Columbia University Press, 2017. | Series:
  Contemporary Asia in the world | Includes bibliographical references
  and index.
Identifiers: LCCN 2016056216 (print) | LCCN 2017032103 (ebook) |
  ISBN 9780231527835 (e-book) | ISBN 9780231157988 (cloth) |
  ISBN 9780231157995 (pbk.)
Subjects: LCSH: Deterrence (Strategy) | United States—Military
  relations—Korea (South) | Korea (South)—Military relations—
  United States. | United States—Military relations—Japan. | Japan—
  Military relations—United States. | Nuclear weapons—Government policy. |
  Nuclear warfare—Prevention.
Classification: LCC U162.6 (ebook) | LCC U162.6 .R64 2017 (print) |
  DDC 355.02/17—dc23
LC record available at https://lccn.loc.gov/2016056216

Cover design: Chang Jae Lee

To my wife Amy and our family, and for a more peaceful world.

Contents

Acknowledgments   ix

Introduction   1

CHAPTER ONE
Extended Deterrence and the Nuclear Umbrella   13

CHAPTER TWO
The Nuclear Umbrella and Extended Deterrence
During the Cold War   38

CHAPTER THREE
The Threats That Drive the Nuclear Umbrella:
China and North Korea   64

CHAPTER FOUR
Japan and the U.S. Nuclear Umbrella   97

CHAPTER FIVE
South Korea and the U.S. Nuclear Umbrella   124

CHAPTER SIX
The U.S. Nuclear Umbrella: Planning, Capabilities,
and Credibility   154

CHAPTER SEVEN
Implications for Security and Extended Deterrence
in Northeast Asia   182

Notes   199
Selected Bibliography   239
Index   255

Acknowledgments

The views expressed in this book are the author's alone and do not represent the official position of the Department of the Navy, the Department of Defense, or the U.S. government.

There are many people I need to acknowledge for their help with this project. I would like to begin by thanking my advisor at the University of Wisconsin-Madison, David Tarr. Many years ago, you helped me to be a better thinker and writer, and I am forever indebted for what you taught me during my time in graduate school. I also want to thank David Cooper and Joan Johnson-Freese for their help and support over the years, Dana Struckman, who graciously offered wise counsel on numerous portions of this project, Uk Heo, long-time friend and collaborator on all things Korea, and Al O'Neill for his assistance during my trips to Washington DC. I am very grateful to the many officials and scholars in Japan, South Korea, and the United States who took time out of their busy schedules to grant me interviews. Your insights and candor were a core element of this book, and I have done my best to protect your anonymity.

From 2012 to 2014, I had the good fortune of spending time as a research fellow at the Belfer Center at Harvard's Kennedy School in the International Security Program and Project on Managing the Atom. My sincere appreciation goes out to Matthew Bunn, Martin Malin, Steve Miller, Hui Zhang, Gary Samore, the late Stephen Bosworth, and all of the outstanding research fellows I had the chance to meet in the program. Your feedback and our many discussions during those two years helped me to think more carefully about these difficult issues and made this a much better book.

I want to express my gratitude to the library staff at the Naval War College. They are all world-class and always very helpful in assisting me in tracking down obscure documents and sources. This project also benefitted from the support of the Ruger Chair at Naval War College lead by Richmond Lloyd and John Cloud, and was also supported by the Academy of Korean Studies grant funded by the Korean Government (MEST) (AKS-2012-AAZ-2101) and administered by the University of Wisconsin-Milwaukee.

I want to thank Anne Routon at Columbia University Press for her support and guidance during this process along with the feedback from the anonymous reviewers. For all who provided comments and advice, your help is greatly appreciated but any errors in the book are mine alone.

Finally, and most importantly, I want to thank and recognize the never ending support I receive from my wife, Amy. Without her encouragement and patience, this project would have never been possible.

*JAPAN, SOUTH KOREA,
AND THE UNITED STATES
NUCLEAR UMBRELLA*

Introduction

Throughout the Cold War, the United States maintained an extended deterrence commitment to protect Japan and South Korea (Republic of Korea [ROK]) as part of a "hub and spoke" system of alliances in East Asia. The guarantee included a mutual security treaty that formalized the U.S. pledge to defend these two allies and the basing of troops in both countries, serving as a sign of U.S. determination as well as providing a U.S. forward presence in the region. The U.S. commitment also entailed the inclusion of the two countries under the U.S. nuclear umbrella, whereby Washington vowed publicly and privately to use nuclear weapons to deter and, if need be, defeat an attack on either of these allies. The United States never renounced the first use of nuclear weapons and continues to maintain that a nuclear response could follow a conventional attack or the use of chemical or biological weapons, as well as a nuclear strike, depending on the circumstances and the countries involved.

The nuclear umbrella also included the deployment of nuclear weapons to both countries as a sign of the nuclear commitment and to have them close should they be needed in a war. For Japan, despite denials to the contrary from both Tokyo and Washington, the U.S. military maintained nuclear weapons on Okinawa until 1972, when the island reverted to Japanese control. Once the nuclear weapons were removed, again despite the public narrative that they would never be present in

Japan, Tokyo and Washington concluded a secret arrangement to allow their return in the event of a crisis in Japan or elsewhere in the region. In addition, U.S. ships carrying nuclear weapons regularly docked in Japanese ports throughout much of the Cold War.

The United States also deployed nuclear weapons to South Korea beginning in 1958 as part of a military modernization effort to bolster deterrence. Washington and Seoul were less secretive regarding these efforts, although the official U.S. position for years was to "neither confirm nor deny" the presence of nuclear weapons. Tactical nuclear weapons remained in South Korea until 1991. Though nuclear weapons were removed from Japan and South Korea, the United States continued to maintain both countries under its nuclear umbrella.

The nuclear umbrella has long been a part of U.S. extended deterrence, yet there have always been some troubling aspects to this strategy, both in Asia and in Europe. Theory maintains that for deterrence to be successful, it must be credible. An adversary must believe that the state threatening retaliation has the military capability and the resolve to follow through on its commitment should deterrence fail. Yet doubts about the credibility of extended deterrence commitments have always been an issue. Though a defender may profess a determined commitment to protect an ally, in a crisis there is no guarantee the commitment will be honored.

For the nuclear umbrella, credibility has been an even more troubling aspect of extended deterrence. Would the United States truly be willing to use nuclear weapons in defense of an ally? If facing a nuclear-armed adversary that could retaliate against U.S. territory, credibility is particularly problematic. As the question went during the Cold War in Europe, would the United States really be willing to use nuclear weapons against the Soviet Union knowing it would likely provoke retaliation against the U.S. homeland? Thus, while few doubted that the United States or any other nuclear state would use nuclear weapons to defend its homeland, many questioned the credibility of the use of nuclear weapons in an extended deterrence situation.

As a result, many leaders and analysts raised fears of "decoupling," whereby the threat of Soviet retaliation on the United States would cause Washington to hesitate in the face of Russian aggression in Europe and weaken the bonds of the NATO alliance. Others have also suggested the dynamics of the stability-instability paradox, whereby the strategic nuclear stalemate of mutually assured destruction would free up Moscow for lower-level actions knowing the United States would fear the consequences of nuclear war and be loath to escalate.[1]

To address these credibility issues, the United States deployed tactical nuclear weapons to Europe and Asia to reassure allies and demonstrate to foes that any aggression on their part always had the chance of triggering a U.S. nuclear response. Nuclear weapons also countered the need to match large Soviet or Chinese conventional forces. Consequently, the adversary faced the possibility of starting down the road to nuclear war by forcing Washington's hand. To further buttress credibility, the United States developed smaller, tactical nuclear weapons that would be easier to use than large strategic weapons. Despite these efforts, doubts remained throughout the Cold War about U.S. willingness to use nuclear weapons to defend its allies.

With the end of the Cold War, concerns for extended deterrence vis-à-vis Russia and China receded, and thinking about nuclear weapons and deterrence in general became less prominent among security thinkers. Even the North Korean nuclear problem appeared to be under control with the conclusion of the 1994 Agreed Framework, which appeared to set a course for denuclearization of the Korean peninsula. Yet by the early 2000s, the Agreed Framework had started to unravel, and in 2002, the Bush administration accused Pyongyang of violating the agreement by pursuing nuclear weapons through enriching uranium.[2] North Korea, formally the Democratic People's Republic of Korea (DPRK), initially denied the accusation but later responded that it had this capability and more but was willing to put all these issues on the table for negotiation. With the situation worsening, the following year the regional players tried to maintain momentum for denuclearization through the Six-Party Talks, and in September 2005 they finalized a deal whereby North Korea agreed to give up its nuclear weapons. However, it soon became clear that the chance for North Korean denuclearization was fading, and on October 9, 2006, Pyongyang formally crossed that redline by detonating its first nuclear device, quickly resurrecting the profile of extended deterrence and the nuclear umbrella.

Though Pyongyang's test produced a yield well below what it likely was expecting, the explosion shocked the region. Soon after, Secretary of State Condoleezza Rice flew to Tokyo and Seoul to reassure these U.S. allies that they remained under the U.S. nuclear umbrella. U.S. efforts were intended to reaffirm its defense commitment while also encouraging allies to forgo developing their own nuclear weapons in the face of this serious disruption of the security environment.

North Korea followed with a second nuclear weapon test in May 2009, during the early months of the new Obama administration. In his first inauguration speech in January 2009, Obama had addressed North Korea and other U.S. adversaries, offering that "we will extend a hand if you are willing to unclench your fist."[3] But the North Korean nuclear test, coming so soon after the inauguration, provided little opportunity for Obama to follow up on his offer. With a new administration now in office, Japan and South Korea were again concerned about the U.S. nuclear umbrella, and Obama moved to calm the waters. Following the test, he called South Korean president Lee Myung-bak and Japanese prime minister Taro Aso to express his anger and assure both leaders of "the unequivocal commitment" of the United States to the defense of their countries.[4] Soon after the test, Washington and Seoul held a previously scheduled summit in June in Washington. The summit concluded by issuing a Joint Vision for the Alliance that declared "the continuing commitment of extended deterrence, including the U.S. nuclear umbrella," providing the formal guarantee at the highest level that South Korea had requested in the run-up to the meeting. In various government-to-government meetings and formal documents, the United States continued to provide regular assurances of the U.S. nuclear umbrella to both Japan and South Korea in the wake of further North Korean weapons tests.

While concerns mount over North Korea and its nuclear ambitions, worries have also increased regarding China. As its economy continues its phenomenal performance, China's defense spending has grown and has provided significant increases in the quantity and capability of its military, the People's Liberation Army (PLA). Over the past ten to fifteen years, China has logged double-digit increases in defense spending, with particular emphasis on its navy, air force, and strategic nuclear forces. The growth of its military capability is even more troublesome given the uncertainties over its strategic direction and fears that it will seek to dominate Asia. However, Japan and South Korea have different perspectives on these assessments.

While both have complicated relationships with China that include extensive economic ties and some degree of wariness for Beijing's future strategic intent, for Japan, the relationship has been far more edgy and competitive. In its 2015 Defense White Paper, Japan acknowledges expectations for China to play a cooperative role in the international community but notes a number of disputes, assertive behaviors, unilateral demands, and "dangerous acts that may invite unintended consequences, raising concerns over China's future direction."[5]

In contrast, the South Korean assessment is more complex and divided. Many South Koreans recognize the importance of maintaining good relations with China. China is South Korea's main trade partner, accounting for more trade volume than its next two partners, Japan and the United States, combined. Trade considerations are essential for South Korea, given the large percentage of its GDP that is dependent on exports. Moreover, China is also a central player in dealing with North Korea, possessing the power and influence that may be able to solve this problem. Throughout 2015, ROK president Park Geun-hye sought to cultivate a close relationship with Chinese president Xi Jinping in hopes of building good ties for trade and security. Park had several meetings with Xi, while North Korean leader Kim Jong-un has yet to meet with the Chinese leader, the first time this has ever happened. However, some in South Korea also have concerns about China's growing power in the region and fear that Beijing will seek to dominate Asia in ways that will hurt South Korea's interests. In addition, there has often been considerable frustration in Seoul over China's apparent reluctance to do much to restrain North Korea.

Thus, Japan sees China as a regional rival while South Korea hopes to maintain friendly ties because of its dependence on the Chinese economy and the recognition that it needs Beijing's help to deal with North Korea. But Tokyo and Seoul agree on the danger of a nuclear North Korea.

One other concern for nuclear weapons and the nuclear umbrella is a resurgent Russia. Over the past decade, Russia, under the leadership of Vladimir Putin, has become an increasingly serious security concern, with rising defense spending and disconcerting actions in Crimea, Ukraine, and Syria. Putin aspires to return Russia to its Cold War status in Asia, but he is largely focused on Europe and the Middle East and faces significant resource constraints to become a major player in all three regions. More important are the threat perceptions of the two U.S. allies in Asia. Japan and Russia have been unable to conclude a formal peace treaty ending World War II, in large part because of their ongoing dispute over the Kuril Islands. Moscow annexed the islands at the end of World War II, but Japan refutes those claims. Until this dispute is settled to Japan's satisfaction, it is unlikely the two will be able to normalize relations, and so far Russia shows no signs of relinquishing the islands it currently occupies. Despite this ongoing row, while Japanese leaders recognize the global concerns over Putin's behavior in Europe and the Middle East, few have serious fears about Russian aggression and are much more worried about China and North Korea.

As for South Korea, Moscow and Seoul established formal diplomatic relations in 1992, and trade and investment between the two countries has grown substantially. Should relations between North and South Korea ever improve, Russia and South Korea have several plans on the drawing board for road and rail links along with oil and gas pipelines that would further facilitate trade and integrate the two economies. Thus, Russia is no longer the security threat to South Korea that it was during the Cold War. As a result, though Japan is warier of Russia than South Korea, neither sees it in the same light as China or North Korea. Consequently, Russia is not included in this study, though it may merit inclusion at a later date, depending on its future trajectory under Putin.

Another issue that has affected the nuclear umbrella and extended deterrence has been the call by President Obama and others to cut the numbers and move toward the eventual elimination of nuclear stockpiles while also reducing the role of nuclear weapons in U.S. security planning. During a speech in Prague in his first year in office, Obama declared, "The United States will take concrete steps towards a world without nuclear weapons. To put an end to Cold War thinking, we will reduce the role of nuclear weapons in our national security strategy, and urge others to do the same. Make no mistake: As long as these weapons exist, the United States will maintain a safe, secure and effective arsenal to deter any adversary, and guarantee that defense to our allies.... But we will begin the work of reducing our arsenal."[6]

Soon after the Prague speech, Obama committed his administration to a reassessment of U.S. nuclear strategy and forces, resulting in the April 2010 Nuclear Posture Review (NPR).[7] The document reemphasized the intention to lessen the role nuclear weapons play in U.S. security strategy and the desire to reduce the number of weapons in the U.S. stockpile. The document also repeated the determination to maintain an effective nuclear deterrent for the United States and its allies so long as others possessed these weapons. Some speculated that the 2010 NPR might include a "sole purpose" statement that limited the role of nuclear weapons to deterring only the nuclear weapons of other states and not conventional, chemical, or biological threats as well. However, the document refrained from giving a "sole purpose" declaration. The Obama NPR also chose to refrain from providing a "no first use" declaration, retaining the option of using nuclear weapons in certain situations.

Instead, the NPR crafted a "negative security assurance" that pledged to refrain from threatening or using nuclear weapons against non-nuclear-weapon states that are in compliance with their obligations under the Nuclear Nonproliferation Treaty (NPT). Any states receiving this assurance that used chemical weapons would face a "devastating conventional military response," and leaders responsible for the attack would be held accountable. However, for states that do possess nuclear weapons or are not in compliance with their NPT obligations, "there remains a narrow range of contingencies in which U.S. nuclear weapons may still play a role in deterring a conventional or chemical/biological attack on the United States or its allies."[8] Obama also hoped that the negative security assurance would encourage those states not in compliance with their NPT obligations to become so. While refraining from adopting a "sole purpose" posture or providing a "no first use" pronouncement, the NPR also contained the caveat that "the United States wishes to stress that it would only consider the use of nuclear weapons in extreme circumstances to defend the vital interests of the United States or its partners."[9]

Obama made some progress on the commitment to reduce the U.S. nuclear arsenal with the April 2010 signing of the New START bilateral arms control agreement with Russia. The treaty reduced the number of deployed nuclear warheads for each to 1,550 from the previous limits of 1,700 to 2,200 in the 2002 Moscow Treaty. However, there were no limits on the number of warheads that could be kept in storage as a strategic reserve. The agreement limited deployed launchers (missiles and bombers) to 700, with a limit of 800 for deployed and nondeployed launchers. New START also provided a system of inspections to verify compliance, replacing the protocol that was contained in the Moscow treaty but was due to expire.[10]

U.S. allies were concerned about these moves and what they might mean for extended deterrence and the nuclear umbrella. To allay their fears, Obama went to considerable lengths to gather and incorporate their input into the final version of the NPR. In the end, leaders in Tokyo and Seoul were relatively satisfied with the NPR, but questions about extended deterrence and the nuclear umbrella remained.

Throughout the years of the Obama administration, the security environment in East Asia has changed significantly with the growth of North Korea's capabilities and a rising China and its accompanying military modernization. These changes, along with Obama's revised thinking about nuclear weapons and changes to the U.S. nuclear force posture, have reenergized concern for and the study of extended deterrence and the nuclear umbrella. As a result, a plethora of studies have examined the issues and offered recommendations for how to buttress these relationships and the concern for credibility.[11]

Finally, remarks by Republican nominee Donald Trump during the 2016 U.S. presidential election campaign added further questions about alliance relations. At several points in the campaign, Trump remarked that Japan and South Korea should contribute more to maintaining the cost of U.S. troops and that if they did not increase their share of alliance expenses, the United States should consider removing its troops. Moreover, Trump also indicated that perhaps it was time for those countries to have their own nuclear weapons.[12] Though most in Japan and South Korea assumed that some of the words were best understood as campaign rhetoric, many nonetheless feared what a Trump presidency could mean for their alliances. Before the final election, one South Korean commentator wondered whether, win or lose, Trump's views might reflect an underlying doubt in the United States regarding the importance of the U.S.-ROK alliance to U.S. interests and a willingness to abandon South Korea.[13] Many in Japan had similar questions about these remarks that undercut the foundations of U.S. alliances in

Asia and Europe.¹⁴ However, once in office, the Trump administration has reaffirmed the U.S. commitment to these two important allies.

The nuclear umbrella is an important element of security relations in East Asia, yet serious questions remain regarding its credibility. These concerns were present during the Cold War and likely will continue on into the future. Allies make known the importance of the nuclear umbrella and call for reassurances that it will remain in place, yet doubts linger, raising crucial questions about the nuclear umbrella and its credibility. What is the role of the nuclear umbrella in northeast Asia? What and whom does the U.S. nuclear umbrella deter? In contrast to the Cold War, in which Washington and Moscow had relatively symmetric nuclear forces, how does the nuclear umbrella operate in asymmetric relationships between states with very different levels of power? What role does the U.S. nuclear umbrella play in regional security and defense planning for Japan and South Korea? How have changes in U.S. force posture, including numbers, types of weapons systems, strategy, and doctrine, affected perceptions of the nuclear umbrella? Finally, how credible is the U.S. nuclear umbrella, and what is the likelihood that the United States would ever use nuclear weapons to defend these Asian allies? Indeed, does a U.S. nuclear umbrella even exist?¹⁵

The central argument of this book is that the United States does indeed possess a nuclear umbrella that has the capability to protect its allies with nuclear weapons should deterrence fail. U.S. leaders have multiple nuclear options, and the military trains to execute that mission should the president give the order. Thus, concerning capability, there is no question the United States has the assets to provide a nuclear umbrella for its allies. The difficulty comes with the other element of credibility—resolve—and there are a number of reasons why a U.S. president would think long and hard and ultimately conclude that using nuclear weapons to defend Japan or South Korea is neither in those countries' interest nor that of the United States. Later chapters will lay out a number of reasons, spanning strategic, operational/military, and moral factors, that make it unwise and unlikely that a U.S. president would ever order a nuclear strike to defend one of its allies and indeed why U.S. allies should not want to be defended with nuclear weapons. Nuclear use in Asia would have a catastrophic effect on civilian populations, and the effects would be likely to spread throughout the region, causing horrendous damage to enemies and allies alike. Moreover, U.S. nuclear use, even in retaliation, weakens norms against their use in future conflicts and makes it easier for other states to cross that redline, which is not in anyone's interest. Instead, while a nuclear response is highly unlikely, the United States has a number of conventional options that it would not hesitate to use to defend Japan and South Korea. Many of these conventional weapons have pinpoint accuracy with similar strategic effects while avoiding the pitfalls of nuclear weapons.

The U.S. alliances with Tokyo and Seoul are solid and credible. There is little doubt Washington would defend these two allies if attacked, but that response is highly unlikely to include nuclear weapons. Though the credibility of the nuclear umbrella is low, the nuclear umbrella remains an important political signal that is an integral part of the regional security architecture and helps demonstrate the U.S. commitment to its allies in Asia. To withdraw the nuclear umbrella would be a serious alteration of the status quo that would disrupt security relations throughout the region. In addition, even if the resolve portion of the umbrella's credibility is very low, the mere existence of the nuclear umbrella along with a small chance it might ever be used may still make an adversary hesitate, given the destructive power of nuclear weapons. Thus, even with the nuclear umbrella's low credibility, it is sufficient to generate a discernible deterrent effect.

Finally, the nuclear umbrella is an important tool for another U.S. goal, limiting the spread of nuclear weapons. The U.S. nuclear umbrella, along with the overall alliance commitment, helps to convince allies to forgo this option and avoid further complications to regional security with the addition of other nuclear weapons states in East Asia. The nonproliferation of nuclear weapons has long been a central element of U.S. foreign policy and is likely to remain so.

The plan of this book is as follows. The theoretical grounding of this study is deterrence theory, and chapter 1 begins with a review of the relevant literature in this area as well as previous work that has been done on nuclear weapons and the nuclear umbrella. Chapter 2 recounts the history of the nuclear umbrella in Japan and South Korea with an examination of the role nuclear weapons played throughout the Cold War in maintaining regional security.

A central question in this book is what type of threats does the nuclear umbrella deter. Chapter 3 reviews the current military capabilities of the two chief adversaries that are the target of the U.S. nuclear umbrella in Asia: China and North Korea. This chapter will review their nuclear and conventional weapons capabilities along with their strategies and doctrines for nuclear weapons. Chapters 4 and 5 analyze the role the nuclear umbrella plays in the defense planning of Japan and South Korea, respectively. These two chapters will review how the United States works with these two allies regarding the nuclear umbrella and provides an assessment of how these alliance partners view the umbrella, both its role and its credibility. An important difference in these two chapters is the threat assessment of Tokyo and Seoul. North Korea's growing nuclear weapon and ballistic missile programs are a clear threat to both, but South Korea must also worry about other elements of the North Korean threat because of its proximity to the DPRK. At the same time, China's rise and the challenges it poses are viewed in a far more threatening manner in Japan than in South Korea.

Chapter 6 shifts to an appraisal of U.S. nuclear force capabilities and its ability to conduct nuclear strikes in defense of its allies. This chapter will also discuss the problem of U.S. resolve, specifically why the United States is unlikely to use nuclear weapons in a conflict to defend these allies and instead would rely on strong, credible conventional options. Chapter 7 will summarize the findings of this study and examine the implications these issues have for extended deterrence theory and policy.

CHAPTER ONE

Extended Deterrence and the Nuclear Umbrella

The U.S. nuclear umbrella that is part of the larger defense commitment to protect Japan and South Korea is grounded in the theory and strategy of deterrence. Deterrence has a long history as a strategy to manage conflict between people and states. Although deterrence has been used for years, its development as a formal theory was largely an effort to find ways of thinking about and utilizing nuclear weapons. It was clear soon after World War II that nuclear weapons were unique, not just weapons with a bigger bang.[1] For the next four decades, scholars and analysts wrote countless studies that examined the workings of deterrence.

When the Cold War came to an end, many people began to reassess the role of nuclear weapons in national security. With the Soviet Union gone, the importance of nuclear weapons in U.S. and global security calculations waned along with interest in deterrence. After the events of September 11, 2001, the perceived usefulness of deterrence faded further as U.S. leaders questioned its relevance when confronting terrorist groups or states, such as Iraq, Iran, and North Korea, that may not be able to be deterred. The 2002 U.S. National Security Strategy observed: "In the Cold War, especially following the Cuban missile crisis, we faced a generally status quo, risk-averse adversary. Deterrence was an effective defense. But deterrence based only upon the threat of retaliation is less likely to work against leaders of rogue states more willing to take risks, gambling with the lives of their people, and the wealth of their nations."[2]

Despite this skepticism in the wake of September 11, interest in deterrence has been resuscitated, and an increasing number of studies have begun to look again at deterrence and the role of nuclear weapons.[3] In what has been dubbed "the second nuclear age," new nuclear weapons states in a variety of regional security environments may think differently about these weapons. Thus, Paul Bracken argues, "a multilateral nuclear order is taking shape," and "as countries acquire these weapons, they consider new ways to use them to advance their strategic purposes."[4] Consequently, deterrence and strategic planning require new thought and research about the role nuclear weapons will play in the future.[5] This chapter will examine some of the important theoretical concepts and issues regarding deterrence theory, particularly extended deterrence whereby a defender seeks to protect allies from attack. Scholars and analysts who study deterrence today have a wealth of knowledge and thinking to draw on from the past. A good deal of this theorizing has stood the test of time. Increasingly, however, studies are pointing out that deterrence is more complex than sometimes recognized and that different dynamics are present today than during the Cold War U.S.-Soviet confrontation.

DETERRENCE THEORY

Deterrence is the use of threats to convince an adversary to refrain from taking an action you do not wish it to take. The central tenet of deterrence is that a threat issued by the defender will raise the costs of a challenger's actions sufficiently high that the challenger will refrain from taking the unwanted action. The defender must alter the challenger's cost/benefit calculus by demonstrating that regardless of what the challenger seeks to obtain, the costs of achieving this objective will outweigh the gains. The defender can seek to raise the costs by threatening to impose a high penalty or deny benefits. At the same time, the challenger must know that restraint on its part will result in an acceptable outcome.[6] If the challenger believes that the punishment is coming regardless of its actions, it has little incentive to show restraint. Deterrence theory maintains that, in the end, if the potential costs outweigh the gains, the challenger will likely be deterred.

Deterrence threats can occur in two ways: deterrence by denial and deterrence by punishment.[7] For centuries, states have tried to deter adversaries by maintaining sufficient military capability to dissuade them from attacking. Defenders built high walls, dug deep moats, and maintained a strong army to persuade their adversaries that the gains from attacking were not worth the costs. Deterrence by denial seeks to defeat an attack or, even if the defender were likely to lose, to make the aggression so costly that it would not be worth attacking in the first place. Thus, the ability to deny an adversary a quick victory while increasing the likelihood of a long war of attrition was an effective deterrence strategy.[8]

Deterrence by denial is closely tied to assessments of the military balance. If the defender allows its military preparedness to remain static while the challenger makes significant improvements to its military capability, deterrence by denial may eventually fail. The attacker may conclude that its force improvements can overcome earlier deficiencies and that an attack will succeed. Thus, the defender's ability to deter by denial is relative to the military capabilities of the attacker. Successful deterrence requires regular assessment of and constant attention to the military balance to ensure the challenger concludes that the balance of forces is not in its favor and that the costs of an attack are too great.

With the advent of airpower, a second route to deterrence became possible. States no longer had to be able to deny an adversary victory to be able to deter, but could do so with threats of punishment. Aerial bombardment allowed countries to bypass the military defenses of enemies and strike directly at high-value targets such as cities, government institutions, and industrial sites.[9] For the first time, states could threaten to inflict severe punishment if attacked without first having to defeat an adversary's ground forces or breach its defenses. Navies also had this capability to a lesser degree, limited by the range of their guns.

Nuclear weapons added further to a state's ability to punish without requiring the defeat of an adversary's military. Nuclear weapons represented a quantum leap in the amount of destruction a state could impose, making it far easier for leaders to threaten unacceptable levels of destruction should an adversary take an unwanted action. With conventional forces, countries can threaten to defend themselves if attacked or seek revenge should they emerge victorious. With nuclear weapons, however, a country can punish its adversary whether it wins or not,[10] and the destruction can occur in a relatively short time, possibly within days or hours.[11] Whereas deterrence by denial relies on careful evaluation of the military balance, nuclear weapons make the assessment simpler because the costs of a nuclear exchange are so much higher and more obvious. As Kenneth Waltz notes, "with nuclear weapons, stability and peace rest on easy calculations of what one country can do to another."[12] If a state possesses only a small number of survivable nuclear weapons, it can potentially threaten an unacceptable amount of damage. Thus, large disparities between adversaries in nuclear or conventional forces may not alter one side's ability to punish the other, so deterrence by punishment is less susceptible to fluctuations in the military balance.[13]

Analysts have given renewed attention to the role of conventional weapons in deterrence. In a deterrence-by-denial strategy, conventional weapons continue to offer the possibility of deterring an adversary, either by raising the costs of victory sufficiently high or by outright denial of victory in a conflict. Thus, despite the advent of nuclear weapons, conventional forces remain an important part of a denial strategy.[14] In addition, with the increase in accuracy and power of some conventional munitions, states have options besides nuclear weapons to punish challengers by hitting strategic targets such as leadership nodes, industrial targets, and hardened/buried targets. Conventional weapons can have the same strategic effects without the collateral destruction of nuclear weapons. During the George W. Bush administration, U.S. strategy became more inclusive of conventional options in the belief that threats of retaliation might be less effective against states like North Korea or Iran. Consequently, U.S. strategy documents began to speak of a "New Triad" and "tailored deterrence" that included conventional strike options along with nuclear retaliation and ballistic missile defense as the chief options for a U.S. response.[15] However, others have argued that conventional weapons may provide only a modest contribution to deterrence because the level of punishment they can inflict is insufficient to deter adversaries, and thus they are no substitute for nuclear weapons.[16]

DETERRENCE SITUATIONS

As deterrence theory has evolved, scholars and analysts have noted the different types of situations that can influence the dynamics of deterrence. These situations include primary versus extended deterrence, immediate versus general deterrence, and symmetric versus asymmetric deterrence. These distinctions are important because states will act differently depending on the type of deterrence situation involved.

Primary Versus Extended Deterrence

In primary deterrence, a state is seeking to protect its homeland; in extended deterrence, a defender is attempting to deter an attack on an ally. The difference is important. Few doubt that a state will respond if it is attacked. However, many doubts arise in a situation of extended deterrence. Would a defender truly come to an ally's aid in a crisis? Is the ally considered sufficiently valuable to warrant the expenditure of troops and money, especially if the challenger is armed with nuclear weapons that may be able to hit the defender's assets in the region, or even the defender's homeland? Defenders have gone to great lengths to demonstrate that they would indeed come to an ally's defense. Treaties and alliances are often used to demonstrate these commitments, but in a crisis there is always a chance that the defender will not follow through on its promise, deciding it is simply not worth the cost. As a result, defenders may resort to more extensive measures, such as positioning its troops on the ally's soil as a way of demonstrating resolve. In that way, its soldiers can not only help to defend the ally but also act as a trip wire to demonstrate the certainty that a larger deployment of forces will follow in the event of war. In the end, however, it is more difficult for a defender to demonstrate its resolve in a situation of extended deterrence than in one of primary deterrence.

Many people confuse and conflate extended deterrence with the nuclear umbrella. Extended deterrence refers to the broad security commitment of one state to defend an ally; it can involve any number of tools that may or may not include nuclear weapons. A strong conventionally armed state can offer an extended deterrence commitment to another state. A nuclear umbrella is thus only one possible feature of an extended deterrence relationship; the two are not interchangeable.

Immediate Versus General Deterrence

Patrick Morgan identified an important distinction in the intensity of deterrence situations.[17] In an immediate deterrence situation, there is an imminent threat of attack from an adversary and the situation is a crisis. The adversary has given notice, either in words or in action, that it is preparing for an attack. To deter the impending aggression, the defender will issue specific counterthreats of retaliation. In general deterrence, two or more states are suspicious of and hostile toward each other. Each side might consider using force against the other if an opportunity arose, but there is no immediate crisis. In this situation, the adversaries undertake general military preparations to defend themselves but do not issue specific counterthreats. Thus, the relationship is relatively peaceful and stable but also characterized by mistrust and animosity. It is important to view immediate and general deterrence as points along a continuum rather than discrete categories. Deterrence situations may shift along the continuum, exhibiting some of the characteristics of both general and immediate deterrence as a situation escalates to a crisis and then returns to the status quo. During the Cold War, U.S.-Soviet relations were largely an example of general deterrence, but at times tensions rose and shifted the relationship to one of immediate deterrence. Eventually, hostilities subsided and moved back toward general deterrence.

The U.S. nuclear umbrella for Japan and South Korea has been part of Washington's general military preparations to defend these two allies. Most of the time, the deterrence situation reflected the characteristics of general deterrence. War was not imminent, and the United States issued only general statements that these two countries were under its nuclear umbrella without making specific counterthreats of nuclear retaliation. One exception involved U.S. efforts to bring an end to the Korean War by threatening to use nuclear weapons.[18] Rather, the umbrella has been part of the general preparations to discourage any adversary from challenging the U.S. commitment, including the mantra that "all options remain on the table." However, if a crisis were to erupt and the situation moved from general to immediate deterrence, the United States might resort to issuing specific threats to use nuclear weapons.

Though an attack was not imminent, North Korea's five nuclear tests in 2006, 2009, 2013, and twice in 2016 triggered an elevated level of concern in the region. The security situation in East Asia was sufficiently disturbed that the United States decided on each occasion to issue pointed warnings that both Japan and South Korea remained under the

U.S. nuclear umbrella. For example, in 2006, while visiting Japan soon after the first North Korean nuclear test, Secretary of State Condoleezza Rice exclaimed, "The role of the United States is to make certain that everybody, including the North Koreans, know very well that the United States will fully recognize and act upon its obligations under its mutual defense treaty (with Japan). The United States has the will and the capability to meet the full range, and I underscore the full range, of its deterrence and security commitment to Japan."[19] The emphasis on "full range" was a clear reference to U.S. nuclear weapons and the nuclear umbrella.

U.S. defense secretary Donald Rumsfeld reinforced the deterrence commitment to South Korea with a more explicit declaration in October 2006: "The United States reaffirms its firm commitment to the Republic of Korea, including continuation of the extended deterrence offered by the U.S. nuclear umbrella consistent with the Mutual Defense Treaty."[20] Although the situation had not shifted to one in which North Korea was actively considering an attack, the nuclear tests were sufficiently unsettling to move the situation away from the status quo of general deterrence. In another example, Washington's high-profile use of B-2 and B-52 bombers in the Key Resolve/Foal Eagle annual spring exercises in 2013 and 2016 can be viewed as a response to an incremental shift from general to immediate deterrence during the tense months that followed North Korea's third and fourth nuclear tests.

Symmetric Versus Asymmetric Deterrence

Finally, deterrence situations may also be characterized as symmetric or asymmetric. A symmetric deterrence situation involves states of relatively equal military strength, such as the United States and the Soviet Union during the Cold War. When the Cold War ended and the U.S.-Soviet confrontation faded, scholars began to examine situations of asymmetric deterrence in which the two opponents had major power differentials.[21]

An asymmetric deterrence situation can occur in two ways. In one type, the defender is a relatively weak state that needs to marshal its power to deter stronger states. Before 1945, a weak state had few options, other than taking whatever defensive measures it could or attempting to form an alliance, to deter an adversary from attacking. However, with a small nuclear force, or chemical and biological weapons, an otherwise weak state may be able to deter a more powerful adversary because it can make threats that pose far greater costs.

In another type of asymmetric deterrence situation, it is the stronger power that is trying to deter an unacceptable action by a weaker state. U.S. efforts to deter Iran or North Korea are examples of this type of asymmetric deterrence situation. As noted earlier, some analysts have questioned whether these so-called rogue states understand the rationale of deterrence or are so risk tolerant that they cannot be deterred. It is argued that the leaders of these countries do not value the same things as the United States and the Soviet Union did during the Cold War, least of all the welfare of their people. Consequently, it becomes difficult to threaten actions that would raise the costs sufficiently for deterrence to succeed. Though some disagreement remains in this debate, it seems clear that even the leaders of so-called rogue states wish to stay in power and value the survival of their regime. Thus, deterrence remains relevant, although it still requires a careful assessment of what the adversary values for deterrence to be successful.

The U.S. defense commitments to Japan and South Korea, including the nuclear umbrella, are examples of extended, asymmetric deterrence, largely in a situation of general deterrence. Chapter 3 will examine the nature of the threats that are being deterred by these U.S. commitments. Almost by definition, the two threats of greatest concern at the moment—North Korea and China—are asymmetric threats when measured against U.S. military power. This could change, however, as Chinese strength continues to grow. Although North Korea remains a serious challenge to regional stability, the security situation in northeast Asia most closely resembles general deterrence, as there is little imminent danger of war.

RATIONALITY

Deterrence theory makes an assumption that state leaders will act rationally. Rational decision making assumes that, when confronted with a choice, leaders collect the necessary information, identify possible options, weigh the costs and benefits of each option, and ultimately choose the one that is likely to produce the greatest benefit for the least cost. Governments and leaders do not act with "perfect rationality," yet states and leaders may be sufficiently rational for the assumption to provide some guidance in assessing state behavior. Moreover, nuclear weapons simplify the associated cost/benefit calculations. Kenneth Waltz argues that "in a conventional world, one is uncertain about winning or losing. In a nuclear world, one is uncertain about surviving or being annihilated. If force is used and not kept within limits, catastrophe will result. That prediction is easy to make because it does not require close estimates of opposing forces."[22]

Critics of the rationality assumption have pointed to several important concerns.[23] Decision makers are human, with a limited ability to retain and analyze information. In addition, determining precise costs and benefits is a difficult task, and decision makers may not agree on the values assigned to various options, pointing to the subjectivity of these types of assessments. Finally, leaders may receive incomplete information because of the difficulty of obtaining the necessary intelligence or time pressures that do not allow the collection of all the necessary data.[24] These issues also affect the challenger's calculations.[25] Consequently, all parties operating within a deterrence situation must deal with information deficiencies and imperfect rational calculations to arrive at their own cost/benefit assessments and those of their opponents.

In northeast Asia, most questions regarding rationality involve assessments of North Korean leadership. In 1977, a U.S. Defense Department report acknowledged that "our intelligence does not pretend to understand the convolutions of Kim Il-sung's mind."[26] A 1999 assessment by the commander of U.S. Forces Korea (USFK) described North Korea as an "unpredictable regime."[27] Kim Jong-il's image as crazy was further enhanced by his portrayal in the media, including his role in the movie *Team America* and his picture on the cover of *The Economist* magazine with the title "Greetings Earthlings."[28] Kim Jong-il and the North Korean regime often relied on provocative rhetoric and actions and brinkmanship to advance their goals, which also helped to confirm the assessments of irrationality.

Analysts have raised similar questions about Kim Jong-un's rationality and unpredictability, along with concerns for his inexperience. U.S. Pacific Command commander Admiral Samuel Locklear commented in a 2014 press briefing, "The young leader, for me . . . is unpredictable.

His behavior, at least in the way it's reported and the way we see it in [a] sense, would make me wonder whether or not he is always in the rational decision-making mode or not. And this is a problem."[29] Some also point to North Korea's apparent obsession in clinging to a failed economic policy, the ideology of *juche* that proclaims self-reliance in the midst of an increasingly interdependent world, and Kim Jong-un's *byungjin* line that calls for simultaneous development of the North Korean economy and nuclear weapons as further evidence of the regime's inability to make rational cost/benefit calculations. While North Korean statements and actions have done much to display a level of irrationality, it is also possible to argue that the regime is, in fact, quite rational in its ability to achieve its objectives with few resources. Andrei Lankov maintains that "their penchant for seemingly irrational and erratic behavior is illusionary: the North Korean leaders actually know what they are doing. They are not madmen nor ideological zealots, but remarkably efficient and cold-minded calculators; perhaps the most perfect Machiavellians of the modern world."[30]

Perceptions of North Korean irrationality may be an important asset for DPRK leaders, demonstrating that they might be quite willing to use force if necessary. Consequently, these perceptions help North Korea deter the United States and South Korea.[31] Denny Roy notes that "if states believe a certain government is prone to impulsive violence, they are more likely to behave passively toward that government, in hopes of avoiding provocation."[32] Being rational does not mean North Korean leaders have not made mistakes, but it does indicate that the regime has a certain level of predictability and is capable of making cost/benefit calculations. However, the cost/benefit calculus may be different from that of other states. North Korea's rigid, collectivist culture allows the leadership to impose tremendous cost on the populace for the good of the state. A South Korean scholar argues that "the individualism on which Western rationality is based is especially sensitive to the loss of human life. As such, even if North Korea were to suffer serious damage during a military conflict with the United States, the consequent political impact would be less significant for itself than for the U.S. administration."[33] It is regime survival that drives the rationality of North Korea, and Kim Jong-un is willing to have his country and people absorb a considerable amount of cost to achieve that goal.

The other target of the U.S. nuclear umbrella, China, is far less problematic. For many years during the Cold War, U.S. leaders were very concerned about the rationality and predictability of Chinese leader Mao Zedong, but today those assessments are different. Certainly, there are concerns about China under Xi Jinping and his goals for China's future, but China is often classified in U.S. government documents as a "near-peer competitor" with hopes to be a "responsible stakeholder," and most analysts assume that China's leaders understand the dynamics of strategic deterrence. U.S. threats are able to hold at risk assets that these leaders value, and Beijing understands the cost/benefit calculations of nuclear deterrence. In the end, many countries in the region are using deterrence strategies, including North Korea to deter the United States and South Korea, and China to deter U.S. involvement in the South China Sea or a future clash over Taiwan. Consequently, all sides seek to understand the rationality and cost/benefit calculations of their adversaries.

CREDIBILITY

For deterrence to be successful, the theory maintains that any threats made must be credible. Credibility requires that a defender have the capability to carry out the threatened action and that the action would impose sufficient cost to make the challenger desist from the unwanted action. It is not necessary that the defender actually possess the capability to impose unacceptable costs but only that the challenger believe it. Indeed, Israel has not conducted a test of nuclear weapons, yet few doubt it possesses them. North Korea could also have chosen to curtail its nuclear program at some point and rely on the ambiguity of an uncertain capability, which would have produced a similar deterrent effect whether or not it was clear that Pyongyang actually had nuclear weapons.

Finally, the defender must convince the challenger of its resolve to carry out the threat should deterrence fail.[34] Resolve is often the most difficult part of an extended deterrence commitment because it is never entirely certain that a defender will stay with an ally in a crisis. Despite professing an undying commitment during peacetime when there are relatively few costs to the commitment, once war breaks out, the defender's assessment of the costs involved may change and the ally find that it is on its own. Regarding extended deterrence and the nuclear umbrella, there is no question the United States possesses the nuclear and conventional capabilities for a credible commitment. The greater challenge comes with resolve.

Defenders use a variety of techniques to demonstrate resolve. States often conclude formal security agreements with allies that provide explicit assurances of the defense commitment. During the Cold War, the United States had numerous security treaties, including bilateral alliances with Japan, South Korea, and the Philippines, as well as larger multilateral agreements such as the North Atlantic Treaty Organization (NATO) and the Southeast Asia Treaty Organization (SEATO). The NATO treaty, concluded in 1949, contained wording that "an armed attack against one or more of them in Europe or North America shall be considered an attack against them all."[35] However, subsequent treaties contained less precise wording; the security clause in the U.S.-ROK treaty, for example, states that each party "would act to meet the common danger in accordance with its constitutional processes."[36] After the NATO treaty, members of the Senate were concerned that the "attack on one" wording usurped its constitutional power to declare war and insisted on different verbiage. The 1960 Japan-U.S. Mutual Defense Treaty contains a similar "subject to their constitutional provisions" clause.[37]

States also demonstrate their commitment through trade ties, along with economic and military aid. Trade and aid signal an investment and common interests with the ally while also helping to build up its capabilities. Bruce Russett has argued that economic ties are very important for successful deterrence, though they do not guarantee it.[38]

A promise to defend an ally can be broken in a crisis. Despite a formal commitment, a defender may hedge its response, particularly if the situation carries great risk and cost. Regarding statements of resolve, Thomas Schelling noted that "saying so, unfortunately, does not make it true; and if it is true, saying so does not always make it believed. We evidently do not want war and would only fight if we had to. The problem is to demonstrate that we would have to."[39] To demonstrate that it "has to," and that it is up to an adversary to either "swerve or collide," the United States has deployed combat troops to Japan and South Korea, including the Fifth Air Force, the Seventh Fleet, and a carrier strike group on the Japanese home islands and the Third Marine Expeditionary Force on

Okinawa, along with the Seventh Air Force and elements of the Second Infantry Division in South Korea.

In addition to helping defend either ally in case of attack, these troops can act as a trip wire to ensure a larger U.S. response should deterrence fail. In the case of Japan, the trip wire function was less important because, as an island state, it had no adversaries on its immediate border that were ready to invade. For South Korea, the trip wire function was critical, so U.S. troops were stationed along the likely invasion routes from the north and close to the demilitarized zone (DMZ). Any invasion from the north was likely to put DPRK forces in contact with U.S. units, which would ensure a vigorous response. Once blood has been shed, the defender is more likely to hold its ground. Moreover, the commitment of ground troops is more difficult to reverse in a crisis, and they provide a direct link to the defender's remaining military power. The U.S. presence in Japan furnished an extensive base infrastructure to allow for a significant forward presence in the region and a visible sign of the commitment to Japanese security. Other methods of demonstrating credibility include appearing to be irrational and oblivious to the costs of any possible retaliation or turning the decision to retaliate over to the ally, which presumably would not hesitate to act if it were attacked.[40]

Finally, if the defender possesses nuclear weapons, it can reinforce deterrence by deploying them to the ally's homeland to deter or, if deterrence fails, fight a war. In addition, the defender may include the ally under its nuclear umbrella, indicating that it might respond with nuclear weapons if its ally were attacked. The presence of nuclear weapons and the declaration of the nuclear umbrella raise the possibility that any conflict could escalate to a nuclear conflagration and increase the costs for an adversary to much higher levels. This is particularly so if the defender has not given a "no first use" pledge, indicating a willingness to be the first to cross the nuclear threshold. While the nuclear umbrella may deter large-scale conflict, it is unclear if it has much effect on lower-level clashes. Yet even a limited conventional conflict would hold out the possibility of escalating to nuclear war.

How certain must the threat to respond be for deterrence to be successful? A defender may make it absolutely certain that it will respond to an attack on an ally, yet the challenger may not be deterred because it is not convinced. Another possibility is that despite strong indicators of resolve, the challenger may believe that the benefits of attacking are sufficiently high that it is willing to accept the costs of certain retaliation, or that a failure to attack carries more costs than showing restraint.[41]

Conversely, a challenger may still be deterred, even in the face of an uncertain or unlikely threat of retaliation, if the costs of retaliation would be very high and leaders are unsure of their ability to limit and control the conflict once hostilities begin. Thomas Schelling notes, "It is the essence of a crisis that the participants are not fully in control of events; they take steps and make decisions that raise or lower the danger, but in a realm of risk and uncertainty." Consequently, Schelling maintained that uncertain deterrence threats can be credible:

> A response that carries some risk of war can be plausible, even reasonable, at a time when a final, ultimate decision to *have* a general war would be implausible or unreasonable. A country can threaten to stumble into a war even if it cannot credibly threaten to invite one. In fact, though a country may not be able with absolute credibility to threaten general war, it may be equally unable with absolute credibility to forestall a major war.[42]

In addition, simply having the capability means there is a possibility of retaliation, even if not a certainty. Thus, resolve cannot be determined through precise calculations of the probability of retaliation and instead relies on shifting assessments of costs and benefits. Determining resolve is an imprecise and continually changing assessment of costs, benefits, risks, and the likelihood of a defender's response.

Resolve will also have different requirements depending on the deterrence situation. During peacetime or in a general deterrence situation, demonstrating resolve is relatively easy. There are few costs involved in extending deterrence, including assertions of a nuclear umbrella, to any number of allies. The test comes when security relations move from general to immediate deterrence, when the situation has become a crisis and an attack is possible. The defender may now be faced with a host of potential costs that begin to alter the earlier cost/benefit calculations for issuing extended deterrence threats, with or without nuclear weapons.

The defender's assessment of the costs it is willing to incur is influenced by a number of factors. The first crucial consideration is the capabilities of the adversary. If the deterrence situation is symmetric, with the power capabilities of the defender and challenger relatively equal, a deterrence failure would pose the likelihood of significant costs for the defender. For example, during the Cold War, U.S. efforts to deter the Soviet Union in Western Europe always meant there was a danger that Washington would have to fight Moscow should it come to the defense of its NATO allies. Confronting the Soviets was particularly menacing because it involved nuclear weapons and the danger of retaliation on the U.S. homeland. As the saying went, would the United States really trade Washington or New York for London or Paris? In 1979, Henry Kissinger protested in a speech that rattled NATO defense ministers, declaring that "it is absurd to base the strategy of the West on the credibility of the threat of mutual suicide" and that our European allies should not continue "asking us to multiply strategic assurances that we cannot possibly mean, we should not want to execute because if we execute, we risk the destruction of civilization."[43] Consequently, there were serious questions about the credibility of the U.S. commitment, particularly the use of nuclear weapons, because this raised the danger of nuclear escalation that could destroy the U.S. homeland. Even in an asymmetric deterrence situation, as is the case with North Korea and China, the possibility of some level of nuclear retaliation injects the prospect of serious costs for the defender should deterrence fail.

Another factor that affects resolve is the interests at stake for both sides of the deterrence situation. Presumably, the state with the greater stakes—the costs and benefits of pursuing its interests—will tend to prevail in the deterrence confrontation. The stakes may include a number of factors, such as access to resources, importance of an ally, geostrategic location, political influence, reputation, or state survival. Concerning the defender in an extended deterrence situation, Huth and Russett argue that "the willingness to run risks or pay costs to defend a protégé will be greater the greater the objective or intrinsic value of the protégé."[44] Thus, the side with the greater interests at stake will likely be able to issue more credible threats.[45] In situations of extended deterrence, this may point to a difficult problem for the defender. Often the challenger and the ally will be in the same region and have interests that may be long established and interlocking. In contrast, the defender may be outside the region but trying to protect an ally who is considered valuable. In these circumstances, the challenger's interests may be quite significant, which may make it easier to issue credible threats should the defender interfere.

The assessment of interests at stake can be a complicated process. How do states gauge whether an adversary has important interests at stake and whether its own interests are stronger, in hopes that the adversary will back down in the end? George and Smoke maintain that the defender's interests, as viewed by the challenger, are central in the challenger's assessment of the deterrence situation. Accordingly, "the opponent is likely to pay more attention to strategic, political, economic, and ideological factors determining the nature and magnitude of those interests than to rhetorical and other signaling devices the defending power may employ to enhance credibility."[46] As noted earlier, Russett makes a similar argument for the importance of economic, political, and military ties, maintaining that, in particular, "economic interdependence may be virtually essential to successful deterrence."[47] These ties do not make successful deterrence a certainty, but they help to demonstrate the depth of the commitment between the allies and support the credibility of the extended deterrence guarantee. Consequently, efforts to send a proper signal to a challenger may be less important than elements of the larger relationship between the defender and the ally and the context of the deterrence situation. With strong signaling from the defender but a lack of close political and economic ties with the ally, the challenger may still conclude that its interests outweigh those of the defender.[48]

Another factor that can influence the credibility of a defense commitment is the past behavior and reputation of the defender and challenger.[49] If either one has a reputation for backing down in a confrontation or deserting an ally in a crisis, logic would indicate that adversaries and friends will be less likely to believe in the credibility of future commitments. In a study of immediate deterrence cases, Paul Huth argued that the "past behavior of the defender in the most recent confrontation with the potential attacker had a significant effect on deterrence outcomes" and "reflects the importance of the interests at stake for the defender."[50] However, Daryl Press maintains that it is current assessments of power and interests that determine a state's credibility:

A country's credibility, at least during crises, is driven not by its past behavior but rather by power and interests. If a country makes threats that it has the power to carry out—and an interest in doing so—those threats will be believed even if the country has bluffed in the past. If it makes threats that it lacks the power to carry out—or has no interest in doing so—its credibility will be viewed with great skepticism.[51]

Yet in the Korean case, Van Jackson maintains that the accumulated set of interactions between the United States and North Korea has had a profound impact on relations. Their perceived reputations, built up over fifty years, demonstrate that "not only do decision-makers often consider the past when assessing the credibility of their rival's threats, but their past word and deed affect the likelihood that a rival will challenge them in the future."[52] Though the debate continues, reputation and past behavior are closely tied to interests. However, concern for reputation can become a goal in itself that skews the overall assessment of interests.

THE CHALLENGES OF CREDIBILITY AND THE NUCLEAR UMBRELLA

Nuclear weapons and the nuclear umbrella raise further questions about credibility, particularly whether threats to use nuclear weapons to defend allies are believable. Since their first use in 1945, nuclear weapons have never again been used in a conflict. State leaders have clearly been reluctant to use nuclear weapons, even against relatively weak states when there was no fear of nuclear retaliation. This has not prevented the maintenance of large, robust nuclear arsenals or the development of detailed nuclear war plans and targeting packages for leaders to have available if war broke out. States also continue to maintain "first use" strategies, indicating a willingness to initiate the use of nuclear weapons in a conventional conflict, often to offset perceived conventional disadvantages. The logic of first use during the Cold War for the United States was to counter Soviet numerical advantages in men and equipment so that Washington did not need to match Moscow's conventional strength.

Traditional realism maintains that the reluctance to use nuclear weapons is due to the success of deterrence. The prospect of mutual nuclear annihilation made it far too dangerous to even chance the possibility of a nuclear exchange. However, others have argued that deterrence does not provide a complete explanation for the nonuse of nuclear weapons.[53] Whether calling it a taboo or a tradition of nonuse, states have refrained from using nuclear weapons, even against nonnuclear adversaries who could not retaliate with nuclear weapons. Nina Tannenwald argues that "a powerful taboo against the use of nuclear weapons has developed in the global system, which, although not (yet) a fully robust prohibition, has stigmatized nuclear weapons as unacceptable weapons—'weapons of mass destruction.' . . . The effect of this taboo has been to delegitimize nuclear weapons as weapons of war, and to embed deterrence practices in a set of norms . . . that stabilize and restrain the self-help behavior of states."[54]

Several factors help to explain the reluctance to use nuclear weapons. First, there is a clear appreciation for the deadly effects of these weapons.[55] Stephen Cimbala notes that leaders are well aware of the tremendous destructiveness of nuclear weapons and the dangers of a nuclear exchange. Consequently, leaders become more cautious and seek to avoid these situations because "leaders will be staring into Nietzsche's abyss, and the abyss will be staring back."[56]

Second, there is what T. V. Paul calls the "reputational costs of nuclear use." Countries that used nuclear weapons, particularly if they were the first to do so in a conflict, would face an outpouring of international condemnation as the state that crossed this line for the first time in decades. As a result, nuclear-armed states are self-deterred from using these weapons against nonnuclear states.[57] Accordingly, Paul argues that "reputational considerations appear to be crucial in explaining self-deterrence in light of the historical record. . . . These reputational considerations derive largely from three sources: the tradition of non-use of nuclear weapons, moral restraints, and legal principles regarding the use of nuclear weapons. Leaders can be directly and indirectly constrained by these factors, even if they do not always publicly acknowledge them."[58]

Finally, there are important military reasons for avoiding the use of nuclear weapons. Nuclear weapons, including tactical nuclear weapons, contaminate the battlefield and greatly complicate the military's ability to conduct follow-on ground operations. The dangers of nuclear fallout for civilians and military personnel, the long-term effects of nuclear explosions, and the impact on neighboring states, including allies, make it difficult to use nuclear weapons, even low-yield tactical nuclear weapons. States may also be reluctant to go nuclear because, as Schelling notes, "senior officials, civilian and military, acknowledged and expected that if the nuclear 'threshold' were ever crossed by either side in a war, the other might feel instantly released from inhibitions, and there might be no telling how far escalation would go."[59] Thus, leaders should be worried about their ability to control events once the first nuclear detonation occurs. Consequently, Schelling argues, "nuclear weapons, once introduced into combat, could not—or probably would not—be contained, restrained, confined, or limited."[60] Nuclear use would also increase the desire of other nonnuclear states to acquire their own nuclear weapons.[61] Thus, Tannenwald concludes that, since the Cuban missile crisis in 1962, "although successive U.S. administrations have worried about the resort to nuclear weapons in a crisis, scarce evidence exists that high-level officials have considered seriously the deliberate use of nuclear weapons to achieve either military or political aims."[62]

Although states have refrained from using nuclear weapons and strong pressure remains on leaders not to do so, under what circumstances might a state be willing to cross the nuclear threshold? No one can say for certain what would trigger a nuclear response, but certainly a state whose survival was threatened would be far more likely to use nuclear weapons to maintain its own existence. This goes to the heart of the difference between primary and extended deterrence, with nuclear threats more credible in primary deterrence. Patrick Morgan notes an important issue regarding the credibility of a threat by a weaker state who is the defender, even in a primary deterrence situation. If the weaker state carried out a threat to respond with nuclear, chemical, or biological weapons, the conflict would likely escalate and provoke an even worse response from its adversary. If the adversary were significantly more powerful than the defender, the result could lead to the end of the defender's regime. Consequently, the stronger state might not consider the defender's threats to be credible and cross the redline regardless. As a result, there can be an inherent credibility problem in an asymmetric deterrence situation in which a weaker state is trying to use nuclear weapons to deter a more powerful state.[63] T. V. Paul notes:

> The awesome destructive power of nuclear weapons gave the basic impetus to the rise of the tradition of non-use, as the potential for total destruction gives nuclear weapons an all-or-nothing character unlike any other weapons invented so far. This means a nuclear state may not use its ultimate capability unless a threshold is crossed, for example, when a vital issue, such as the survival of the state itself, is threatened.... Breaking the tradition would elicit the revulsion of generations to come, unless it was for a question of extremely vital importance, such as the physical existence of the nuclear state or its key allies.[64]

In extended deterrence, it becomes more difficult for the defender to demonstrate that it is willing to accept these costs and that the interests are truly vital. Given the pressure to not use nuclear weapons, defenders may still balk, even when a key ally's security is at stake, not only because of the restraints of the "nuclear taboo" but also because of the potential costs of the adversary's likely retaliation. Moreover, if the defender possesses conventional options that can be used in place of a nuclear response, a defender may go to great lengths to avoid escalating to a nuclear conflict.

The credibility of the nuclear umbrella may also be affected by efforts to reduce the role and size of nuclear arsenals with the possibility of moving to zero, which would eliminate the nuclear umbrella. During the past decade, a movement to eliminate all of the world's nuclear weapons was reenergized by four high-profile advocates—George P. Shultz, William J. Perry, Henry A. Kissinger, and Sam Nunn—who wrote in 2007:

> Nuclear weapons were essential to maintaining international security during the Cold War because they were a means of deterrence. The end of the Cold War made the doctrine of mutual Soviet-American deterrence obsolete. Deterrence continues to be a relevant consideration for many states with regard to threats from other states. But reliance on nuclear weapons for this purpose is becoming increasingly hazardous and decreasingly effective.... We endorse setting the goal of a world free of nuclear weapons and working energetically on the actions required to achieve that goal.[65]

Short of the goal of nuclear disarmament, these advocates and others have called for drastically reducing nuclear stockpiles and reserving nuclear weapons for the "sole purpose" of deterring the nuclear weapons of other states, arguing that the more nuclear weapons there are in the world, the greater are the problems of proliferation and the possibility of their falling into the hands of terrorists. These advocates dismiss the utility of nuclear weapons for any other purpose. In his April 2009 Prague speech, President Obama committed his administration to move in this direction, and with the 2010 Nuclear Posture Review and the New START agreement, he reduced the role and number of U.S. nuclear weapons. It is unlikely the goal of zero can ever be met, but the call has had an impact on discussions about the future of the nuclear umbrella.

Some in the United States have argued that the remedy for this credibility problem is to develop smaller yield nuclear weapons that would be more accurate, generate less damage, particularly collateral civilian casualties, and be easier for political leaders to use. With regard to the current U.S. nuclear arsenal, Lieber and Press argue:

> Of course, a deterrent threat also needs to be credible—that is, an adversary needs to be convinced that a retaliatory threat will actually be executed. If not backed by the capability and the credibility to execute threats, deterrence is merely a dangerous bluff. A deterrence force should therefore provide decision-makers with options they would conceivably execute if their redlines were crossed. Otherwise, allies will question U.S. assurances, adversaries will doubt U.S. threats, and a U.S. president may confront an escalating crisis without any acceptable options.[66]

A 2015 CSIS report led by Clark Murdoch concurs that the United States needs a range of "discriminate nuclear options" because its arsenal of large Cold War–era nuclear weapons is ill suited for future nuclear conflicts.

> The United States needs to develop and deploy more employable nuclear weapons, ones that enable the United States to respond directly and proportionately to an adversary's employment of a nuclear weapon. This is not about "nuclear warfighting," but demonstrating

the resolve to match an adversary's escalation of a conflict to the nuclear level. By doing so, the United States sends a powerful political message—"You can't win this conflict by going nuclear"—and, in effect, makes nuclear escalation a less attractive option.[67]

However, in a 2007 interview, General James Cartwright, vice chairman of the Joint Chiefs of Staff and former head of U.S. Strategic Command, noted that any U.S. president would be very reluctant to use nuclear weapons in a conflict: "I don't want to put myself in the shoes of a president, but who is not going to take [as] incredibly serious the use of a nuclear weapon." General Cartwright also maintained that lowering the yield of nuclear weapons is not the issue, noting that "it is not just a little bit [of] a weapon of mass destruction. It is a weapon of mass destruction. It is going to change not just that country's future, but all of our futures when we start using these things, big or little."[68]

Another dimension of making credible threats is the conventional military power available to a defender. If the deterrence situation is asymmetric and the defender possesses significant conventional military capability, the defender may not need to issue nuclear threats to deter a challenger. Given the restraints of the nuclear taboo, conventional retaliation may be far more credible. If the defender's conventional weapons can inflict unacceptable damage, the strategic effect on the challenger will be the same. Defenders may still issue nuclear threats as extra guarantees to deter challengers and assure allies, in part for political reasons, even though the conventional retaliatory options are more credible. However, even retaliating with conventional weapons raises the possibility that the challenger will respond by striking at an ally, hitting any assets the defender might have in the region, or possibly attacking the defender's homeland. A crucial factor is whether the challenger perceives the defender's retaliation as an existential threat aimed at regime change or simply as a proportional response to some action it has taken. If the challenger possesses even a small survivable nuclear force, the defender risks a nuclear detonation on its homeland, particularly if the challenger feels it has no other options. If the defender chooses to retaliate, therefore, it will go to great lengths to ensure that there is no surviving nuclear force, but it may not be certain of hitting all nuclear weapon targets. Thus, while conventional retaliation by the defender is more credible, it is not without potential risks. In a situation of primary deterrence, there is little doubt that a defender will accept this risk, but in extended deterrence, this is not a certainty.

EXTENDED DETERRENCE AND THE ALLY

Much of the literature on extended deterrence focuses on the actions, interactions, motivations, and decision making of the defender and the challenger. Far less attention has been paid to the role played by the ally in the relationship. During the early days of the Cold War, these deterrence relations often involved a strong defender such as the Soviet Union or the United States and an ally that was relatively weak. Many of these allies were recovering from the destruction of World War II or the Korean War. As the years passed, however, these relationships changed. Japan and South Korea, supported by U.S. military and economic aid and extended deterrence, rebuilt their economies, developed capable and technologically advanced militaries, and became important players in the global economic system.[69] Thus, the U.S. alliances with Japan and South Korea have evolved into relationships that resemble partnerships rather than the patron-client relations of old.[70] Moreover, both allies contribute far more to the alliances than was the case in the past. As a result, the role played by the ally has become central to the issue of deterrence.

One of the primary motivations of the ally in an extended deterrence relationship is to obtain protection from the defender. For a variety of reasons, the ally may be too weak to secure its own defense, or it faces a challenger that is a global power that only an alliance with another global power can balance. Most of the time, the situation may be one of general deterrence, with adversarial relations between the defender/ally and challenger but no imminent threat of attack. On occasion, however, the situation may shift toward one of immediate deterrence, prompting the defender to issue specific warnings and counterthreats to buttress its security commitment. The ally will watch closely the actions of the defender and may lobby it for more robust assurances of the defense commitment. Thus, while the defender seeks to protect its ally and provide credible threats to the challenger, it is also working to reassure and demonstrate the credibility of its commitment to its protégé.

This raises an interesting issue about the nuclear umbrella. As noted previously, there is significant evidence that states are very reluctant to use nuclear weapons, except possibly when their own survival is at stake. In extended deterrence, the defender may be much more reluctant to use nuclear weapons because their use might severely damage its reputation and escalate the conflict while bringing destruction to the region and possibly to the defender's homeland. Thus, proclamations to include an ally under its nuclear umbrella and threats to use nuclear weapons if deterrence fails have serious credibility problems. Allies must have similar questions about the credibility of these commitments, yet are likely to continue to ask to be included under the nuclear umbrella. Indeed, given the uncertainties inherent in extended deterrence, allies may be overbearing in their calls for reassurance so that defenders can never say "I love you" often enough to fully assure allies.

The answer may lie in the different arenas in which the nuclear umbrella operates. While there may be significant questions in the security realm about the credibility of the commitment, in the political and psychological realms the nuclear umbrella may continue to provide important elements of reassurance for alliance partners. Providing a nuclear umbrella is a commitment of considerable magnitude, and not all allies receive such a pledge. Thus, even though the nuclear umbrella may have credibility problems, it is a significant indicator of the overall importance of an ally to a defender. Particularly if the security commitment has been in place for a long time, the nuclear umbrella may become part of the alliance security architecture. To remove the umbrella based on the lack of credibility may be a serious negative political signal and a modification of the status quo that would be very disturbing to allies.

An alliance and the defender's nuclear umbrella may play another important role as well. The presence of important interests with high stakes for the defender is a crucial element of a credible extended deterrence commitment. Yet the interests of the defender and the ally may not be the same. While the defender's chief goal is to protect the ally, the ally may have other, more offensive ambitions against the challenger. With a credible alliance in place, the protégé may believe it has the cover to be aggressive, knowing the defender will come to its rescue should any provocative venture go badly.[71] However, the alliance also gives the defender leverage to exert some degree of restraint over the ally. Consequently, the security guarantee may play dual roles of both protecting the ally and restraining it from taking actions that could unsettle the region.

One of the key aspects of a nuclear umbrella is its contribution to nonproliferation goals. The defender may hope that so long as the ally remains under its nuclear umbrella and overall security commitment, the ally will not feel the need to acquire its own nuclear weapons capability. Failure to prevent a state from acquiring nuclear weapons could also create a domino effect, pushing others in the region to develop their own nuclear capability. For example, in East Asia, one of the chief concerns regarding North Korea's nuclear weapons program is that it could prod South Korea or Japan to go nuclear as well. Moreover, even if only one of these U.S. allies made the decision to go nuclear, the other would likely follow. Similar concerns are present for a nuclear Iran and the possibility of further proliferation in the Middle East. More nuclear-armed states would greatly complicate security relations, so from the U.S. vantage, the nuclear umbrella is as much about restraining the spread of nuclear weapons as it is about protecting its allies.

CONCLUSION

This chapter has addressed some of the important theoretical considerations regarding extended deterrence and the U.S. nuclear umbrella for Japan and South Korea. The U.S. commitment and the nuclear umbrella have long been a part of the regional security architecture, yet some questions about the credibility and dynamics of the U.S. nuclear umbrella remain. This chapter provides a framework for pursuing answers to these questions in subsequent chapters. In chapter 2, we turn to a historical overview of the nuclear umbrella in East Asia throughout the Cold War. While the nuclear umbrella was applied to both Japan and South Korea, the details of its implementation were very different, and these differences are critical to understanding the nuclear commitment today.

CHAPTER TWO

The Nuclear Umbrella and Extended Deterrence During the Cold War

Nuclear weapons were an important part of security calculations throughout the Cold War. The United States held a monopoly on nuclear weapons until 1949, when the Soviet Union conducted its first nuclear test. Eventually, Washington and Moscow developed nuclear arsenals that exceeded 10,000 nuclear warheads each, based on strategy and doctrine grounded in mutually assured destruction. Both countries relied on the "triad"—land-based intercontinental ballistic missiles (ICBMs), submarine-launched ballistic missiles (SLBMs), and bombers—to deliver their nuclear weapons, along with an array of tactical nuclear weapons that included nuclear artillery shells, nuclear-tipped missiles, land mines, and depth charges. These weapons were intended to deter an attack on each other's homeland but also to defend allies through extended deterrence and the maintenance of a nuclear umbrella.

For those under the U.S. umbrella, Washington sought to deter their adversaries while reassuring allies that the United States would use nuclear weapons for their defense. In addition to the nuclear weapons available in the United States, nuclear weapons were sometimes based on the ally's home territory, as was the case with Japan, South Korea, and Europe. This chapter will examine the role nuclear weapons played in Japanese and South Korean security during the Cold War, including the origins of the U.S. nuclear umbrella and the role it played in Cold War security planning.

JAPAN

Japan's experience with nuclear weapons has been unique, intimate, and horrible. During World War II, Japan embarked on a small-scale clandestine effort to develop nuclear weapons. The program was not a priority for military leaders and did not receive sufficient funding and attention to be successful.[1] However, on August 6 and August 9, 1945, the United States dropped atomic bombs on Hiroshima and Nagasaki to bring an end to the war. Though no one knows for certain, the initial effects of the bombing are believed to have killed approximately 130,000–150,000 in Hiroshima and another 60,000–70,000 in Nagasaki. Thousands more died in later years from burns, radiation poisoning, and other long-term effects.[2] These remain the only two instances in which nuclear weapons have been used in wartime.

Japanese are well aware of the long-term radiation effects that endure far beyond the blast. The *Hibakusha*, literally the "explosion-affected people," are those who survived but carry with them the effects of the explosion and radiation and have passed them on to succeeding generations. The Japanese government recognizes more than 227,500 *Hibakusha*, of whom approximately 1 percent have been afflicted with diseases caused by radiation.[3] The atomic bombs dropped on Hiroshima and Nagasaki left an indelible mark on Japan, creating a "nuclear allergy" that has affected the thinking of many Japanese about nuclear weapons ever since.

After World War II, the United States occupied Japan, determined to demilitarize and democratize the country. Measures included implementation of a "peace constitution"; in Article 9, Japan forever renounced "war as a sovereign right" and pledged that "land, sea, and air forces, as well as other war potential, will never be maintained."[4] As the Cold War intensified, Article 9 was interpreted to allow Japan to possess a self-defense force restricted to defending the homeland while focusing on rebuilding its economy after the devastation of World War II. The United States assumed the bulk of Japan's external defense in return for maintaining a number of bases on the main islands and on the island of Okinawa. On September 8, 1951, Washington and Tokyo codified these arrangements in the U.S.-Japan Security Treaty, which allowed the United States considerable latitude in how it used these facilities. Article I of the treaty stated:

Japan grants, and the United States of America accepts, the right, upon the coming into force of the Treaty of Peace and of this Treaty, to dispose United States land, air and sea forces in and about Japan. Such forces may be utilized to contribute to the maintenance of international peace and security in the Far East and to the security of Japan against armed attack from without, including assistance given at the express request of the Japanese Government to put down largescale internal riots and disturbances in Japan, caused through instigation or intervention by an outside power or powers.[5]

The signing of the security agreement occurred on the same day as the signing of the peace treaty with Japan, also known as the San Francisco Treaty.

In 1955, Prime Minister Ichiro Hatoyama's response to a reporter's question indicated that the U.S. defense commitment could permit the deployment of U.S. nuclear weapons to Japan. Indeed, the United States regularly maintained nuclear weapons in Okinawa until the islands reverted to Japanese sovereignty in 1972.[6] Hatoyama's controversial remarks launched a heated debate about the issue. Politicians from the ruling Liberal Democratic Party (LDP) quieted the uproar when they announced an understanding they believed they had with U.S. authorities that Tokyo would be consulted before any such deployments took place. U.S. officials dismissed the idea of an understanding but accepted the need for the statement to calm domestic opposition.[7]

As the years passed, antinuclear sentiment grew among the Japanese public, though not among certain leadership circles. In 1954, the United States had conducted its first test of a hydrogen bomb at Bikini Atoll in the Marshall Islands. Code-named Castle Bravo, the test generated nuclear fallout that poisoned the crew of a Japanese fishing boat, the *Lucky Dragon*, raising serious concerns in Japan and internationally about nuclear testing and nuclear weapons. In 1955, the Japanese Diet passed the Atomic Energy Basic Act, which stated that "research, development, and utilization of atomic energy shall be limited to peaceful purposes."[8]

Despite strong public opposition to nuclear weapons, conservatives believed that Japan should consider acquiring its own nuclear arsenal. Prime Ministers Ichiro Hatoyama (1954–1956), Tanzan Ishibashi (1956), and Nobusuke Kishi (1956–1960) wanted Japan to rearm but faced strong public opposition and serious budget constraints.[9] They believed the solution to this problem was for Japan to build up other facets of its national strength and address conventional shortfalls by acquiring nuclear weapons. In 1957, Prime Minister Kishi told the Diet that because nuclear weapons were defensive in nature, Japan could acquire them without violating Article 9.[10]

In 1959, U.S. and Japanese officials began discussions on revising the 1951 security treaty. During these meetings, the Ministry of Foreign Affairs asserted that Japan should not rule out the possibility of acquiring nuclear weapons sometime in the future. However, the new agreement, the Treaty of Mutual Cooperation and Security Between the United States and Japan, signed January 19, 1960, made no mention of extended deterrence or the U.S. nuclear umbrella. Despite his personal opposition, Prime Minister Hayato Ikeda considered acquiring nuclear weapons based largely on budget considerations and criticism he received from French president Charles de Gaulle for Japan's overreliance on Washington for its security.[11] However, he decided not to pursue the matter.

The nuclear issue surfaced again in October 1964 when China conducted its first nuclear test. Beijing followed with its first nuclear-capable missile test in October 1966 and its first hydrogen bomb test in June 1967. Japanese leaders were very concerned for their security, given the continued rivalry with China, but also that Beijing had passed them by in the military and technological competition represented by nuclear weapons. In November 1964, the China Division in the Japanese Foreign Ministry wrote a memorandum that stated "China will possess nuclear weapons earlier than expected, and its military implications are being reevaluated internationally. [China] has gotten to the stage of being capable of exerting pressure on neighboring countries not only psychologically, but also militarily."[12]

Soon after China's test, Prime Minister Eisaku Satō raised the issue of Japan's acquiring nuclear weapons with U.S. ambassador Edwin O. Reischauer. The issue was sensitive because some Japanese feared entrapment in a U.S. war, including a possible nuclear exchange with the Soviet Union or resumption of hostilities in Korea. Given the number of U.S. bases and personnel located in Japan, leaders in Tokyo feared the likelihood of a preemptive strike on these facilities, along with any Japanese nuclear weapons sites, should Washington ever go to war against Moscow or Beijing. In December 1964, a telegram from the U.S. Embassy in Tokyo recounted a meeting in which Prime Minister Satō told the U.S. ambassador to Japan

> if [the] other fellow had nuclear [weapon]s it was only common sense to have them oneself. Japanese public he realized was not ready for this but would have to be educated to this point, and he felt younger generation showed hopeful signs of going this way. Nuclear [weapon]s he had discovered were much less costly than was generally assumed and Japanese scientific and industrial level was fully up to producing them. He then hastily added that, of course, Japan had none of the "imperialistic" ambitions of past so U.S. should not be worried by what he said.[13]

The following month, in a meeting with President Lyndon Johnson and Secretary of State Dean Rusk, Satō stated that the Japanese public believed that Japan should never possess nuclear weapons and that "although he could see why it might be argued that if China has nuclear weapons, Japan should also, this was not Japan's policy."[14]

Extending the U.S. Nuclear Umbrella Over Japan

While Japan continued its commitment to not possessing nuclear weapons, it did seek assurances from the United States that Washington would use nuclear weapons to defend it against an attack from China. During his January 1965 visit to the United States and meeting with President Johnson, Satō asked Johnson for a commitment of the U.S. nuclear umbrella. According to a U.S. memorandum from the meeting:

> The President said in reply to a question that Prime Minister phrased about defense that, since Japan possesses no nuclear weapons, and we do have them, if Japan needs our nuclear deterrent for its defense, the United States would stand by its commitments and provide that defense. The President asked whether that struck at the heart of the Prime Minister's question. The Prime Minister

confirmed that that is what he would like to ask but said that he is unable to say so publicly. The President said that his reply on the defense of Japan is affirmative.[15]

The joint statement that followed the meeting made no mention of the nuclear umbrella but stated "that it is essential for the stability and peace of Asia that there be no uncertainty about Japan's security" and affirmed the U.S. "determination to abide by its commitment under the Treaty to defend Japan against any armed attack from the outside."[16]

In all likelihood, Satō was not serious about acquiring nuclear weapons, but Washington was surprised to hear the prime minister express this possibility. Indeed, Satō's ruminations about Japanese nuclear weapons may have been intended to assist in drawing out Johnson's nuclear commitment.[17] It was clear that the Johnson administration would oppose any attempt by Japan to acquire nuclear weapons, and after the meeting Satō gave a speech at the National Press Club in Washington, DC, where he declared Japan would not go nuclear. His earlier intimations were more an indication of what he and subsequent Japanese leaders would do to ensure a solid U.S. security guarantee.[18]

In 1967, Prime Minister Satō again sought reassurance of the nuclear umbrella from the Johnson administration, reminding the president of his 1965 commitment. According to a meeting memo between Satō and Johnson on November 15:

> At present Japan is secure under the U.S.-Japan Security Treaty, which provides that the United States will defend Japan against external attack. However, Communist China is developing nuclear weapons and Japan may soon be threatened by a nuclear attack. More than two years ago, the President assured the Prime Minister that the United States would live up to her commitment to defend Japan "against any form of attack." He said he wished to ask the President to reconfirm this assurance at this time because of the concern expressed by the Emperor and in view of the discussions on the status of Okinawa. The President [Johnson] said the United States is committed and as long as he is President we would carry out this commitment.[19]

Again, the joint statement that followed the 1967 summit was silent on the nuclear umbrella, noting only that "Communist China is developing its nuclear arsenal and [the United States and Japan] agreed on the importance of creating conditions wherein Asian nations would not be susceptible to threats from Communist China" and that it was "the fundamental policy of both countries to maintain firmly the Treaty of Mutual Cooperation and Security between the United States and Japan in order to ensure the security of Japan and the peace and security of the Far East."[20]

Thus, despite the existence of a formal security alliance that pledged the United States to defend Japan, Prime Minister Satō continued to seek the reassurance of the U.S. nuclear umbrella. He believed the nuclear umbrella helped allay fears that a nuclear-capable China would be a psychological threat pushing Japan toward a neutral position in the region.[21] In 1975, President Gerald Ford provided the first public commitment of the nuclear umbrella in a joint statement with Japanese prime minister Takeo Miki, in which "they recognized that the United States nuclear deterrent is an important contributor to the security of Japan."[22] However, the U.S. commitment remained a relatively quiet, informal guarantee between U.S. and Japanese leaders.

Establishing Japan's Formal Position on Nuclear Weapons

While the nuclear umbrella was established behind closed doors, in December 1967 Prime Minister Satō made a formal pronouncement to the Diet establishing Japan's public position on nuclear weapons, as outlined in the Three Non-Nuclear Principles. These principles became the cornerstone of Japan's nuclear policy, declaring that it would not possess, manufacture, or allow nuclear weapons on Japanese territory. A few months later, fearing the prime minister might have gone too far,[23] the Satō government expanded these principles into the Four Pillars. The first pillar encompassed the three nonnuclear principles; the remaining three were the promotion of nuclear power for peaceful purposes, support for global nuclear disarmament, and reliance on the U.S. nuclear umbrella for protection against nuclear threats. This last pillar was Japan's first public acknowledgment of the role of the U.S. nuclear umbrella in its security.

While Satō proclaimed publicly Japan's determination to forgo nuclear weapons and its reliance on the U.S. nuclear umbrella, his private views were different. In a 1969 meeting with Prime Minister Satō and others, U.S. ambassador Alexis Johnson reported that, to the "astonishment of Hori (Chief Cabinet Secretary) and Togo (chief of the Foreign Ministry Security Affairs Department), who were also present, he [Satō] said that GOJ's 'three nuclear principles' (non-possession, non-production and non-introduction) were 'nonsense'. However, this should not be interpreted to mean Japan wants to have nuclear weapons."[24]

Prime Minister Satō was likely influenced by the results of a secret study that concluded its work in September 1968. The Study Group on Democracy, commissioned in 1966 to assess Japan's nuclear policy, was composed of government officials, journalists, and academics. Its report concluded that Japan's civilian nuclear power program provided the option of developing nuclear weapons at some point in the future but that, for a number of reasons, it was not prudent to pursue that option at this time.[25] Among the reasons noted were the technical, geographic, and economic difficulties of maintaining a credible nuclear force; the dangers of a divisive domestic debate, given the continued strength of the "nuclear allergy"; the negative impact nuclear weapons might have on regional relations and the military balance; the international condemnation and isolation that would likely follow; and the possibility of some type of preemptive action by China or the Soviet Union. Given International Atomic Energy Agency (IAEA) oversight of its civilian nuclear program, any attempt to develop weapons was likely to be detected, precluding the possibility of a clandestine nuclear program. Moreover, if Japan developed nuclear weapons, it would not be able to sign the recently concluded Nuclear Nonproliferation Treaty (NPT); as a result, Tokyo would be cut off from U.S. assistance in developing its civilian nuclear energy program and would lose the U.S. nuclear umbrella.[26]

Thus, the report concluded that developing nuclear weapons had a number of serious potential costs and would do little to enhance Japanese security. Other government studies followed and reached similar conclusions. One such effort was commissioned in the early 1970s by then defense chief Yasuhiro Nakasone, who supported Tokyo's efforts to explore a nuclear weapons option. The study concluded that the U.S. nuclear umbrella remained the most viable alternative because developing nuclear weapons would be costly, consuming close to 40 percent of Japan's defense budget. Moreover, Japan lacked the geographic size to test nuclear weapons, the basing facilities to house them, and the proper technology for delivery systems.[27] Consequently, Japan's best route was to maintain its security relationship with the United States, including the commitment of the U.S. nuclear umbrella, while keeping a latent capability to develop nuclear weapons should future circumstances warrant.

In 1970, the Japanese Defense Agency, which transitioned to a cabinet-level Ministry of Defense in 2007, published its first White Paper, in which the Japanese government publicly acknowledged its hedging strategy.[28] A Japanese press report described the "gist" of its nuclear policy as follows: "as for defensive nuclear weapons, it is considered that Japan may have them in theory, without contradicting the Constitution. In view of the danger of inviting adverse foreign reactions and large-scale war, Japan will follow the policy of not acquiring nuclear weapons at present."[29] In addition, the White Paper noted, "Japan relies on the U.S. deterrent for defense against nuclear wars or large-scale wars."[30] Japan repeated its reliance on the U.S. nuclear umbrella in the 1976 National Defense Program Outline, the first document of this sort published by Japan and one of the foundation documents of Japanese defense planning.[31] Most recently, the 2014 National Defense Program Guidelines call for Japan to take a more active role in its own defense and deterrence while maintaining the importance of the Japan-U.S. alliance and U.S. extended deterrence.[32] Thus, Japanese leaders cemented the importance of the U.S. nuclear umbrella for Japanese security but maintained the potential for breaking out with its own nuclear weapons program, in part to hedge against any serious changes in the international security environment and also to tie down the U.S. nuclear umbrella.

The NPT, Okinawa, and the U.S. Nuclear Umbrella

Japanese leaders faced two other issues that affected their decision making on nuclear weapons during the Cold War: the NPT and the reversion of Okinawa to Japanese sovereignty. Both issues were closely tied to Prime Minister Satō's promulgation of the three nonnuclear principles and together were part of a complex policy on nuclear weapons.

Nuclear Nonproliferation Treaty

Drafts of the NPT began to circulate in 1966, and criticism of the agreement quickly surfaced in Japan from several quarters—concerns that were echoed by other U.S. allies in Asia. Those who opposed nuclear weapons supported the NPT in principle but believed it did not go far enough in committing the nuclear weapons states to disarmament. Article VI of the treaty contained only vague language that called on all parties "to pursue negotiations in good faith on effective measures relating to cessation of the nuclear arms race at an early date and to nuclear disarmament, and on a Treaty on general and complete disarmament under strict and effective international control."[33] For these opponents, the treaty was too weak to effectively lead to the abolition of nuclear weapons.

Many in the ruling LDP and the Satō administration had other misgivings. Because Japan would be signing as a nonnuclear state, critics feared the NPT would relegate Japan to a second-class position relative to other world powers. The NPT would also foreclose the option of Japan's developing nuclear weapons in the future. In December 1967, Takeo Fukuda maintained, "the majority of the Liberal Democrats see the need to outgrow the 'nuclear allergy.'"[34] Others feared that the NPT might also place restrictions on Japan's growing civilian nuclear power program.[35] In 1966, Vice Foreign Minister Shimoda lamented that "Japan cannot agree to such a big power–centered approach, implying as it does that the nuclear powers would not be required to reduce their capabilities or stockpile, while the non-nuclear powers would be barred in this treaty from having nuclear weapons."[36] Later in 1966, the foreign affairs minister, Ushiba Nobuhiko, complained to the State Department's country director for Japan that the NPT was based on an inherent inequality that locked Japan into a second-tier status.[37]

Despite these reservations, Satō signed the NPT on February 3, 1970, after Germany had signed in December 1969. Japan was one of the last countries to do so and took another six years to ratify the agreement. In fact, it is likely Satō concluded that he had little choice but to sign, because Japanese participation was important to U.S. leaders and Japan remained heavily dependent on Washington for its own security. However, Satō announced Japan's intention to sign shortly before Tokyo and Washington began talks on another key issue with nuclear implications, the reversion of Okinawa.

Reversion of Okinawa

When Japan signed the formal surrender documents in September 1945, all Japanese territory came under the control of the U.S. occupation. In September 1951, close to fifty countries signed the San Francisco Treaty with Japan. Article 3 of the treaty placed the Ryukyu Islands, which included Okinawa, under U.S. authority, and the Pentagon proceeded to establish several important military bases there. These facilities included the deployment of nuclear weapons so that, according to one source, Japan became a major logistics hub for U.S. nuclear weapons in Asia.[38] Nuclear weapons were also stored in Iwo Jima and Chichi Jima, two islands in the Bonin chain that were also Japanese but under U.S. administrative control.[39] Though an "open secret" for years, in February 2016 newly declassified documents acknowledged that the United States had maintained nuclear weapons on Okinawa for years prior to the 1972 reversion.[40] U.S. officials understood that storing nuclear weapons on the Japanese main islands would have been a problem for the ruling LDP. Consequently, one report noted that the United States also had "nuclear bombs (sans their fissile cores) stored on the mainland at Misawa and Itazuki airbases (and possibly at Atsugi, Iwakuni, Johnson, and Komaki airbases as well)."[41]

In a meeting with U.S. ambassador Alexis Johnson in July 1967, Japanese foreign minister Takeo Miki presented a memorandum that strongly urged the United States to consider the return of Okinawa. The communication recognized the importance of U.S. bases remaining intact but noted that growing domestic pressure in Japan and Okinawa necessitated resolving the issue. Failure to do so, according to the document, entailed "a risk that it may be taken advantage of by forces bent on driving a wedge in Japanese-U.S. relations. There is also a risk that it may cause trouble to the operation of bases on Okinawa."[42] Talks began to address the return, but a key sticking point was the U.S. wish to retain nuclear weapons on Okinawa after it reverted to Japan. The Nixon administration and the Pentagon voiced strong opposition to the removal of U.S. nuclear weapons. A State Department briefing document produced for Secretary of State William Rogers prior to his trip to Japan in July 1969 called on the secretary to "reiterate our need to retain nuclear weapons on Okinawa in order to avoid diminishing the credibility of our deterrent and to permit us to fulfill our security commitment to Japan and other countries in the area. We understand the Japanese attitude toward nuclear weapons but believe they are an important element in our deterrent posture."[43]

Though not entirely certain, it appears that Satō decided sometime in 1968 that he needed to insist on the reversion of Okinawa without the presence of U.S. nuclear weapons. In March 1969, he announced to the Diet his position that Okinawa would be viewed the same as the Japanese main islands and that the United States must not maintain nuclear weapons there. Satō declared that he had instructed his ambassador to the United States, Takeso Shimoda, to start talks with Washington from that position.[44]

Though Satō would have personally supported the retention of U.S. nuclear weapons in Okinawa, domestic opposition to this move was strong, and it was a battle Satō did not want to fight. Moreover, the U.S.-Japan Mutual Security Treaty was up for renewal in 1970, and he did not want a repetition of the massive demonstrations that occurred when the treaty was approved in 1960, something that was sure to occur if the United States retained nuclear weapons in Okinawa. As a result, Satō appears to have announced his willingness to sign the NPT shortly before Okinawa talks began to gain concessions from Washington on the Okinawa issue. In addition, Japanese leaders noted that the retention of nuclear weapons on Okinawa would be inconsistent with the three nonnuclear principles and likely to provoke a strong negative reaction from several sectors of the Japanese public.

Satō journeyed to Washington in November 1969 for a summit meeting with Richard Nixon. In their joint communiqué, the two leaders agreed to "immediately enter into consultations regarding specific arrangements for accomplishing the early reversion of Okinawa," hopefully by 1972.[45] The communiqué also noted Prime Minister Satō's concern for "the particular sentiment of the Japanese people against nuclear weapons and the policy of the Japanese Government reflecting such sentiment."[46] While this was the communiqué released to the public, in secret the two leaders were adding an important rider to the reversion of Okinawa. During summit discussions, Nixon acknowledged that Okinawa "would be placed on 'homeland level' as reversion took place," an indication that U.S. nuclear weapons would not remain, but queried "what would happen in an emergency?"[47] Both leaders agreed that a formal mention of nuclear weapons in the joint statement would be problematic.

To support the language contained in the joint statement, Satō and Nixon signed a secret "agreed minute" in which Nixon requested that "in time of great emergency the United States Government will require the re-entry of nuclear weapons and transit rights in Okinawa with prior consultation with the Government of Japan. The United States Government would anticipate a favorable response." Satō replied that the government of Japan "will meet these requirements without delay when such prior consultation takes place."[48] In June 1971, the Japanese government signed the agreement with the United States that certified the reversion of Okinawa to Japan, and the Diet ratified it in November 1971. On May 17, 1972, Okinawa formally reverted to Japanese administrative control.

Though Okinawa was settled, U.S.-Japan relations remained difficult during the Nixon years. As the Japanese economy continued its phenomenal growth, trade friction increased. The Nixon Doctrine, calling for a reduction of the U.S. presence in the region, was announced with no consultation with Tokyo and accompanied by greater demands for Japanese burden sharing. Some U.S. officials indicated that Japan should consider acquiring its own nuclear weapons, possibly in an effort to encourage Japanese leaders to spend more on their own defense—an interesting reversal of Japan's frequent use of the "nuclear card" to extract greater assurances from the United States. In Japan, the "nuclear allergy" and public sentiment to refrain from acquiring nuclear weapons remained strong, but not among some Japanese conservatives, who continued to chafe at the second-class status this implied. Kiichi Miyazawa, former minister of international trade and industry, lamented in December 1971:

> Recent events have been influenced by distinctions between "first-rate" and "second-rate" nations, using nuclear capabilities and atomic stockpiles as yardsticks.... If the major nations of the world who have nuclear capabilities try to be too assertive and push Japan

around too much and too far, they may run the risk of opening up what they most want to avoid. There is already a body of opinion in Japan which feels that dependence on the US nuclear umbrella is basically incompatible with our national sovereignty. When the coming generations assume a greater role in the society, they may want to choose the lesser of two evils and opt to build their own umbrella instead of renting their neighbor's, if only to satisfy their desire to be their own masters. This may become likelier as time passes and memories of Hiroshima and Nagasaki recede.[49]

Much of the debate regarding nuclear weapons and the U.S. nuclear umbrella quieted down after Japan ratified the NPT on June 8, 1976. Concerns for North Korea's nuclear ambitions, along with its ballistic missile tests and growing tensions with China, would raise the profile of the U.S. nuclear umbrella in the years ahead.

SOUTH KOREA

Nuclear Weapons and the Korean War

Nuclear weapons first played a major role in ROK security during the Korean War. North Korean forces rolled across the thirty-eighth parallel on June 25, 1950, in a bid to reunify the peninsula after it was divided at the conclusion of World War II. Pyongyang almost succeeded as it pushed South Korean forces and a small remnant of U.S. troops and advisers to a perimeter in southeastern Korea around the city of Busan. The defenders within the "Busan perimeter" hung on until U.S. and UN forces joined the war and began to push North Korean soldiers back up the peninsula. On September 15, 1950, General Douglas MacArthur, the commander of the United Nations Command (UNC) that led U.S./UN troops, landed an invasion force at Incheon on the western coast of Korea, leading to a hasty retreat of North Korean forces back across the thirty-eighth parallel. U.S. leaders now faced a difficult decision. Should they be content with restoring the status quo of a divided Korea or continue north to reunify the peninsula and eject the communist government of Kim Il-sung? President Truman concluded that this was an opportunity that should not be passed up, and U.S./UN troops continued their advance. As U.S./UN forces moved closer to the Yalu River that forms the border between North Korea and China, Beijing warned, through Indian intermediaries, that it would not tolerate the presence of these troops so close to the border and in late October began moving forces into North Korea. General MacArthur and U.S. officials dismissed the warning and continued the drive to reunite the peninsula. As U.S./UN troops approached the Yalu—Amnok to Koreans—on November 26, 1950, Chinese "volunteers" launched a massive assault that drove U.S./UN soldiers into a hurried retreat south. By spring 1951, the war had ground to a stalemate along a front that was close to the war's starting position along the thirty-eighth parallel. The war continued for another two years before leaders concluded an armistice agreement in July 1953.

U.S. leaders considered using nuclear weapons at three points during the conflict: in June 1950, immediately following the attack on South Korea; in November 1950, when Chinese troops entered the war in earnest and drove U.S./UN forces back down the peninsula; and in spring 1953, when armistice negotiations dragged on, greatly increasing U.S. frustration at the apparent communist intransigence.[50] When the invasion began, U.S. leaders were convinced the attack was instigated by the Soviets and the Chinese.[51] After the war, Secretary of State Dean Acheson maintained that the invasion of Korea had confirmed that "the USSR was willing to use forces in battle to achieve objectives."[52] An intelligence estimate prepared by the State Department maintained that "the North Korean Government is completely under Kremlin control and there is no possibility that the North Korean's acted without prior instruction from Moscow."[53] As a result, U.S. leaders feared the possibility of escalating the conflict and drawing the Soviets in further. Washington gave some initial consideration to using nuclear weapons, with extensive debate among members of the Truman administration along with the Departments of State and Defense, and did some initial planning for nuclear operations. However, the State Department was vociferous in its concerns about using nuclear weapons because of the moral outrage that would likely be directed against Washington and the diminution of U.S. global leadership that would result from their use. A State Department report completed in early November 1950 argued that if the United States were to use atomic weapons instead of conventional ones, even for the same goal, "the effect on world opinion will be vastly different. The A-bomb has the status of a peculiar monster conceived by American cunning, and its use by us in whatever situation would be exploited to our serious detriment."[54] Any use of atomic weapons in Korea, the report continued, would damage the "moral position" of the United States if it were undertaken unilaterally without UN sanction. Such use would likely destroy the unity of the UN coalition, and "U.S. use of the A-bomb would be deplored and denounced by a considerable number of nations who had up to that time supported the action in Korea."[55] Finally, dropping an A-bomb on the Chinese would elevate "fears that we reserve atomic weapons exclusively for Japanese and Chinese."[56] In the end, based on moral concerns and tactical issues, President Truman chose not to employ atomic weapons.

When Chinese "volunteers" joined the war in November 1950, Truman again considered using nuclear weapons to stem the tide. In a session with reporters on November 30, 1950, Truman declared that using nuclear weapons in Korea had always been a consideration and that the decision to do so rested with commanders in the field. Shortly after, the administration clarified that the decision to use nuclear weapons remained with the president. Strong messages of disapproval, even after the clarification on authorization, came from Britain and France, among others.[57] In a press conference with reporters, Truman was asked a question about possible U.S. use of atomic weapons in Korea. After first implying that MacArthur might be given the authority to order their use, he maintained that we would use "every weapon that we have." Responding to the reporter's follow-up question, Truman continued: "There has always been active consideration of its use. I don't want to see it used. It is a terrible weapon, and it should not be used on innocent men, women, and children who have nothing whatever to do with this military aggression. That happens when it is used."[58] Soon after, the White House issued another clarification that only the president is authorized to order the use of nuclear weapons and that "naturally, there has been consideration of this subject [using nuclear weapons] since the outbreak of the hostilities in Korea, just as there is consideration of the use of all military weapons whenever our forces are in combat."[59] Taking the war to China also raised the possibility of drawing the Soviets into the conflict. In February 1950, Beijing and Moscow signed the Sino-Soviet Treaty of Friendship, Alliance, and Mutual Assistance. Some feared that nuclear strikes against

China might prod the Russians to invoke the treaty and come to their ally's assistance. However, there was disagreement over whether Russian intervention was likely and might be worth chancing.[60]

President Truman's pronouncements raised a good bit of concern, particularly among some U.S. allies and others in the international community. In December 1950, British prime minister Clement Attlee traveled to Washington for a meeting with U.S. officials to obtain, among other things, a clarification on the U.S. intent to use nuclear weapons. British officials were determined to receive a pledge from Washington that it would only use nuclear weapons in consultation with London. In the communiqué that followed the December 8 meeting, Truman noted "that it was his hope that world conditions would never call for the use of the atomic bomb" and "that it was also his desire to keep the Prime Minister [Atlee] at all times informed of developments which might bring about a change in the situation."[61] After further deliberations, including consensus between the Departments of State and Defense, the administration decided to postpone any use of nuclear weapons. Despite some tactical and military arguments, Truman was greatly disturbed by the moral dimensions of ordering another nuclear strike. In his memoirs, Dean Rusk details the following story:

> More fundamentally, Harry Truman was not a man who would use nuclear blackmail. Truman's abhorrence of nuclear weapons is well illustrated by an incident during the Korean War when he was meeting with the Joint Chiefs of Staff to discuss military plans.
>
> One of the chiefs remarked, "If the Chinese enter the war, this will mean the use of atomic weapons." Harry Truman came out of his chair, turned to the general, and said, "Who told you that?" The general said, "That's part of our strategic doctrine." Truman said, "you are not going to put me in that position. You'd better go back and get yourself some more strategic doctrine!"[62]

According to T. V. Paul,

> Truman's reluctance to use nuclear weapons in Korea was thus caused largely by two fundamental factors: the concerns regarding creating a bad reputation worldwide if Washington used nuclear

weapons again in Asia, and the tactical/strategic unsuitability of the weapon for the particular military goal. A close reading of the documents and statements, however, show [sic] that the reputation concerns were more prominent than tactical considerations.⁶³

Nina Tannenwald concurs with Paul's assessment, noting, "Moral concerns on the part of some officials about using such a disproportionate weapon and perceived opposition from world publics and leaders, including accusations of racism, had an inhibiting effect on Truman and his advisors during the war."⁶⁴

In January 1953, Dwight Eisenhower entered the White House determined to bring an end to the conflict in Korea. Though Eisenhower had several concerns about using nuclear weapons—the reaction of U.S. allies, drawing the Soviets into the war, and the vulnerability of Japanese cities to possible retaliation—he believed that threats to use nuclear weapons could speed up armistice talks at Panmunjom. Consequently, in May 1953, Secretary of State John Foster Dulles informed Indian prime minister Jawaharlal Nehru that the United States would not be responsible for using nuclear weapons in Korea if a successful truce could not be arranged, with the understanding that this message would be communicated to leaders in Beijing.⁶⁵ Similar messages indicating U.S. willingness to use nuclear weapons, possibly against the Chinese homeland, were conveyed through officials at the talks in Panmunjom.⁶⁶ Eisenhower and many in his administration were convinced that the nuclear threats had worked to prod Chinese and North Korean compliance at the talks, but studies have disputed this causal link.⁶⁷ In the end, despite several opportunities to use nuclear weapons to achieve military and political goals, Presidents Truman and Eisenhower declined to do so.

The U.S. decision to refrain from using nuclear weapons during the Korea War raises an intriguing question. Did this U.S. reluctance affect South Korea's or Japan's later assessments of the credibility of the U.S. nuclear umbrella? The research collected for this project found no indication to suggest that it did. Though evidence may exist to the contrary, it seems likely that in the early days of the alliances, the credibility of the U.S. nuclear umbrella was superseded by larger concerns for the overall alliances, with or without U.S. nuclear weapons. In South Korea, later U.S. actions such as Nixon's reduction of U.S. ground forces and closer relations with China would raise concerns for the larger strategic relationship, but U.S. nuclear restraint during the Korean War appeared to add little more to the worry ROK leaders were already feeling. Moreover, with nuclear weapons already deployed in Korea, the credibility of the nuclear umbrella may have seemed less important than the larger alliance relationship. In Japan's case, there appeared to be little concern for U.S. nuclear credibility based on the Korean War.

Nuclear Weapons, Deterrence, and the Cold War in Korea

Though nuclear weapons were never used during the Korean War, it was not long after the conflict that the United States began to consider deploying nuclear weapons to the peninsula to enhance U.S. extended deterrence for South Korea. When the war ended, U.S. leaders believed they had done a poor job signaling U.S. determination to defend the Republic of Korea. To remedy this situation, Washington extended a formal security guarantee to Seoul through a Mutual Security Treaty, signed in October 1953 and approved by the Senate in January 1954. In addition, the United States stationed a significant number of combat troops close to the demilitarized zone (DMZ) and along the major invasion routes from the north to the south. These troops, the Seventh and Second U.S. Infantry Divisions, acted as a trip wire so that a North Korean attack would contact U.S. troops and ensure a U.S. response to the invasion. The United States also supplied significant military and economic aid to build South Korea's own defense capabilities and demonstrate the importance of this alliance. All of these measures were intended to demonstrate a credible extended deterrence commitment to dissuade North Korea from attacking again.[68]

Two years after the Korean War ended, U.S. leaders began to deliberate the possibility of deploying nuclear weapons to buttress the American commitment. Consideration of this measure was part of a larger concern with communist violations of the 1953 armistice agreement. Subparagraph 13(d) of the agreement prohibited the introduction of military equipment not present at the time of its signing. However, obsolete weapons could be replaced "on the basis of piece-for-piece of the same effectiveness and the same type."[69] U.S. leaders believed the military balance on the peninsula was slowly tipping as a result of arms shipments from the Soviet Union and China in violation of the agreement.[70]

To address the imbalance, U.S. officials considered broadening the interpretation of subparagraph 13(d) to allow for new weapons systems, or simply scrapping this portion of the armistice altogether. The decision was made more difficult by indications from the Pentagon that modernization of U.S. forces in Korea would include the deployment of nuclear-capable systems such as 280 mm artillery and Honest John missiles.[71] In fact, in November 1956, the U.S. Far East Command had developed a standard operating procedure for two locations in South Korea (Uijongbu and Anyang-Ni) that were suitable to receive nuclear weapons if the deployment occurred.[72]

After a debate that lasted more than a year, the Eisenhower administration chose to suspend subparagraph 13(d). On June 21, 1957, UNC authorities informed North Korea that the UNC was "relieved of corresponding obligations under the provisions of this paragraph [13(d)] until such time as the relative military balance has been restored and your side, by its actions, has demonstrated its willingness to comply."[73] However, U.S. officials deferred the decision to deploy nuclear weapons to a later date because there was little consensus on the wisdom of this action.

Disagreement came largely from two sources. The State Department was hesitant to deploy nuclear weapons as part of the modernization process. Secretary of State John Foster Dulles feared that they would be "very conspicuous weapons" and "resented throughout Asia," with too many political costs. Dulles agreed that the modernization of U.S. forces needed to occur, but if it included nuclear weapons, this would hand a propaganda victory to the communists.[74] The State Department did recognize that the introduction of nuclear weapons would permit a reduction in ROK troop strength from twenty to sixteen divisions, four fewer divisions for U.S. assistance to support. Accordingly, ROK President Syngman Rhee should implement the reductions before the U.S. introduced nuclear weapons.[75]

Vehement counterarguments were made by the Joint Chiefs of Staff and the Department of Defense. Modernizing U.S. forces in Korea was a "package deal" that required dual capable weapons such as Honest John Missiles in Pentomic divisions. The Korean War demonstrated that ROK and U.S. troops were vulnerable to a sudden massive DPRK assault across the border. The Pentagon believed a North Korean assault would eventually be brought to a halt by U.S.-ROK forces, but given Seoul's proximity, an invasion could not be allowed to progress far beyond the DMZ. Consequently, the Defense Department maintained "our number one reason" for deploying nuclear weapons in Korea was to prevent U.S.-ROK forces from being overrun in the initial phases of an attack.[76] U.S. defense planners believed 280 mm "dual capable" cannons were especially important because they provided "pinpoint means of delivering atomic munitions under all conditions of weather, and it is also an excellent conventional artillery piece."[77] These weapons would reassure ROK leaders of the U.S. commitment and encourage the South to maintain a smaller standing military, leading to cost savings for the United States. Introducing nuclear weapons at the same time as other modernization measures would draw less attention than if they were deployed separately at a later date.

President Eisenhower chose to proceed with modernization plans but delayed the deployment of nuclear weapons. Within a few months, he changed his mind and decided that nuclear weapons were indeed necessary but conditioned their deployment on South Korean troop reductions. President Rhee refused to reduce ROK force levels, and nuclear weapons were deployed despite Rhee's intransience. In January 1958, the first U.S. nuclear weapons—Honest John Missiles and 280 mm cannons with nuclear shells—arrived in Korea.[78]

Tactical nuclear weapons in Korea were part of the Eisenhower administration's "New Look" approach to defense. When the Korean War ended, Eisenhower was determined to bring the federal budget back under control from the excesses of wartime spending. Yet the United States also confronted an expanding Soviet conventional threat that was costly to match. Eisenhower's solution to this dilemma was greater reliance on nuclear weapons, both tactical and strategic. U.S. policy became known as "massive retaliation"; according to Dulles, the United States would respond to an adversary's aggression with its "great capacity to retaliate instantly and by means and at places of our own choosing."[79] As the Soviets began to acquire their own nuclear capability, U.S. massive retaliation threats, particularly to defend allies, became less credible. While the United States continued to depend on strategic nuclear weapons and "massive retaliation" for defense of the U.S.

homeland, deterring attacks on other areas relied on tactical nuclear weapons. Consequently, the deployment of tactical nuclear weapons to Europe and Korea became a central part of U.S. defense strategy.

U.S. officials considered the possibility of using nuclear weapons in Korea on two more occasions during late 1960s. In January 1968, North Korean gunboats seized the U.S. intelligence-gathering vessel *USS Pueblo* in international waters off the North Korean coast. After several frustrating months, in May 1968, the Pentagon developed a set of possible responses, code-named Operation Freedom Drop, that included "planning of a nuclear contingency plan against North Korea." [80] The following April, North Korea shot down a U.S. EC-121, an early warning and surveillance aircraft that was flying well away from DPRK airspace, killing all thirty-one Americans on board. In a report to Henry Kissinger, Richard Nixon's national security adviser, the Pentagon included, among a number of possible responses, three options for a "Nuclear Contingency Plan for North Korea," again named Operation Freedom Drop.[81] However, both Johnson and Nixon opted against a nuclear response.

For the next two decades, the United States adopted a "neither confirm nor deny" posture regarding nuclear weapons in Korea, but it was conventional wisdom that Washington had these weapons on the peninsula. In June 1975, Secretary of Defense James Schlesinger confirmed what most had assumed, acknowledging "we have deployed in Korea tactical nuclear weapons, as is, I believe, well known."[82] The acknowledgment was in part intended to reassure South Korean leaders following Nixon's 1971 withdrawal of a combat division from Korea and warming relations with China, as well as to ensure that Seoul did not pursue its own nuclear weapons. Though exact numbers are classified, sources estimate that the number of nuclear weapons in Korea during the 1960s and 1970s ranged from 600 to 800 warheads.[83] By the late 1980s, that number may have fallen to around 250.[84] U.S. nuclear weapons in Korea consisted of nuclear-tipped missiles (Honest John, Nike-Hercules, Matador, and Sergeant), nuclear artillery munitions, atomic demolitions mines (ADMs), and gravity bombs.[85] Nuclear artillery was the chief element of U.S. nuclear forces in Korea because it offset the numerically superior North Korean forces. A 1981 Defense Department report maintained that "because [nuclear munitions] are controllable and usable, their presence provides a real threat to enemy forces, reducing their effectiveness in massing to conduct a conventional battle."[86]

In a 1979 Defense Department report, the United States articulated its overall rationale for deploying tactical nuclear weapons:

> The U.S. theater nuclear forces have a symbolic importance that transcends their direct military value. They are the visible evidence of the broader U.S. commitment and of the linkage between our deployed posture and the strategic nuclear forces.... It continues to be U.S. policy that we will resist attacks on the United States and its allies by whatever necessary means, including nuclear weapons....
> They [nuclear weapons] also dramatize to a potential attacker that any conventional attack could set off a chain of nuclear escalation, the consequences of which would be incalculable.[87]

For the first two decades, U.S. nuclear weapons in South Korea were positioned close to the DMZ, allowing them to be moved forward rapidly in wartime. Artillery shells and ADMs were to be moved forward by truck and helicopter in case of hostilities.

By the 1970s, some U.S. officials began to recognize the problems associated with deploying U.S. nuclear weapons to Korea. One U.S. missile system, the Nike-Hercules, was forward deployed and designed to hit targets in North Korea. However, the missiles were so far forward that one Defense Department official who was touring the sites proclaimed "they [Nikes] were on hilltops within artillery range of the North Koreans. We were all just appalled. They were like tiny little outposts within spitting distance of the North Koreans, like little castles on hilltops."[88] Soon after, the Pentagon dismantled the missiles, expressing shock that no one had previously recognized the danger of a nuclear deployment so close to the DMZ.[89]

The deployment of ADMs also raised serious concerns. The U.S. Army intended to use ADMs between the DMZ and Seoul to stop or disrupt a North Korean invasion before it moved too deeply into ROK territory. According to a press report, ADMs would

> block avenues of approach by cratering defiles [narrow valleys] or creating rubble; sever routes of communication by destroying

tunnels, bridges, roads, and canal locks; create areas of tree blow-down and forest fires; crater areas including frozen bodies of water subject to landings by hostile airmobile units, [and] create water barriers by the destruction of dams and reservoirs.[90]

However, it became clear, particularly as the metropolitan Seoul city limits expanded, that those weapons could not be used in proximity to the capital, given the blast damage and fallout that would likely occur. Moreover, ADMs were most likely stored at Kunsan Air Force Base, 140 to 150 miles from the DMZ. Strategic warning would be needed to move these weapons to forward positions which, given their role, would need to be close to the DMZ. Yet given these forward locations, ADMs would likely have to be used early in a conflict or risk being overrun by DPRK forces. In 1987, General Louis Menetry, Commander, U.S. Forces Korea, declaring that it was "pretty dumb" to deploy these weapons along the DMZ, had them dismantled and removed in the late 1980s.[91]

If deterrence should fail, U.S. military strategy intended early use of nuclear weapons to blunt a North Korean invasion by refusing to trade territory for time. Yet early use of nuclear weapons required that they be forward deployed. These positions made the weapons a likely target for a preemptive attack and generated a dangerous "use or lose" situation should U.S.-ROK forces fail to contain a North Korean advance, creating an unintended need for escalation to a nuclear conflict.

Finally, the use of tactical nuclear weapons in Korea would endanger U.S. and ROK military personnel and the South Korean people and might possibly drift over the Soviet Union, China, or Japan, contaminating battle zones and heightening tension between the United States and others in the region. Thus, by the late 1980s, as the Cold War was winding down, there was growing unease with the presence of U.S. nuclear weapons on the peninsula. In 1987, General Menetrey declared, "I do not envision any circumstance which . . . would require the use of nuclear weapons."[92] The following year, Lieutenant General John Cushman, commander of I Corps, which protected crucial approaches to Seoul, maintained that "nuclear weapons are no longer necessary for the defense of Korea" and that "actual use would be an appalling catastrophe even to the victor."[93] These assessments were followed by others that nuclear weapons were no longer necessary to counter a DPRK invasion and not worth the trouble.[94]

With few defending the military necessity of maintaining nuclear weapons in Korea, in October 1991 President George H. W. Bush revealed that the United States had begun the process of removing all U.S. nuclear weapons from the Korean peninsula. Bush hoped this move would encourage Pyongyang to forgo its nuclear weapons ambitions and comply with IAEA inspection demands that it had rebuffed. President Bush remarked in a news conference, "I think it's evidence of our good faith. I am convinced that the next move should be up to North Korea to meet the international standards to comply with the IAEA and other rules. But the main thing is they've got to dispel the mistrust that exists regarding North Korea and the way to do that is to be open, openness in terms of inspections."[95] The removal of nuclear weapons from Korea was also part of a larger effort to ensure the security of tactical nuclear weapons during the breakup of the Soviet Union. President Bush hoped that if the United States agreed to pull in its nuclear weapons from deployments abroad, it would encourage Soviet President Mikhail Gorbachev to do the same, making it more difficult for nuclear weapons to "stray" out of Soviet control.[96] In mid-December 1991, ROK President Roh Tae-woo announced that nuclear weapons were no longer present in South Korea.[97]

Throughout the time the United States deployed nuclear weapons to Korea, it also maintained a declared nuclear umbrella over South Korea. Since the late 1960s, Washington and Seoul have held the annual Security Consultative Meeting (SCM) where the U.S. secretary of defense and the ROK minister of defense meet to assess regional security threats, review defense cooperation, and reaffirm the importance of the alliance. Beginning in 1978 and every year after, the SCM joint communiqué has included language that reaffirms South Korea's inclusion under the U.S. nuclear umbrella.

CONCLUSION

The U.S. nuclear umbrella has been in place for many decades to support the U.S. security guarantee to Japan and South Korea, forming one part of a commitment that included a security treaty, economic and military aid, and troop deployments. The nuclear umbrella took different forms in both countries but had similar credibility problems.

The United States clearly had the capability to support a nuclear security commitment with a large arsenal of strategic and tactical nuclear weapons. Yet, as Soviet forces reached parity and China began to expand its nuclear forces, the umbrella became increasingly less credible. The effort to bridge the capability gap with tactical nuclear weapons that would presumably be easier to use also had serious problems. These weapons were eventually withdrawn from Japan and Korea, but the commitment of the nuclear umbrella remained.

The role of nuclear weapons in extended deterrence commitments in the early years of these alliances raises an interesting theoretical question. In the case of both Japan and South Korea, the U.S. nuclear umbrella was kept quiet, and even secret, for a number of years. For deterrence to be successful, deterrence theory maintains that adversaries must know that a particular capability is in play and the defender is willing to use it. In Japan's case, the commitment was made in secret between Johnson and Satō and remained so until Gerald Ford made the first public commitment, and the presence of nuclear weapons and the agreement to return them in a crisis remained secret for years. The nuclear commitment to South Korea was better known, but for years it was hardly a forceful pronouncement intended to deter adversaries.

In the case of Japan, there was always a need to account for domestic political sensitivities and the "nuclear allergy." Thus, while the overall Japan-U.S. alliance helped to reassure the Japanese public and deter its enemies, the U.S. nuclear umbrella had to remain quiet for many years and provided reassurance only for its leaders. In South Korea, the United States already had a large troop presence to act as a trip wire and deterrent. In the early years, tactical nuclear weapons were viewed more as an actual warfighting tool than a deterrent and thus did not require the same level of public knowledge. South Korean leaders likely knew of the presence of nuclear weapons, even though the U.S. did not confirm this publicly until 1975. Overall, it is safe to say that the messaging of the early years of the nuclear umbrella was muddled and remains open to debate and further research.

CHAPTER THREE

The Threats That Drive the Nuclear Umbrella

China and North Korea

An important starting point for examining the U.S. nuclear umbrella for Japan and South Korea is an assessment of the threats this commitment is intended to counter. During the Cold War, the United States extended a nuclear umbrella over Japan and South Korea to protect these regions from the Soviet Union, China, and North Korea. Since the end of the Cold War, Russia has been considered less of a threat, though a resurgent Russia under Putin remains a concern. Today, the chief threats are China and North Korea; however, Tokyo and Seoul have different assessments and prioritization of these threats.

For Japan, China is a serious, long-term strategic concern that could threaten its position in the region. While the possibility of a major war or invasion of the home islands is very remote, conflict in gray zones—areas of neither peace nor war—is of greater concern, along with the possibility that a small-scale or accidental clash could escalate. In particular, Japan worries about Chinese intimidation in contested areas such as the Senkaku islands (Diaoyu to the Chinese) and overall Chinese dominance in the region, enhanced by Beijing's growing military capabilities and lack of transparency.[1] North Korea is a more immediate threat to regional stability and security but is less concerning for Tokyo's long-term strategic interests and future.

For South Korea, the Democratic People's Republic of Korea (DPRK), with which it is still technically in a state of war, is an immediate and menacing security threat with significant military capabilities poised across the DMZ. North-South tensions have ebbed and flowed over the years, but strategic stability remains solid and there is little likelihood that North Korea would come across the DMZ in another Korean War–style invasion. However, Pyongyang's willingness to conduct lower-level provocations remains a serious worry, and the DPRK's growing nuclear weapon and ballistic missile programs continue to rattle nerves in both South Korea and Japan.

China is a different matter for South Korea. Seoul and Beijing maintain a vibrant economic relationship and growing political ties. President Park Geun-hye met with Chinese president Xi Jinping on several occasions, including Park's attendance at China's 2015 celebration of the seventieth anniversary of the end of World War II. Some in South Korea have been wary of China's rising power and have been upset with Beijing's willingness to protect Pyongyang following weapons tests and other provocative behavior. Despite these concerns, however, South Korea has a very different and sometimes more benign perception of China's growing power than Japan. This chapter will examine the capabilities of the People's Liberation Army (PLA) and Korean People's Army (KPA), along with the strategy and doctrine that are the focus of the U.S. nuclear umbrella.

CHINA'S MILITARY CAPABILITIES

China began a gradual but determined modernization of its armed forces after its 1979 invasion of Vietnam. Defense spending increased throughout the 1980s, but Chinese leaders believed that the threat of a major war was low, allowing China to focus on all four modernizations first proclaimed by Zhou Enlai and later championed by Deng Xiaoping: agriculture, industry, national defense, and science and technology. For most of the 1980s and early 1990s, Chinese concern was focused on Moscow as its chief threat. However, the Taiwan crisis of 1995–96 and Taiwan's apparent move toward independence forced Chinese leaders to shift their attention. From July 1995 to March 1996, China conducted a series of missile tests and military exercises designed to express its displeasure with Taiwanese president Lee Teng-hui's efforts to push independence from the mainland. In March 1996, Chinese actions sought to intimidate the Taiwanese electorate as Lee ran for a second term, an election he won, while also sending a message to Washington to mind its own business concerning China-Taiwan relations. During these months, the Clinton administration sent two carrier battle groups to the region as a show of support for Taiwan. Moreover, Chinese authorities were furious when after initially refusing to grant Lee a visa to visit Cornell University, his alma mater, Clinton relented and approved the visit.

Outraged that Washington could operate with such impunity so close to its shores, especially on an issue as vital as Taiwan, Beijing sped up its modernization efforts to demonstrate to Taiwan and its supporters in Washington that Beijing's determination to prevent Taiwanese independence, with military force if necessary, was credible. The intensified modernization effort was aided by the resources generated from China's booming economy, a growing industrial and technological base that allowed China to develop its own weapons, and a failing post–Cold War Russian economy that made Moscow all too happy to sell Russian weapons systems to China.[2] The modernization effort placed particular emphasis on the navy, air force, and strategic missile forces. The army, though still a formidable force, received less attention and has been reduced in size over the past decade.

China's economic rise over the past forty-plus years has provided the resources for a large and steady increase in its military spending and capabilities. After China embarked on the path of economic reform in 1978, the annual average increases to the defense budget were as follows: 1978–1987, 3.5 percent; 1988–1997, 14.5 percent; and 1998–2007, 15.9 percent.[3] From 2008 to 2014, the defense budget grew from $58.8 billion to $132 billion, with average annual increases of close to 15 percent. In 2015, Chinese authorities announced that defense spending rose to $145 billion, a 10.1 percent increase from the previous year.[4] However, for 2016, Beijing reported an increase of only 7 to 8 percent, the first single-digit increase since 2010. This was in part a reflection of a slowing economy but also, as others have indicated, a sign of greater efficiencies in the military along with reorganizing efforts that allowed for decreased spending without any reduction in military capability.[5]

Many assessments also maintain that the defense spending reported by the Chinese government is significantly lower than the amount that is actually spent. For example, in its 2016 annual report, the Pentagon

TABLE 3.1 Top Ten Military Spenders in 2015

Rank	Country	Spending ($billion)	Change 2006–2015 (%)	Share of GDP 2015 (%)	World Share (%)
1	USA	596	−3.9	3.3	36
2	China	[215]	132	[1.9]	[13]
3	Saudi Arabia	87.2	97	13.7	5.2
4	Russia	66.4	91	5.4	4.0
5	United Kingdom	55.5	−7.2	2.0	3.3
6	India	51.3	43	2.3	3.1
7	France	50.9	−5.9	2.1	3.0
8	Japan	40.9	−0.5	1.0	2.4
9	Germany	39.4	2.8	1.2	2.4
10	South Korea	36.4	37	2.6	2.2

Source: Perlo-Freeman, et al., "Trends in World Military Expenditure, 2015" (SIPRI).

Note: [ ] = estimated

maintained that Chinese defense spending for 2015 was more than $180 billion, citing China's lack of transparency along with differences over what items are included.[6] In a 2015 report, the Stockholm International Peace and Research Institute (SIPRI) gives an even higher estimate of $215 billion. SIPRI estimates that the increase in Chinese defense spending from 2006 to 2015 was 132 percent (see table 3.1), the largest percentage increase for that period among the ten highest military spenders.[7]

These consistent, hefty increases in defense spending have raised concerns in the region and in Washington. Japanese leaders have been increasingly alarmed by growing Chinese defense budgets along with more aggressive behavior, particularly Beijing's actions concerning the Senkakus. Japan's 2015 Defense White Paper maintains: "While advocating 'peaceful development,' China, particularly over maritime issues where its interests conflict with others,' based on its own assertions incompatible with the existing international legal order, continues to act in an assertive manner, including coercive attempts at changing the status quo, and is poised to fulfill its unilateral demands without compromise."[8] In 2016, Admiral Harry B. Harris, Jr., Commander, U.S. Pacific Command, noted in congressional testimony: "China's military modernization program is transforming its forces into a high-tech military to achieve its dream of regional dominance, with growing aspirations of global reach and influence. Given China's economic rise, the goal may be natural; however, the lack of transparency on China's overall strategic intent behind its military investments and activities creates instability and regional anxiety."[9] In 2015, the Obama National Security Strategy noted that "the United States welcomes the rise of a stable, peaceful, and prosperous China," but "we will closely monitor China's military modernization and expanding presence in Asia."[10] However, while the aggregate amount of Chinese defense spending has increased dramatically, as a percentage of GDP it has remained relatively consistent at roughly 2 percent.

Conventional Forces

China has the largest standing military in the world with 2.333 million in its armed forces. The largest branch by far is the People's Liberation Army (PLA) at 1.6 million, followed by the air force (PLAAF) at 398,000, the navy (PLAN) at 235,000, and the strategic missile forces at 100,000. Another 660,000 personnel are part of various paramilitary units, including internal security forces, border defense, coast guard, and several maritime police organizations.[11] Since the 1980s, the overall PLA has been cut several times—by 1 million in 1985, 500,000 in 1997, and 200,000 in 2003—to reach its current size of 1.6 million. In September 2015, Chinese president Xi Jinping announced another round of cuts, reducing the PLA by 300,000. Though a significant reduction and presented as a signal of China's peaceful intent, it likely had more to do with ongoing efforts to streamline and modernize the force while reducing costs and, thus, will have little effect on the overall effectiveness of the PLA. Moreover, the announcement came in conjunction with China's 2015 military parade to commemorate the end of World War II, which was an important display of China's military strength. A large share of these cuts is likely to be borne by the ground forces, but other areas will be cut as well.[12]

The army has been the lowest priority of China's modernization efforts, but it remains an impressive fighting force that is also improving, though more slowly than the other branches. The PLA maintains a number of large weapon systems, including 6,540 main battle tanks and 650 light tanks. Of these, 3,050 are T-59 tanks, old systems based on the Soviet T-54, though some have received important upgrades to their armor and fire control systems. The most modern components of China's tank force, 2,200 T-96 and 790 T-98/99 tanks, represent major improvements with further enhancements to their armor and firing systems. The T-98A/99 models are the most advanced tanks but also the most costly, which has limited production and deployment to elite units. The tank, based on Russian and Western designs, entered into service in 2001.[13] The PLA also maintains more than 13,000 artillery and multiple rocket launcher systems, along with more than 5,000 armored infantry fighting vehicles and armored personnel carriers.[14]

Chinese airpower has received considerable attention in Beijing's modernization efforts. Since the early 1990s, the PLAAF has improved its capabilities as a modern, all-weather force capable of conducting joint offensive and defensive operations. In the past, Beijing relied extensively on the importation of Soviet aircraft designs so that in 2000, all but ninety-five of its estimated 3,200 fighter aircraft were based on vintage 1950s MiG-19 and MiG-20 design aircraft. These planes lacked electronic warfare capability, did not possess the stealth technology of U.S. aircraft, and relied mostly on gravity bombs or missiles that lacked beyond-visual-range capability.[15] Increasingly, however, China is building its own more modern airframes that are capable of all-weather, offensive, defensive, and joint operations.[16] The PLAAF has thus increased the quality and quantity of more advanced planes within its current force of 2,306 combat aircraft.[17]

In addition, China is recapitalizing several of its older airframes, such as the J-10 and J-11, while also building newer, more modern versions of these planes. As a result, more of its fighters will have air-to-air refueling capability, advanced avionics, the ability to carry beyond-visual-range missiles and precision-guided munitions (PGMs), and improved electronic warfare capability. *Jane's* predicts that by 2017, half of China's tactical combat aircraft will be more advanced fourth-generation planes. However, the PLAAF will still have 700 J-7 legacy fighters.[18] China is also working on other advanced combat aircraft, including the carrier-based J-15, the J-16 strike fighter, the fifth-generation J-20 stealth fighter, and the FC-31 (J-31) stealth fighter, a plane that may be able to match the U.S. F-35. China introduced the FC-31 at its 2014 International Aviation and Aerospace Exhibition in Zhuhai, and analysts have noted that the plane, which bears a striking resemblance to the U.S. F-35, is likely based on stolen plans.[19]

In addition to improvements in its fighter and attack forces, the PLAAF is also modernizing its bomber force. The H-6K bomber received major upgrades to its propulsion, electronics, and weapons systems and now carries cruise missiles, anti-ship missiles, and other precision-guided munitions. The plane can be refueled in midair to increase its range, but it lacks stealth capability.[20] Modernization has also included efforts to increase its lift and air-to-air refueling capabilities, both of which will advance the reach and power projection of the Chinese military. Finally, China is devoting considerable effort to developing unmanned aerial vehicles (UAVs) that are comparable to the U.S. Predator and Global Hawk drones.

With the improvements China has made in the past two decades, *Jane's* notes that Beijing is "shifting the air balance of power in the Taiwan Strait and placing the PLAAF in a better position to challenge US and Japanese regional domination."[21] Another analyst notes that the "pace of modernization of the PLAAF's inventory has increased since 2010 and is now broadening in scope beyond its initial focus on tactical aviation. . . . Success in achieving this latter transformative goal now appears central to progressing the modernization process from a focus on inventory recapitalization and towards true strategic modernization."[22] Thus, the 2016 DoD report on China's military notes that "the PLAAF is rapidly closing the gap with western air forces across a broad spectrum of capabilities from aircraft and command-and-control (C2) to jammers, electronic warfare (EW), and datalinks."[23]

The navy (PLAN) has been undergoing one of the most significant modernization efforts within the Chinese military. According to *Jane's*, the PLAN "is in the midst of a concerted modernization that is turning the force into a leading regional naval power able to secure maritime control against smaller opponents while striving to deter more powerful foes." As a result, "the PLAN is becoming a force containing major combatants that is capable of independent action and power projection along the country's periphery and into the Pacific Ocean."[24] China has invested heavily in improving its platforms, training, personnel, and manufacturing base to transform its small coastal force into a regional and, by 2050, a global blue water navy.

The growth of China's maritime forces has been based on several goals. First, the PLAN is committed to preventing or reversing any attempt by Taiwan to move toward independence from the mainland. In addition, China seeks to deter and defeat the United States should it provide any assistance to Taipei's independence ambitions. After the 1996 Taiwan Strait crisis, in which the United States sent unimpeded two carrier battle groups to support Taipei, China began a concerted effort to prevent that from ever happening again. This effort, labeled "anti-access/area denial" or A2/AD, has sought through more advanced ships and weaponry to make it difficult for U.S. surface vessels to operate within the near seas or the first island chain.[25] With increased naval capabilities and other force improvements, "China's military as a whole is on the verge of obtaining a credible sea denial capability against the U.S. Navy (USN) in the Western Pacific and an ability to undertake offensive operations against Japan and Taiwan, with the absence of US military support."[26] Finally, the PLAN's growth is designed to protect Beijing's growing economic and maritime interests as well as its territorial claims in the South and East China Seas.

The PLAN is composed of seventy-four surface combatants (one aircraft carrier, destroyers, and frigates), more than 200 patrol and coastal combatants (corvettes, mine warfare, and amphibious ships), 171 logistics and support vessels, and a submarine force of sixty-one boats. China has four ballistic missile submarines that are capable of firing strategic weapons and fifty-seven attack submarines.[27] The PLAN is also supported by a large contingent of coast guard, fishing patrol, and other coastal patrol forces.[28] In addition, China has used a unique maritime militia force that Erickson and Kennedy describe as "ships that appeared to be crewed by civilians, but in all likelihood were actually controlled by state-sponsored forces taking orders from China's military."[29]

Of particular interest for defense watchers are Beijing's efforts to develop an aircraft carrier program. In 1998, China purchased the *Varyag*, a Soviet carrier from Ukraine, and after extensive renovations, the ship entered service in 2012 renamed the *Liaoning*. China continues to conduct training exercises and integration of the carrier air wing, composed of the J-15 airplane. Beijing has begun building its first indigenous carrier and has plans to build several of these ships by 2030. However, according to the DoD China report, the *Liaoning* will not have the same power projection capability as a U.S. carrier: "Liaoning's smaller size limits the number of aircraft it can embark, while the ski-jump configuration limits aircraft fuel and ordnance loads."[30] The platform is more appropriate for "fleet air defense" and will continue to be a training platform for pilots, crews, and commanders as they train and develop tactics for later generation carriers.[31] Even with new, more modern carriers, China has a long way to go to master difficult carrier and task force operations that took the U.S. Navy years to learn. Despite these near-term limits on China's aircraft carriers, one Asian defense attaché in Beijing remarked: "An aircraft carrier symbolises the ambition to move far beyond your own shores. It is a tool for power projection. China's navy is still a dwarf compared with the US, but this makes it official that they will be rivals."[32]

Chemical and Biological Weapons

Official Chinese sources regularly declare that China does not possess or manufacture chemical or biological weapons and supports their abolition. Beijing declared in its 2010 Defense White Paper that "China sincerely fulfills its obligations under the Chemical Weapons Convention (CWC)" and "supports multilateral efforts to strengthen the effectiveness of the Biological Weapons Convention (BWC) and is committed to the comprehensive and strict implementation of the Convention."[33] China acceded to the BWC in 1984, signed the CWC in 1993, and ratified it in 1997.

Despite these commitments, some questions remain about China's chemical and biological weapons programs. In July 2010, a U.S. State Department report on global compliance with arms control and disarmament agreements noted that "available information does not allow the United States to confirm whether China has fully declared or explained its historical CW activities, including CW production, disposition of produced CW agents, and transfer of CW agents to another country."[34] However, the 2016 compliance report noted no concerns regarding China's adherence to the CW agreement.[35]

Regarding biological weapons (BW), the 2010 report noted that "the voluntary BWC CBM [Confidence Building Measures] declarations China has submitted have neither documented the offensive BW program it possessed prior to its accession to the BWC in 1984, nor documented that China has eliminated the program or any remaining biological munitions in accordance with the BWC."[36] The 2015 report noted: "Available information indicates China engaged during the reporting period in biological activities with potential dual-use applications. However, the information did not establish that China is engaged in activities prohibited by the BWC."[37] Thus, a degree of uncertainty surrounds its chemical and biological weapon programs.

Ballistic Missiles, Cruise Missiles, and Nuclear Weapons

Another emphasis of Chinese defense spending has been its strategic forces. According to *Jane's*, "China now maintains one of the world's most active strategic nuclear and missile weapon modernisation programmes, encompassing land-, sea-, and air-launched weapons."[38] The effort is largely to modernize old systems with newer capabilities but also includes an expansion of the overall quantity of its strategic forces. China's nuclear and missile forces were reorganized in December 2015 with the termination of the Second Artillery Corps and its replacement with the PLA Rocket Force. Strategic forces have been a high priority for funding over the last fifteen to twenty years, and the development of a number of new ballistic and cruise missile systems demonstrates a significant commitment of resources. While much of this effort has been undertaken with an eye toward the United States, Russia, and India, a growing and more modern Chinese force is of increasing concern to Japan and, to a lesser extent, South Korea. Moreover, among the five original nuclear weapons states—the United States, Russia, China, the United Kingdom, and France—China is the only one that has been expanding its nuclear weapons force, though at a slow pace.[39]

Exact counts of the Chinese nuclear arsenal are difficult to obtain as Beijing does not make such information public. Estimates of China's nuclear stockpile vary between 170 and 260.[40] Chinese warheads are not actively deployed on missiles but are maintained in storage during peacetime. In a crisis, the warheads would be mated with ballistic missiles for deployment. However, a new report indicates that some in China's military may be considering placing its nuclear forces on a higher state of alert to be able to launch a retaliatory strike more quickly. Military leaders worry about maintaining a credible deterrent that is not vulnerable to a U.S. first strike, U.S. precision-guided conventional munitions, and ballistic missile defense.[41]

China has approximately 165 land-based ballistic missiles of various ranges capable of delivering nuclear payloads.[42] One of the oldest is the DF-4, a liquid-fuel ICBM with a range of more than 5,500 kilometers that is capable of reaching India, Guam, and parts of Russia but not the continental United States. This missile is in the process of being replaced; only about ten DF-4s remain in the Chinese arsenal.[43]

China's largest and longest range missile capable of carrying nuclear payloads is the DF-5, with a range of more than 13,000 kilometers. The DF-5 is a liquid-fuel, silo-based missile and, given its extended range, is likely used to target the United States and Russia. Though most Chinese missiles are believed to be equipped with a single warhead, some of the DF-5s are MIRVed [multiple independently targetable reentry vehicles].[44] These missiles are slowly being replaced with the more modern DF-31A, but it is not clear if all the DF-5s will be scrapped. China maintains approximately twenty DF-5s, in part because they are reliable and relatively low-cost systems.

In 2006, the PLA introduced its most advanced ICBM, the DF-31, a two-stage, solid-fuel missile deployed on a road-mobile, transporter erector launcher (TEL) with a single warhead and a range of 7,250 kilometers. The range of the DF-31 is insufficient to reach the continental United States. Production of this system has stopped, and the number of DF-31s is likely to remain at ten. Instead, production has shifted to a variant, the DF-31A, a three-stage solid-fuel missile also mounted on a road-mobile TEL system but with an increased range of more than 11,200 kilometers that allows it to reach most of the continental United States.[45] The DF-31A most likely is equipped to carry a single warhead, but in 2011 *Jane's* indicated it may be capable of carrying one maneuverable reentry vehicle (MRV) or a MIRV system of three to four warheads.[46] Estimates indicate that China has ten DF-31s and twenty-five DF-31As.[47] All of these missiles have sufficient range to hit Japan and South Korea, and the DF-31 and 31A are expected to replace the DF-4 and DF-5 for all regional targets. The DF-5 and DF-31A have range sufficient to reach the United States.

Work continues on other more advanced systems. One is the longer-range and likely MIRVed ICBM, the DF-41.[48] This is a solid-fuel, road-mobile missile with the range to reach all of the continental United States. China has conducted several tests of the DF-41 but has yet to deploy the missile.[49] Another is a hypersonic glide vehicle, the DF-ZF, that has been tested several times and is capable of maneuvering while traveling at speeds of Mach 5. The vehicle is likely to carry a nuclear warhead and will allow China to evade existing ballistic missile defense systems.[50]

The PLA also maintains a number of other ballistic missiles at intermediate and medium ranges (IRBM and MRBM) that are capable of delivering a nuclear payload and reaching regional targets. The bulk of its MRBMs are the eighty to ninety DF-21 missiles, a system developed from China's JL-1 SLBM. First introduced in the late 1980s, DF-21 missiles are of several types with different capabilities. The DF-21A has a range of 1,750 kilometers and greater accuracy than the basic DF-21, which never entered service.[51] The missile carries a single warhead, possibly maneuverable, and is capable of carrying a conventional or nuclear payload. The DF-21B is capable of carrying a nuclear warhead. The DF-21C is armed with a conventional warhead and has improved accuracy for use in precision strike operations.[52] Mixing nuclear and conventional payloads on similar systems can be very dangerous. If a conventionally armed DF-21C were deployed in a crisis, it would not be clear if this were a conventional or nuclear version, creating the possibility of a preemptive strike should an adversary mistake it for a nuclear-tipped missile.

The United States Navy is particularly concerned about the DF-21D, a solid-fuel missile with a range of 1,500 kilometers and armed with a maneuverable warhead.[53] The missile and warhead are equipped with their own sensors to allow for course corrections in the terminal phase of flight. This missile would be able to sink large maneuvering surface vessels, including aircraft carriers, greatly enhancing China's anti-access, area denial capability. The DF-21D has been tested against land-based targets, but its ability to hit moving targets in the open ocean is uncertain.[54] China is also working on an improved version of this system in the DF-26.

The vast majority of China's ballistic missile force is composed of two types of short-range ballistic missiles (SRBM), the DF-11 and DF-15, which have a range of less than 1,000 kilometers. The Chinese initially developed these missiles for export, but during the early 1990s, they became increasingly concerned about Taiwan's independence ambitions. Consequently, these missiles were redirected against Taiwan to deter the island from declaring independence and to provide a strike capability should it attempt to do so. China has deployed 300 to 400 DF-15s and 700 to 800 DF-11s, with most of this force targeting Taiwan. Both types of missiles have a range of 500 to 600 kilometers and are configured to carry various payloads, including high-explosive conventional warheads, cluster bombs, or earth-penetrating warheads. The DF-15 can be armed with a nuclear payload, but it is unclear if China has done so.[55]

Finally, China is working on a "long-range 'strategic' stealth bomber" that would likely be designed to carry nuclear weapons. If China were to reach this goal, it would have a legitimate "triad" of long-range nuclear delivery systems.[56]

Impressed with the accuracy and effectiveness of the Tomahawk cruise missile in the 1990–91 Persian Gulf War, China has devoted considerable effort and resources to the development of an advanced cruise missile force.[57] The PLA has several models, including the YJ-63 (Ying Ji, or Eagle Strike), the CJ-10 (Chang Jian, or Long Sword), and the YJ-62. The YJ-63, China's first land attack cruise missile, is launched from H-6 bombers and has a range of 200 to 300 kilometers. China has fifty of the more advanced CJ-10 cruise missiles, which have a range of 1,500 kilometers. These missiles are deployed on TEL vehicles, which carry three missiles in separate launch tubes. The missile is likely able to carry a conventional or nuclear payload, though there is some uncertainty regarding the nuclear mission. Work also continues on a more advanced version, the CJ-20, an air-launched cruise missile with a range of 2,700 kilometers, allowing it to reach Guam, which would likely be nuclear capable.[58]

In addition to land-based missiles, China maintains a small submarine-based ballistic missile force of four Jin-class (Type 094) SSBNs. Sources indicate that China is likely to build one more Jin-class boat before turning to a third-generation submarine and a more advanced JL-3 SLBM sometime in the next decade. Jin-class submarines can carry twelve single-warhead JL-2 [JuLang, or Great Wave] SLBMs. The JL-2, based on designs of the DF-31 missile, is believed to have a range of 7,200 kilometers and be capable of carrying nuclear or conventional payloads. All Jin-class submarines are based on Hainan Island, indicating "a desire to ensure a nuclear 'second-strike' capability against India, as well as possible southern hemisphere strike options against the United States that would complicate the latter's missile defences."[59]

China is expected to begin conducting deterrence patrols sometime in the near future, and according to the Pentagon, the Jin-class submarine with JL-2 SLBMs "represents China's first credible, sea-based nuclear deterrent."[60] However, deterrence patrols are difficult to conduct and will require improved command and control (C2) capabilities, along with advanced intelligence, surveillance, and reconnaissance (ISR). The Chinese central government maintains tight control over its nuclear forces, and dispersing these assets, along with its large mobile land-based missile force, in peacetime or in a crisis will create significant C2 challenges.[61]

A key dimension of China's military capabilities is its ability to project power beyond its borders. In the 2010 report on China, the Pentagon maintained that by 2015 to 2020, "China will be able to project and sustain a modest sized force—perhaps several battalions of ground forces or a naval flotilla of up to a dozen ships—in low-intensity operations far from China. It is unlikely, however, that China will be able to project and sustain large forces in high-intensity combat operations far from China until well into the following decade."[62] However, five years later, the Pentagon report noted, "Current trends in China's weapons production will enable the PLA to conduct a range of military operations in Asia far from China's traditional territorial claims."[63] Thus, China's military power, both conventional and nonconventional, continues to grow and will remain a concern for regional security planners.

CHINESE NUCLEAR STRATEGY AND DOCTRINE

Little specific information is available regarding China's nuclear strategy and doctrine, which are closely held by the Chinese government. China has a relatively small nuclear weapons arsenal of approximately 170 to 260 warheads, a bit smaller than France (300) and larger than the United Kingdom (215) if the lower estimates are correct.[64] China continues to maintain a minimum deterrence posture with what it believes are the fewest nuclear weapons for a secure, survivable second strike capability that can ride out an attack and retaliate, imposing unacceptable costs on any attacker.[65] Fravel and Medeiros argue that Chinese leaders going back to Mao "embraced the idea of deterrence through assured retaliation, in which a small number of survivable weapons would be enough to retaliate and impose unacceptable damage on an adversary."[66] However, debate continues over whether Chinese force modernization indicates continued adherence to minimum deterrence, but with improvements to ensure survivability, or a shift to a more powerful second strike capability that is moving beyond minimum deterrence and may also contemplate a warfighting posture.[67]

Minimum deterrence necessitates the adoption of a countervalue targeting strategy, retaliating against cities to inflict unacceptable costs, rather than a counterforce strategy that seeks to hit military targets. However, these distinctions would be largely irrelevant in a nuclear war. While China could opt in the future for matching the size of the U.S. and Russian arsenals, it appears for the moment to be maintaining a minimum deterrent posture, but one that is adapting to changing strategic conditions. Thus, given the size of its arsenal, the PLA has made a concerted effort to improve the survivability of its force, ensuring a secure second strike capability, by developing improved mobile land-based missiles and ballistic missile submarines. In addition, Chinese leaders have been concerned that ballistic missile defense capabilities and other technology countermeasures may degrade the deterrence value of its relatively small force. U.S. moves to increase its strategic nuclear capability along with expanded missile defense may be the impetus for Beijing to alter its minimum deterrence posture should it fear its forces might no longer survive to retaliate. Of course, these arguments could simply be used as an excuse by those wishing to move beyond minimum deterrence. Time will tell if China decides to move away from minimum deterrence and seek parity with the United States and Russia.

Along with its minimum deterrent posture, the Chinese government continues to declare a "no first use" policy regarding nuclear weapons.[68] The 2015 Defense White Paper maintained: "China has always pursued the policy of no first use of nuclear weapons and adhered to a self-defensive nuclear strategy that is defensive in nature. China will unconditionally not use or threaten to use nuclear weapons against non-nuclear weapons states or in nuclear-weapon-free zones, and will never enter into a nuclear arms race with any other country."[69] Thus, in addition to a no-first-use pledge, China also provides a negative assurance that it will not use nuclear weapons against countries that do not possess these weapons. However, some in the Chinese military have raised doubts, especially regarding a willingness to use nuclear weapons in a war over Taiwan or for a conventional attack that threatened the Communist Party, its nuclear forces, or the Chinese homeland. A high-level official at the Nanjing Army Command College told a Hong Kong newspaper in January 2008 that

> the policy of not to use nuclear weapons first is not unlimited, without conditions, or without premises. China will never use nuclear weapons first, especially not to use nuclear weapons against non-nuclear countries. . . . When big powers equipped with nuclear arms disregard the completeness of sovereignty and territory of [the] Chinese people and make frequent moves that are unconventional and hurt fundamental interests of Chinese people, however, it is not impossible to break such a strategy on tactical issues.[70]

While some of these sentiments have come from PLA leaders, the Pentagon's 2016 China report notes "there has been no indication that national leaders are willing to attach such nuances and caveats to China's NFU doctrine."[71] Though political leaders have held firm to China's no-first-use commitment, this position is to some degree ambiguous. Indeed, all no-first-use doctrines, while contributing to some level of predictability and stability in the strategic environment, can be easily reversed.

How do the Chinese view the U.S. nuclear umbrella, and how has it affected planning regarding nuclear weapons? These assessments are difficult, both because evidence is hard to come by and because of the inherent difficulty in determining why deterrence was successful. It is often very hard to ascertain the degree to which a defender's commitment, in this case the extension of the U.S. nuclear umbrella, has influenced the perceptions and actions of the challenger. Moreover, the U.S.-China deterrence situation is largely one of general deterrence, not even at the same level of rivalry as U.S.-Soviet relations during the Cold War, though some people believe it is headed in that direction. Each side maintains a nuclear arsenal as part of its overall defense preparations, but rarely have relations moved toward a crisis of immediate deterrence in which the United States has issued pointed counterthreats to deter Chinese actions. As a result, the nuclear umbrella has been far less conspicuous in U.S.-China relations than in the case of North Korea.

China is certainly concerned about the existing U.S. strategic force posture and plans to modernize these forces. Though the Obama administration reduced the number of deployed nuclear forces in the New START treaty and called for deemphasizing the role of nuclear weapons, Chinese leaders and analysts continue to fear that Washington is seeking primacy in this domain.[72] President Trump's calls for expanding the U.S. nuclear arsenal have added to these concerns.[73] A particular worry is the growing scale and effectiveness of ballistic missile defense (BMD), not only U.S. capabilities but also Washington's efforts to construct a regional BMD architecture in Asia. Japan is already an enthusiastic member, and there are fears that other U.S. allies, especially South Korea, may join. Though U.S. leaders maintain that BMD is directed at North Korea and not China, Beijing is not convinced, and this concern will become even more troublesome as BMD technology improves. When combined with U.S. conventional global strike capabilities and improved ISR, Chinese analysts fear this could seriously degrade their own nuclear deterrent.[74] Yet, in the end, Cunningham and Fravel argue, "Chinese strategists are relatively and perhaps, unexpectedly optimistic about U.S.-China crisis stability, now and in the future. . . . Chinese strategists believe that the interests at stake would be too low in any U.S.-China scenario for either side to create risks of nuclear escalation."[75] Thus, Chinese thinking about the U.S. nuclear umbrella appears to be rolled into larger issues of the broader strategic nuclear relationship.

NORTH KOREA'S MILITARY CAPABILITIES

North Korean military capabilities are considerably different from those of China. While China has a larger and vastly more modern military force and its future strategic direction and intent are uncertain, it shares many common interests with the United States and there remains a possibility of crafting a relatively stable and cooperative relationship with Beijing.[76] North Korea, on the other hand, is an immediate security problem, certainly for South Korea but also for Japan. The DPRK has succeeded in rattling nerves in East Asia on many occasions. North Korea maintains a large conventional capability, but it is one that has been deteriorating with age. The KPA has upgraded some of its conventional systems, and the overall size and capability of the military make it a dangerous force, but the lack of investment and modernization over the years has degraded its effectiveness. In part to offset its aging conventional capabilities and to avoid the costly arms race necessary to keep up with a modern ROK military and U.S. forces in Korea, the DPRK has undertaken extensive efforts to build its asymmetric capabilities, including nuclear, chemical, and biological weapons, ballistic missiles, special forces, and an offensive cyber capability that are serious threats for South Korea, Japan, and the United States.

Conventional Forces

North Korea is often touted as the world's most militarized society, fielding an active duty armed force of 1.19 million along with more than 7.7 million reservists in various national defense groups.[77] The DPRK military ranks fourth globally in the number of personnel, behind China, the United States, and India. These numbers represent a significant portion of North Korea's total population of almost 25 million. North Korea's economy has been in dismal shape since the 1990s, but the government continues to devote a significant share of GDP to defense spending. According to a U.S. State Department report, from 2002 to 2012 North Korea spent an average of $4 billion annually, or 24.8 percent of GDP.[78] Despite these numbers, *Jane's* notes that North Korea's conventional capability has slipped considerably, and "due to financial problems, severe deficiencies in equipment remain—problems that have been further hindered by a lack of extended, comprehensive, and realistic training for most ground force units, especially the mechanised and armoured forces."[79]

North Korea maintains the capability to attack across the DMZ with as little as twelve to thirty-six hours' warning. However, its forces would have a difficult time sustaining combat operations for more than two to three months. Readiness of the KPA is uncertain and "uneven." The struggle for food that has plagued the DPRK economy has also affected the KPA. *Jane's* notes "frequent reports of serious shortages of food, fuel, winter clothes, and other military supplies for KPA troops. Soldiers, who have historically spent part of their time engaged in agricultural work to supplement their food supply, have been reported to be spending greater amounts of time engaged in these activities and also in KPA enterprises in order to earn foreign currency."[80] Though KPA members tend to be better fed than the general population, many remain undernourished, causing low morale in some units.

The army is by far the largest of the DPRK's services, with 1.02 million soldiers making it one of the largest armies in the world. Approximately 200,000 of these are special operations forces (SOF), whose role is to "cover infiltration into the forward and rear areas to strike major units and facilities, assassinations of key personnel, disruption of rear areas and hybrid operations."[81] A 2015 Pentagon assessment of DPRK SOF notes they "are among the most highly trained, well-equipped, best-fed, and highly motivated forces in the KPA. As North Korea's conventional capabilities decline relative to the ROK and the United States, North Korea appears to increasingly regard SOF capabilities as vital for asymmetric coercion."[82]

North Korea maintains a large force of 4,060 tanks, a dimension of the KPA that conjures up memories of the North's 1950 invasion when these forces poured across the thirty-eighth parallel. While the number of tanks surpasses that of the South, the quantity is offset by their increasing age as most are based on old Soviet model T-34, T-54/55, T-59, and T-62 tanks and Chinese-designed light tanks.[83] North Korea has modernized a portion of its tank force with the addition of 900 Chonma-ho and Songun-ho tanks to replace the T-54s and T-55s.[84] These new, indigenously produced models are variants of the T-62 tank and are equipped with advanced turret guns and fire control systems.[85]

Despite these improvements, a North Korean armored assault would face a plethora of deadly obstacles. The geography along the North-South border is a series of mountain ranges that run in a north-south direction. As a result, there are only a few suitable invasion corridors between the mountain ranges that would support a massive conventional assault.

ROK and U.S. defense planners are well aware of these routes and have fortified these positions with mines, anti-armor precision-guided munitions, artillery, and air support.[86] A 1998 study noted that "a traditional armored assault by North Korean forces would amount to putting metal in a metalgrinder, and be fairly straightforward for the allies to stop."[87] The realities of this assessment have not changed.

One of North Korea's conventional force strengths is the number of artillery tubes and multiple rocket launcher (MRL) systems along with their proximity to the DMZ, putting Seoul within range of a massive bombardment. The DPRK has 8,500 self-propelled and towed artillery pieces and 5,100 MRL systems.[88] Pyongyang has upgraded this capability with the apparent addition of a new 300-mm MRL that carries eight launch tubes and increases the range of its previous launchers. In addition, many of these artillery and rocket assets are positioned in hardened, underground facilities and tunnels dug into nearby mountains, affording protection and the ability to strike with little warning. Should a conflict break out, suppression of these weapons would be an important task, but they would be difficult to take out before doing serious damage to the Seoul metropolitan area.

The KPAF has a large force of 545 combat aircraft, but its capability is reduced significantly because of its age. Only 108 of these planes are the more advanced MiG-23, MiG-29, or Su-25.[89] The remainder are largely older Soviet and Chinese designs that would have a difficult time squaring off against more modern ROK and U.S. planes. The bomber fleet consists of 80 H-5 aircraft that are capable of carrying conventional, chemical, or nuclear bombs. The bombers are based on old Soviet designs and fly at slow speeds, making them vulnerable to air defense systems, surface-to-air missiles, and fighter aircraft. Because of a lack of fuel and spare parts, along with other maintenance challenges for an aging fleet, North Korean pilots train on average only 20 hours per year in their aircraft.[90] North Korea also has an extensive and capable air defense system composed of several types of surface-to-air missiles and antiaircraft guns.[91]

The KPAF has worked to modernize its force with the growth of UAVs. Interest in UAVs began in the 1970s, and after acquiring a Chinese model, Pyongyang began its own program in the 1990s. In subsequent years, North Korea also received help from Syria, Egypt, Iran, and

Russia. Estimates place its total UAV force at approximately 300 drones, but most are fairly primitive, unable to fly long distances and equipped with camera systems incapable of transmitting photographs in real time while in flight. UAVs are used as intelligence and reconnaissance platforms but could also be equipped with conventional explosives as well as chemical or biological weapons.[92]

The Korean People's Navy (KPN) is one of the world's largest, but most of its ships are small, with only three frigates and no ships of larger classes. The KPN is a brown water coastal force with three primary missions: defend the country's coastal waters; secure coastal shipping and fishing; and insert special operations forces. The bulk of the navy consists of 383 patrol and coastal combat ships and twenty-four mine warfare vessels, providing North Korea with little oceangoing capability.[93] The KPN also has Landing Craft Air Cushions (LCACs) and high-speed landing craft for support of SOF insertion and amphibious operations. Pyongyang has devoted some efforts to modernizing its fleet with improved fire control systems, automated command and control, and some new vessels, but these efforts have been limited.

The large numbers of KPN vessels is deceptive for other reasons.[94] First, given North Korea's geography, the KPN must split its ships into east and west fleets and would have a very difficult time bringing the two fleets together for combined operations during combat. The U.S. and ROK navies would easily be able to block the transit of North Korean surface vessels from one coast to another. Second, because of resource constraints and maintenance challenges, close to 10 percent of the fleet is laid up at any one time for repair. Third, an additional 10 to 20 percent of the fleet is in land storage, and reviving these vessels would require significant time, effort, and resources. Finally, if fighting broke out, the KPN surface fleet would be in serious difficulty because "the advanced weaponry and combined operations capabilities of the U.S. Navy and RoKN, combined with air supremacy, would quickly neutralize the vast majority of the KPN's surface combatants."[95] Moreover, South Korea has undertaken several efforts to improve its naval capabilities, including building new patrol-killer guided missile boats designed specifically to protect ROK coastal waters, a new line of frigates to replace the aging Ulsan-class ships, and plans for the construction of three additional Aegis-class destroyers.

A more serious concern is the North's submarine force, which numbers approximately seventy-three, including twenty Romeo-class attack submarines, thirty-two Sang-O class submarines, and more than twenty midget submarines, one of which was likely responsible for firing the torpedo that sank the ROK's *Cheonan* in March 2010. North Korea is also working on a ballistic missile submarine called the Sinpo class, along with the KN-11 SLBM. KPN boats are tasked with several missions, including "to disrupt sea lanes of communication, lay mines, attack surface vessels, and support the infiltration of special operation forces,"[96] and these boats are "at a higher state of readiness than other KPN assets."[97]

Chemical and Biological Weapons

North Korea is believed to have an extensive chemical weapons program, with stockpiles of approximately 2,500 to 5,000 tons,[98] making it the third largest arsenal in the world behind the United States and Russia. Pyongyang is not a party to the Chemical Weapons Convention, one of six countries who have not joined. North Korea claims that during the Korean War, the United Nations Command used chemical and biological weapons against the North, and consequently it would never use either of these weapons and supports their abolition. However, North Korea has never provided any official declarations about its program or allowed international inspections of any of its chemical facilities.[99] The KPA may have twenty different types of chemical agents but has focused most of its production on sulfur, mustard gas, chlorine, phosgene, sarin, and V-agents.[100] The assassination of Kim Jong-nam, the half-brother of North Korean leader Kim Jong-un, was done with a VX nerve agent that provided a link to the DPRK's chemical weapons stockpile. The chemical agents are produced indigenously and are deliverable with ballistic missiles, artillery, and rocket systems; some of these weapons are deployed close to the DMZ for early use in a conflict. ROK sources indicate that 30 percent of DPRK artillery and half of its missile force are capable of delivering chemical munitions. Most of its chemical weapons are "unitary munitions," consisting of a single canister of a deadly chemical, rather than the more modern and stable "binary" weapons in which two or more chemicals are combined when ready for use.¹⁰¹ It is believed that corps commanders have been granted launch authority to use these weapons should contact be lost with the leadership in Pyongyang.¹⁰²

The details of a North Korean biological weapons program are less certain. North Korea acceded to the BW Convention in 1987 and, as with chemical weapons, maintains that it would never use biological weapons and supports their abolition. The KPA is believed to maintain up to thirteen different biological agents, including anthrax, botulism, cholera, hemorrhagic fever, smallpox, and typhoid fever. North Korea is also a serious proliferation concern, having worked in the past with Syria, Iran, Egypt, and Libya on biological weapons. Some reports indicate that DPRK efforts to weaponize biological weapons have received far less attention than work to develop offensive chemical weapons and may be focused largely on the need to defend against an adversary's biological weapons. While estimates vary regarding the nature and scope of North Korea's biological weapons program, "the DPRK possesses a range of pathogen samples that could be weaponized, and the technical capabilities to do so, rather than deployed, ready-to-use biological weapons."¹⁰³

Nuclear Weapons and Ballistic Missiles

The most serious dimensions of North Korea's military capabilities and the ones the U.S. nuclear umbrella confronts directly are its nuclear weapon and ballistic missile programs. North Korea has conducted five nuclear tests, in October 2006, May 2009, February 2013, and January and September 2016. Pyongyang declared that the January 2016 test was a hydrogen bomb and proclaimed that "the DPRK proudly joined the advanced ranks of nuclear weapons states possessed of even [the] H-bomb and the Korean people came to demonstrate the spirit of the dignified nation equipped with the most powerful nuclear deterrent."¹⁰⁴ Estimates placed the yield of the test explosion at six to nine kilotons, which is well below the explosive power of most H-bombs. Consequently, experts believed the test was either a failed H-bomb test or, more likely, a boosted fission device that used a small amount of fusion material to increase its yield.¹⁰⁵ While the test did not match North Korea's declaration, it did demonstrate continued progress in its nuclear weapons program.

Within the same year, North Korea conducted another test on September 9, the national holiday that celebrates the founding of the DPRK, demonstrating a pace of testing that was far more rapid than previously. This test was the largest of the five, with an estimated yield of fifteen to twenty kilotons, but still smaller than many previous tests by the United States and the old Soviet Union as they developed their nuclear capabilities.[106] In announcing the test, the Korean Central News Agency cited North Korean scientists who said that the test will allow the DPRK to produce "a variety of smaller, lighter and diversified nuclear warheads" and will improve the "technology of mounting nuclear warheads on ballistic rockets."[107] Given the yield, the test was likely not a hydrogen bomb but rather again some type of boosted fission device, but North Korea's announcement, if true, indicates continued progress toward weaponizing a nuclear warhead.

In February 2015, North Korea's arsenal was believed to have approximately ten to sixteen nuclear weapons, an increase from the estimates of four to eight that had been the standard for several years. Approximately six to eight of these weapons originate from reprocessed plutonium produced by the reactor at Yongbyon and another four to eight from North Korea's uranium enrichment facilities.[108]

The plutonium estimates are based on material from previously produced spent fuel manufactured at its research reactor in Yongbyon. North Korea closed down the reactor in 2007 and blew up the cooling tower in what was largely a symbolic act. However, in March 2013 Pyongyang declared it would restart the old reactor, and by February 2016 the director of national intelligence James Clapper reported, "North Korea has been operating the reactor long enough so that it could begin to recover plutonium from the reactor's spent fuel within a matter of weeks to months."[109] Estimates indicate that the resuscitated reactor may be able to produce enough spent plutonium for one bomb per year.

Highly enriched uranium is another path North Korea is pursing for nuclear weapons. In November 2010, Stanford physicist and former Los Alamos director Siegfried Hecker was shown a modern facility he estimated to contain 2,000 centrifuges for enriching uranium. While Hecker noted that the "facilities appear to be designed primarily for civilian nuclear power, not to boost North Korea's military capability," he cautioned that "the uranium enrichment facilities could be readily converted to produce highly-enriched uranium (HEU) bomb fuel."[110] Later reports indicated North Korea was likely to have a second HEU facility that would double its capacity to enrich uranium.

Other assessments of the potential size of the North Korean nuclear arsenal have painted an even grimmer picture. An April 2015 story in the *Wall Street Journal* cited an estimate by Chinese scientists that placed the DPRK arsenal at twenty warheads. The study indicated that the stockpile was evenly divided between plutonium- and uranium-based warheads and was expected to double by 2016.[111] In June 2016, David Albright and Serena Kelleher-Vergantini reported that the arsenal had increased, but only to thirteen to twenty-one warheads.[112] The previous year, Albright published a study that examined three potential scenarios in a future North Korean program and projected that the force could grow to twenty, fifty, or one hundred nuclear weapons by 2020, depending on certain variables.[113]

The future size and scope of the North Korean force remains a point of speculation. However, it is likely that North Korea will opt for a small nuclear arsenal of approximately 100 to 150 warheads that gives it a force similar in size to that of Pakistan or India.[114] While Pyongyang could seek a larger force, it may decide that this is sufficient for its needs. Another factor is the cost to build and maintain a larger arsenal. The North Korean economy continues to struggle and will be further pressed by the sanctions regime that is in place. The expense of building nuclear weapons and maintaining the necessary infrastructure to support them is considerable and may work to limit the size of the nuclear stockpile that North Korea is willing and able to maintain.

North Korea has also devoted significant effort and resources to the development of a robust ballistic missile program. Pyongyang began its efforts to acquire missile technology in the 1960s with the acquisition of Soviet surface-to-air missiles. In 1965, Kim Il-sung founded the Hamhung Military Academy to assist in the development of advanced weapons, noting that "if war breaks out, the United States and Japan will also be involved. In order to prevent their involvement, we have to be able to produce rockets that fly as far as Japan."[115] Eventually, North Korea obtained Soviet FROG (Free Rocket Over Ground) missiles and later began to produce its own version by reverse engineering these Soviet designs. North Korea now has twenty-four FROG missiles of various types that are capable of carrying conventional or chemical warheads.

Sometime in the early 1980s, Pyongyang obtained the Scud B missile from Egypt and later produced an improved Scud C, a short-range ballistic missile with an enhanced range of 500 kilometers, which covers most of South Korea. Work has also progressed on another short-range ballistic missile, the Toksa or KN-02. An upgraded variant of the Soviet SS-21, it uses a solid-fuel propellant, an important advancement over North Korea's many liquid-fuel missiles. It has a range of approximately 120 kilometers, making it capable of reaching Seoul and other targets south of the capital. At some point, it might be outfitted to carry nuclear weapons, but it is more likely to carry conventional or chemical payloads. The KN-02 has been tested on several occasions and is believed to be North Korea's most reliable and accurate missile.

In 1988, North Korea pursued further enhancements to the Scud and produced the Nodong missile, a one-stage MRBM with a range of 1,200 to 1,500 kilometers, depending on the variant and type of warhead. The first Nodong was flight tested in 1993, and several others have been launched over the years, often as a protest to ROK-U.S. military exercises that are held twice annually during the fall and spring. The accuracy and reliability of the Nodong are uncertain, but it is likely that this missile is configured to carry a nuclear payload along with its conventional and chemical capabilities. The Nodong's range brings all of Japan and U.S. bases there, including Okinawa, within range. North Korea is believed to have close to 800 to 1,000 short- to medium-range ballistic missiles, including 500 Scuds of different types and 150 to 200 Nodongs.[116] While North Korea thus has a large cache of short- and medium-range missiles, the number of launchers is significantly less, reducing the number of missiles it can deploy at any given time without reloading.

Finally, North Korea is also working on other longer-range systems, including the Musudan missile, believed to have a range of 3,000 to 4,000 kilometers, making it capable of reaching Guam, and the KN-08, an intercontinental missile that can target most of the United States. Both of these missiles are mounted on mobile launchers and have been deployed and appeared in parades. The Musudan has been flight tested on several occasions, but only one test, in June 2016, was deemed anything close to a success.[117] The KN-08 has yet to be flight tested, raising important concerns about the capability and reliability of both missiles. North Korea is also working on an upgraded version of the KN-08, the KN-14, and they tested an IRBM in February 2017, a modified Musudan that used solid fuel. The missile, called the Pukguksong-2 by North Korean media, is an improved model of an earlier SLBM. However, some analysts argue that other countries have tested variations of these systems, making them more reliable than some people believe. Moreover, even if they are not reliable, they may possess what Wit and Ahn have called "emergency operational capability," so that even if the chance of working is low, deployment in a crisis would nonetheless generate deterrence benefit for North Korea.[118]

Work also continues on the Taepodong, an intercontinental ballistic missile capable of reaching the U.S. mainland. North Korea has conducted several tests of this missile, including its use as a space launch vehicle. On several occasions, Pyongyang has attempted to put a satellite into orbit. The most recent effort occurred in February 2016 with the launch of the Unha-3, which achieved orbit but is reportedly not functioning properly. North Korea maintains that these launches are part of a legitimate space program, but they are also a cover for its ICBM program because both use almost identical technology. Moreover, the launches are banned under previous UN Security Council resolutions that followed earlier launches and nuclear weapon tests.

In addition to land-based missiles, North Korea has also been working to develop a submarine-launched ballistic missile (SLBM). Pyongyang appears to have begun the program in the early 1990s in cooperation with Soviet/Russian scientists, though the central government in Moscow may not have been aware of it.[119] In 2014, evidence surfaced of a North Korean submarine equipped with a vertical launch tube, a Sinpo-class submarine (named after the Sinpo South Shipyard where it was discovered), followed by satellite imagery of a ground-based test stand for missile ejection tests.[120] North Korea has conducted several vertical launch tube missile ejection tests for an SLBM from a ground-based platform, a submerged platform, or a submarine.[121] These tests have had mixed results, and it is not clear how far North Korea has progressed or when it will have an operational ballistic missile submarine. Given the attention the SLBM program has received, including Kim Jong-un's attendance at some of the tests, the program seems to be a high priority of the regime. Indeed, an SLBM capability would increase the survivability of North Korea's nuclear deterrent while allowing movement of these weapons closer to intended targets. Though Pyongyang has considerable work to do before it has a functioning SLBM and submarine, along with the necessary expertise to conduct deterrence patrols, it will continue working on this capability.

North Korea's nuclear weapon and ballistic missile programs continue to grow, but they also face some significant hurdles. Most important, North Korean scientists must be able to miniaturize a warhead to fit on a ballistic missile. Pyongyang has yet to provide definitive evidence to demonstrate that capability, but increasingly, analysts are concluding it has mastered the task, in part based on circumstantial evidence. For example, Pyongyang may have received assistance in warhead design from the AQ Khan network, and the relatively small yield of North Korea's first nuclear test may have been an effort to determine how to miniaturize a warhead.[122] In March 2016, Admiral William Gortney, head of NORAD and commander of U.S. Northern Command, stated in congressional testimony that "while the KN-08 remains untested, modeling suggests it could deliver a nuclear payload to much of the Continental United States."[123] One day before Gortney's statement, Kim Jong-un appeared with DPRK scientists next to a silver globe that was likely a mockup of a nuclear warhead.[124]

Second, most of North Korea's missile force uses liquid fuel for its engines. Liquid fuel is dangerous, unstable, and corrosive. Missiles can only be fueled for a relatively short period of time; within two or three days, either the missiles must be fired or the fuel must be emptied. Each time this is done, the possibility of accidental explosions increases significantly, creating serious risks for land- or submarine-based systems. Moreover, North Korea's goal is to maintain a survivable and reliable nuclear deterrent. Every time it pulls in launch systems for refueling, it takes these weapons offline, making them unavailable for use and reducing their deterrence effect.

Third, while North Korea has developed reentry vehicles (RVs) for its short- and medium-range ballistic missiles, it has not developed RVs for its long-range missiles. It is a difficult task to design a long-range RV capable of surviving a violent reentry through the earth's atmosphere to deliver a warhead on target and detonate it where intended.

Furthermore, DPRK missiles are known to be inaccurate, requiring improvements in their long-range guidance systems.

Finally, once North Korea has developed its nuclear weapons force, there will be further challenges and expense in maintaining it. Guidance systems, engines, parts, and other components need to be replaced periodically, a task that is a difficult for any state, much less North Korea, which would need to do so while under the weight of sanctions.[125] All of these hurdles will be difficult to overcome, and it is unclear when North Korea will reach these goals. However, it is clear that it will continue working to build an effective and reliable nuclear deterrent.

NORTH KOREAN NUCLEAR STRATEGY AND DOCTRINE

As with China, there are no clear indications of North Korea's thinking on the role of nuclear weapons. Pyongyang has not made pronouncements regarding its strategy and doctrine, though it has made a number of statements that provide some idea of its thinking. In addition, several studies have sought to piece together the available information to develop tentative estimates of DPRK strategy and doctrine.[126] The most important role for North Korea's nuclear weapons is likely deterrence, addressing what it sees as serious security threats. Pyongyang fears the possibility of a U.S.-ROK regime change operation or political intimidation. Several accounts cite North Koreans concluding that the regimes in Iraq, Libya, and Afghanistan would not have been ousted if they had had nuclear weapons.[127] Thus, nuclear weapons have become a central part of DPRK security strategy to ensure the survival of the regime. For example, on February 10, 2005, North Korea, in formally declaring itself a nuclear power, noted that "the United States disclosed its attempt to topple the political system in the DPRK at any cost, threatening it with a nuclear stick. This compels us to take a measure to bolster its nuclear-weapons arsenal in order to protect the ideology, system, freedom, and democracy chosen by its people." Consequently, North Korean nuclear weapons "will remain [a] nuclear deterrent for self-defense under any circumstances."[128] In 2014, the *Rodong Sinmun*, the official paper of the Korean Workers Party Central Committee, declared, "A nuclear war has not broken out on the peninsula entirely because the DPRK has steadily bolstered up its war deterrence. The reality clearly proves once again how farsighted the DPRK was when it took such self-defensive steps as reacting to a nuclear threat in kind. Even a nuclear weapons state can never slacken its vigilance as long as there are such nuclear warmongers as the United States."[129] Finally, in its announcement of the January 2016 "H-bomb" test, North Korea noted that "nothing is more foolish than dropping a hunting gun before herds of ferocious wolves." Thus, "there can neither be suspended nuclear development nor nuclear dismantlement on the part of the DPRK unless the United States has rolled back its vicious hostile policy toward the former. The army and people of the DPRK will steadily escalate its nuclear deterrence of justice both in quality and quantity to reliably guarantee the future of the revolutionary cause of Juche for all ages."[130] Pyongyang has made similar declarations regarding nuclear weapons and deterrence on many occasions during the past decade.

In addition to deterrence, nuclear weapons also play a role in domestic politics, providing an important achievement for a regime that has few economic successes to claim. As well, Pyongyang likely believes that it gains international prestige and greater political leverage in dealing with South Korea and the United States as a result of developing nuclear weapons.

Another role that nuclear weapons might play in North Korean behavior is what Cold War analysts called the "stability-instability paradox" whereby the U.S.-Soviet nuclear standoff maintained stability at the strategic level but freed up both sides for destabilizing actions at lower levels. The threat of nuclear annihilation ensured that conflicts would not escalate, allowing for more lower-level mischief. It is plausible that North Korea may view its nuclear capability as a shield to conduct more lower-level provocations, as it did in 2010 with the sinking of the *Cheonan* and the shelling of Yeonpyeong Island. However, North Korea has long been tolerant of high levels of risk, and its weapons tests and abrasive rhetoric are more accurately read through the lens of deterrence than that of the paradox.[131] So far at least, nuclear weapons do not appear to have emboldened DPRK behavior beyond its past willingness to take risks. South Korea's determined pronouncements after Yeonpyeong Island that it will respond next time North Korea conducts a military operation, along with increased U.S.-ROK planning and preparation as demonstrated in the Combined Counter-Provocation Plan, may have been important factors in restraining kinetic North Korean provocations. However, the influence that nuclear weapons may have on North Korean behavior bears close watching.

Finally, a focus on deterrence means that North Korea will seek to achieve a survivable second strike nuclear force able to retaliate after an attack. A small nuclear arsenal will likely be sufficient to achieve these needs. However, it is also possible that Pyongyang may move toward a warfighting strategy that entails the early first use of nuclear weapons to stop an invasion by striking massed ROK and U.S. forces, military bases in South Korea and Japan, and possible invasion routes.[132] This would necessitate developing smaller tactical nuclear weapons and adopting a posture Vipin Narang labels "asymmetric escalation"—one "explicitly designed to deter primarily ground conventional attacks by enabling a state to respond with rapid, asymmetric escalation to first-use of nuclear weapons against military and/or civilian targets."[133] North Korea has given a "no first use" declaration, but these are always suspect, especially when a state's survival is at stake, and Pyongyang would not hesitate to use nuclear weapons if it believed that were the case.

U.S. nuclear weapons and the nuclear umbrella have no doubt gotten North Korea's attention, though it remains unclear how they have affected Pyongyang's thinking and planning. Though the same caveats apply regarding the inability to determine the factors contributing to successful deterrence, North Korea regularly issues statements of concern over U.S. nuclear weapons and the likelihood that the United States might start a nuclear war on the peninsula. In part signals of North Korean concerns, they are also efforts to criticize the U.S. policy of extended deterrence and justify its own nuclear program. North Korea's determination to acquire a nuclear weapon with a long-range missile that can reach the continental United States is no doubt an indicator of its belief that it needs to be able to threaten the U.S. homeland to counter the U.S. nuclear umbrella. On many occasions, the United States has issued pointed counterthreats to reinforce deterrence against North Korea and to reassure the South because the situation had shifted toward one of immediate deterrence. Some people have argued that rather than deterring North Korea, these actions have actually provoked Pyongyang and worsened security relations. Indeed, as strategic deterrence has held in Korea for the past six decades, it is difficult to ascertain what role the nuclear umbrella has played, but it is clear that it has had an impact on North Korean strategy and doctrine.

The future of North Korea's nuclear weapons program is uncertain, not only in how Pyongyang's strategy and doctrine will develop but also in the type of force it intends to build. U.S. intelligence officials may have gotten it correct in February 2011:

> Because of deficiencies in their conventional military forces, the North's leaders are focused on deterrence and defense. The Intelligence Community assesses Pyongyang views its nuclear capabilities are intended for deterrence, international prestige, and coercive diplomacy. We judge that North Korea would consider using nuclear weapons only under certain narrow circumstances. We also assess, albeit with low confidence, Pyongyang probably would not attempt to use nuclear weapons against U.S. forces or territory unless it perceived its regime to be on the verge of military defeat and risked an irretrievable loss of control.[134]

Thus, strategic deterrence is likely to hold in Korea as it has for the past six decades. The DPRK's primary goal is maintaining the survival of the Kim family regime, and an offensive strike across the DMZ with nuclear or conventional weapons would bring its downfall. However, a growing North Korean nuclear capability and the dangers of miscalculation and escalation will severely complicate security relations in the region and will keep leaders in Seoul and Tokyo attentive to the U.S. nuclear umbrella.

CONCLUSION

The primary concerns of the U.S. nuclear umbrella in Asia are China and North Korea. Both have military capabilities, conventional and unconventional, that pose serious concerns for U.S. allies in East Asia. Yet threat perceptions by Seoul and Tokyo are very different. Both U.S. allies see North Korea as a serious, immediate threat that is doing a lot to disrupt regional security. In some respects, leaders and analysts in Japan fear a North Korean nuclear strike more than do those in South Korea, but Seoul's proximity to the DMZ and North Korea's penchant for provocative behavior place them on the immediate firing line should deterrence fail. North Korea's determination to develop nuclear weapons destabilizes regional peace and stability, which could have a serious impact on both countries.

China is another matter. Japan sees China as a serious long-term challenge to its security and to regional stability. Beijing's aggressive actions in the maritime domain and efforts to push the United States out of Asia would have a serious impact on Japanese interests. Tokyo and Beijing are locked in a struggle for regional influence that is closely tied to the U.S.-Japan alliance. China's military modernization efforts, including its strategic nuclear forces, are deeply concerning, possibly indicating Beijing's intentions to dominate the region. The Japan-U.S. alliance, along with the nuclear umbrella, remains a fundamental element of Japanese security vis-à-vis China.

South Korea is in a more difficult position concerning China. Sino-ROK economic ties are crucial for South Korea's economic development; ROK trade with China is more than with the United States and Japan combined. South Korean leaders also recognize that China plays a central role in dealing with North Korea, adding another motive for maintaining good relations with Beijing. However, South Koreans in some quarters are becoming increasingly wary of China's actions and future strategic intent. Thus, although economic ties with China are important, security will always dictate a close relationship with the United States, and South Koreans are painfully aware of the possibility of being caught in the middle. Consequently, relations with China and security assessments that involve the nuclear umbrella are more complicated for South Korea. In the end, the U.S. nuclear umbrella is a tool that must address an increasingly complicated security environment for both Japan and South Korea.

CHAPTER FOUR

Japan and the U.S. Nuclear Umbrella

During the Cold War, Japan conducted several assessments regarding the feasibility of developing its own nuclear weapons. Each time, these studies concluded that although Japan had the technology and materials to produce nuclear weapons, the economic, political, and security costs were prohibitive and it would remain a nonnuclear state. However, these studies often contained an important caveat: Japan would not develop nuclear weapons "at present," leaving the door open for this path should there be drastic changes to the security environment or deterioration of the U.S. extended deterrence commitment. Thus, while much of the Japanese public had a "nuclear allergy," many of Japan's conservative leaders did not and actively considered a nuclear option. Japanese leaders also made it clear that the U.S. alliance and the nuclear umbrella were vital to Japan's security.

While Japan decided not to develop nuclear weapons, it also largely relinquished strategy and management of the U.S. nuclear umbrella to Washington.[1] Though maintaining a public position that supported nuclear disarmament, "consecutive Japanese governments adopted a posture of being a reluctant recipient of the U.S. extended nuclear deterrence, which was regarded as a 'necessary evil' particularly during the Cold War."[2] The third of the nonnuclear principles committed Japan to keeping U.S. nuclear weapons out of Japan, but it is now clear that U.S. ships carrying nuclear weapons were allowed to dock in Japanese ports.

The United States maintained a large nuclear arsenal in Okinawa until 1972, and Japanese officials continued to seek reassurances regarding the nuclear umbrella. For years, Japanese leaders had relatively little dialogue with U.S. officials over the details of the nuclear umbrella, including what would trigger a U.S. nuclear response and U.S. plans for how to use nuclear weapons. Over the past decade, U.S. and Japanese defense planners have significantly increased their collaboration toward a more shared understanding of the role of the nuclear umbrella in Japanese security. In the end, the nuclear umbrella became an important part of the overall Japan-U.S. and regional security architecture. Despite the inherent credibility problems of the U.S. commitment to defend Japan with nuclear weapons, the nuclear umbrella helped to maintain regional stability, was an important political signal to Japan of the importance of the alliance, and convinced Japanese leaders that they need not have their own nuclear capability.

This chapter will examine the role of the U.S. nuclear umbrella in Japanese defense planning, including Tokyo's assessment of its security environment, Japan's security strategy and the role of the U.S. nuclear umbrella in that strategy, Japanese efforts to enhance extended deterrence, and finally, the obstacles to and likelihood of Japan's ever developing its own nuclear weapons capability.

UNDER THE NUCLEAR UMBRELLA: JAPANESE PLANNING AND SECURITY CALCULATIONS

Nuclear weapons and the U.S. nuclear umbrella are a central part of Japanese security considerations and defense policy. Japanese leaders quietly thought about the merits of acquiring nuclear weapons but ultimately decided to forgo them, relying on the U.S. nuclear umbrella instead, while retaining a latent capability through its civilian nuclear program.

In the early days of the U.S.-Japan alliance, there was little discussion about the U.S. nuclear umbrella. The 1960 Treaty of Mutual Cooperation and Security made no mention of extended deterrence or the nuclear umbrella, noting only that Tokyo and Washington would maintain and develop "their capacities to resist armed attack"

(Article III), consult from time to time and "whenever the security of Japan or international peace and security in the Far East is threatened" (Article IV), and "an armed attack against either Party in the territories under the administration of Japan would be dangerous to its own peace and safety and declares that it would act to meet the common danger in accordance with its constitutional provisions and processes" (Article V).[3]

Japan's nuclear worries increased dramatically with China's first nuclear test in 1964, followed by nuclear-capable missile tests and Beijing's first H-bomb test. To address these fears, in January 1965, Japanese leaders made a formal request to President Lyndon Johnson for the U.S. nuclear deterrent to defend Japan. Johnson provided the commitment, but did so quietly. Johnson made a general public commitment in 1966 regarding China's nuclear weapons, declaring that "the leaders of China must realize that any nuclear capability they can develop can—and will—be deterred. We have already declared that nations which do not seek national nuclear weapons can be sure that they will have our strong support, if they need it, against any threat of nuclear blackmail."[4] In 1967, Satō asked for confirmation during his summit meeting, and Johnson gave the same reply, reassuring him of the U.S. nuclear commitment. Satō believed that the nuclear umbrella, in addition to the formal alliance, was essential to address the fears that a nuclear-armed China could intimidate Japan and be a psychological threat that pushed Japan to neutrality in the region.[5]

In 1968, Satō promulgated the Four Pillars, with the last pillar publically acknowledging Japan's reliance on the U.S. nuclear umbrella. Japan continued to study the possibility and implications of going nuclear but decided to maintain its security through the alliance with the United States and the nuclear umbrella while maintaining a latent capability to develop nuclear weapons should future circumstances warrant.[6]

Since that time, Japan has reasserted the importance of the U.S. nuclear commitment in its most important defense planning document, the National Defense Program Guidelines. Japanese officials have produced this document on five separate occasions, in 1976, 1995, 2004, 2010, and the latest version in 2013 (the first two were called the National Defense Program Outline).

The National Defense Program Guidelines

The first National Defense Program Outline, published in 1976, stated that while there was little likelihood of full-scale military conflict involving Japan, "against [the] nuclear threat Japan will rely on the nuclear capability of the United States."[7] In the context of the Cold War, Tokyo's chief security concerns were the Soviet Union and China. Japanese leaders were also concerned about a possible U.S. retrenchment from Asia following the Vietnam War. North Korea had yet to test a nuclear weapon and had little capability to reach the Japanese home islands.

Following the end of the Cold War, in 1995 Tokyo issued another National Defense Program Outline, which reiterated its reliance on the U.S. nuclear deterrent in wording similar to that of 1976.[8] With the collapse of the Soviet Union, Moscow had receded as a threat but was replaced by North Korea, which now possessed medium-range Nodong missiles capable of reaching most of Japan with conventional and chemical warheads as well as a nascent nuclear program, though one that was constrained by the 1994 Agreed Framework.

The 2004 document, now called the National Defense Program Guidelines (NDPG), followed in the wake of the September 11 attacks on the United States and acknowledged that the security environment was changing with a broader array of threats, particularly that of international terrorism. Though the Russian threat continued to recede, North Korean military activities "constitute a major destabilizing factor to regional and international security, and are a serious challenge to international non-proliferation efforts." Regarding China, the NDPG warns, "we will have to remain attentive to its future actions."[9] The 2004 NDPG stressed the importance of the Japan-U.S. alliance and, after affirming adherence to the three nonnuclear principles, stated that "to protect its territory and people against the threat of nuclear weapons, Japan will continue to rely on the U.S. nuclear deterrent."[10]

Liberal Democratic Party (LDP) leaders were preparing to release a revised NDPG in 2009. However, after a crushing defeat of the LDP in the historic election of August 2009, the Democratic Party of Japan (DPJ) delayed final approval and released its own NDPG in December 2010. The new NDPG outlined the growing North Korean threat following its second nuclear weapons test in May 2009 along with ongoing work on various missile programs. Relations with China were also continuing to deteriorate, particularly over the Senkaku/Daioyu islands, in what Japanese officials and analysts called gray zones, where tensions persist over unresolved territorial disputes that are neither peace nor war.

The 2010 NDPG marked an important shift in Japanese defense strategy. Instead of relying, as in the past, on a "Basic Defense Force Concept" that "places priority on ensuring deterrence through the existence of defense forces per se," the Japan Self-Defense Force (JSDF) shifted to a " 'Dynamic Defense Force' that focuses on [the] 'operation' of defense forces, and . . . increasing SDF activities as well as ensuring the quantity and quality of equipment." Regarding "dynamic deterrence," the 2010 NDPG asserts that Japan will ensure "deterrence by showing Japan's will and high-performance defense capabilities through timely and appropriate conduct of various activities."[11] A Japanese report preparatory to the NDPG noted that the new security environment "increased the importance of 'dynamic deterrence' through which a defense force demonstrates high operational performance in normal circumstances by conducting timely and appropriate operations, such as surveillance and preparation against airspace violation, in contrast to the traditional 'static deterrence' focused on quantities and size of weapons and troops."[12] Thus, Japan committed to demonstrating its deterrence capability rather than relying solely on the possession of certain capabilities.

The document reaffirmed Japan's commitment to the three nonnuclear principles along with support for international efforts to achieve nuclear disarmament and a nuclear-free world, but noted "at the same time, as long as nuclear weapons exist, the extended deterrence provided by the United States, with [a] nuclear deterrent as a vital element, will be indispensable."[13] In addition, in the wake of the two North Korean nuclear tests in 2006 and 2009, Japan pledged to play a greater role in supporting the U.S. security guarantee: "In order to maintain and improve the credibility of the extended deterrence, Japan will closely cooperate with the United States, and will also appropriately implement its own efforts including ballistic missile defense and civil protection."[14] Thus, Japan sought to increase its contribution to U.S. extended deterrence rather than simply rely on Washington's security guarantee.

In December 2012, the LDP regained control of the Japanese Diet vaulting Shinzo Abe back into the prime minister's office, a position he had held for a year in 2006–07. To distance itself from the previous DPJ government, the Abe administration released a revised NDPG in December 2013. The document repeated similar themes from the past, including concern for "gray zone" issues and identification of North Korea as "a serious and imminent threat to Japan's security," along with elevated concern for China's growing and more modern military capabilities accompanied by its uncertain intentions. Regarding China's actions in the maritime and air domains, because "Japan has great concerns about these Chinese activities, it will need to pay utmost attention to them."[15] However, planners believed "the probability of a large-scale military conflict between major countries . . . presumably remains low" and the alliance with the United States continued to be a "cornerstone."[16]

Regarding nuclear weapons, Japan restated its commitment to the three nonnuclear principles and that it would continue to "play a constructive and active role in international nuclear disarmament and non-proliferation efforts" to assist in "creating a world free of nuclear weapons." However, "extended deterrence provided by the U.S. with nuclear deterrence at its core, is indispensable."[17] In some respects, this language is stronger than previous iterations, placing the nuclear umbrella at the center of U.S. extended deterrence. Moreover, to "maintain and enhance the credibility of extended deterrence," Japan would closely cooperate with Washington and undertake its own measures, such as ballistic missile defense and civil defense measures.[18]

U.S. Assurances of the Nuclear Umbrella

Since the 1960s, the United States has periodically, but quietly, provided assurances to Japanese leaders of the U.S. nuclear umbrella. Given Japan's past experience with nuclear weapons, formal public acknowledgment of the umbrella was more difficult than was the case for South Korea. For Japan, statements affirming the U.S. nuclear umbrella were contained in the 1978 and 1997 Guidelines for U.S.-Japan Defense Cooperation, a document that provides the outline of alliance roles and missions. In both cases, the documents include a terse and somewhat vague statement that "the United States will maintain its nuclear deterrent capability."[19] Other public pronouncements began to appear in the joint statements of the Security Consultative Committee (SCC) meetings that included the U.S. secretaries of defense and state along with their Japanese counterparts. The 1997 and 2000 SCC joint statements did not contain a specific reference to the nuclear umbrella, but the 2002 statement noted, "The Ministers stressed that North Korean use of weapons of mass destruction, such as nuclear, chemical, and biological weapons would have the gravest consequences."[20] Though a veiled reference to the use of U.S. nuclear weapons, the statement was not a clear indicator of nuclear extended deterrence.

In 2005, the joint statement was more specific: "U.S. strike capabilities and the nuclear deterrence provided by the U.S. remain an essential complement to Japan's defense capabilities in ensuring the defense of Japan and contribute to peace and security in the region."[21] There was no mention in the May 2006 statement, but in 2007, after North Korea's first nuclear test in October 2006, the joint statement was explicit: "U.S. extended deterrence underpins the defense of Japan and regional security. The U.S. reaffirmed that the full range of U.S. military capabilities—both nuclear and non-nuclear strike forces and defensive capabilities—form the core of extended deterrence and support U.S. commitments to the defense of Japan."[22] After North Korea's test, Secretary of State Condoleezza Rice had used similar wording when she declared, "The United States has the will and the capability to meet the full range—and I underscore full range—of its deterrent and security commitments to Japan."[23] Throughout the Cold War, the nuclear umbrella had been part of the general deterrence preparations to defend Japan from the Soviet Union and China. With North Korea's first nuclear test and its disruptive impact on regional security, deterrence shifted toward an immediate deterrence problem, prompting more pointed statements of the nuclear umbrella.

In subsequent years, the SCC statements contained similar declarations. The April 2015 communique, after reaffirming the U.S. "rebalance" to the region, noted that "central to this is the ironclad U.S. commitment to the defense of Japan, through the full range of U.S. military capabilities, including nuclear and conventional."[24] In addition, in response to the third North Korean nuclear test in February 2013, President Obama pledged to Japanese prime minister Abe in a phone call that "the United

States remains steadfast in its defense commitments to Japan, including the extended deterrence offered by the U.S. nuclear umbrella," according to a White House summary.[25] The explicit statements of the nuclear umbrella also provided reassurances in the face of more aggressive Chinese behavior. As a result, the U.S. nuclear umbrella has taken on a more public and prominent position in the alliance and in U.S. extended deterrence for Japan.

THE ROLE OF THE NUCLEAR UMBRELLA
IN JAPAN'S SECURITY PLANNING

Since the mid-1960s, the U.S. nuclear umbrella has been an important element of Japanese security planning, but Japanese leaders gave little thought to the details. In its early years, the nuclear umbrella was relatively informal, with little direct Japan-U.S. coordination. With growing concern over North Korea's nuclear and ballistic missile capabilities followed by increasing hostility with China, Japanese defense planners have been very concerned with the implementation and credibility of the U.S. nuclear umbrella. Given these regional threats, there is a sense that Japan is more vulnerable with an "eroding security position," requiring increased attention to the umbrella.[26]

In many respects Japan and South Korea are linked through the U.S. nuclear umbrella and their bilateral alliances with the United States. However, when it comes to assessments of the role of the nuclear umbrella, there is some divergence in their views. For South Korea, addressed in Chapter 5, the focus is on the immediate military threat from North Korea. In Japan, the immediate security concern is also the DPRK, but China is seen as a long-term security problem. We now turn to a specific discussion of the roles the nuclear umbrella plays for Japan in addressing these security concerns.

First, the U.S. commitment to defend Japan with nuclear weapons has been a tool to address the growing nuclear weapons and ballistic missile capability of North Korea. One Japanese official believed that North Korea would likely not launch against the South but rather that Japan or a U.S. base in Japan was the most likely target of a North Korean nuclear strike.[27] According to a U.S. analyst, North Korea is an immediate military threat and a direct operational challenge to Japanese security.[28]

In 1998, North Korea launched a long-range Taepodong missile that traveled over Japanese airspace and unnerved Japanese citizens. The test outraged Japan, and according to one U.S. analyst, "the Japanese public recognized for the first time that someone was out to get them."[29]

The 2006 North Korean nuclear weapon test added to Japanese anxiety. North Korea has 150 to 200 intermediate-range Nodong missiles that can reach most of Japan, and this may be the first missile system Pyongyang has outfitted with a nuclear weapon. The Nodong can also be used with conventional, chemical, or biological munitions. Since 1993, North Korea has conducted multiple tests of the Nodong, which could reach Japan within seven to ten minutes, causing horrendous damage to Tokyo or other Japanese cities with little notice.[30] There is serious concern in Japan about the rationality of North Korean leader Kim Jong-un, including whether he understands deterrence theory or the credibility of the U.S. defense commitment. The U.S. nuclear umbrella provides a direct deterrent threat by promising overwhelming destruction should North Korea ever use conventional, chemical, biological, or nuclear weapons.

Second, the U.S. nuclear umbrella addresses the longer-term and perhaps more serious security concerns associated with Sino-Japanese rivalry.[31] China's nuclear weapons program in the 1960s was the impetus for the first formal, though secret, U.S. statement on the nuclear umbrella. In the years since, the likelihood of a Chinese, or for that matter Russian, attack on the Japanese home islands has become negligible. Instead, concerns have shifted south to the maritime environment of the East China Sea and Japan's southernmost islands, the Senkakus.

Worries regarding China are less about an overt military threat than in the case of North Korea. Indeed, some U.S. experts and officials maintain that when Japanese officials talk about North Korea, they are really talking about China. According to one U.S. official, China is the big existential threat, and there is a "deeply ingrained hostility" between China and Japan.[32] There is also a sense of frustration that little can be done to deter North Korea, so it is better to concentrate on China. Japanese analysts fear that China will use its nuclear weapons capability to intimidate and blackmail Japan on issues such as the Senkakus in ways that are more troublesome than a direct military attack.[33] Fears continue to grow that China will act more aggressively in the maritime arena, and dangers of an inadvertent clash or conflict through miscalculation continue to grow. According to one Japanese analyst, China will not use nuclear weapons against Japan, but the U.S. nuclear umbrella is needed to neutralize Beijing's political power and influence.[34] Thus, China is more of a long-term political and security concern of general deterrence than Pyongyang, which is an immediate military threat. The U.S. nuclear umbrella is seen as helping to counter Beijing's political and military leverage and reduce any intimidation by China, allowing for greater freedom of action in the face of growing Chinese power. Contrary to views about North Korea, there is greater confidence that Chinese leaders are rational, understand deterrence, and desire stability to support their need for continued economic growth.

Finally, the U.S. nuclear umbrella is an important political signal with crucial implications for the Japan-U.S. alliance and the regional security architecture. The U.S. defense commitment and the overall alliance relationship has many political, economic, and military dimensions. The nuclear umbrella is one part of a large and complex alliance relationship. Not only does the credibility of the nuclear umbrella support the alliance, but the overall health of the alliance in turn helps to bolster the nuclear umbrella. One former U.S. official noted that Japanese concerns are not specifically about the credibility of the nuclear umbrella but more about the overall state of the alliance. If the larger alliance were unreliable, that would be a problem for the nuclear umbrella.[35] The nuclear umbrella, he notes, is an article of faith. Don't remove it or test it; it has to be a given. While it is "soothing," it is not entirely clear that the United States would use nuclear weapons. Rather, it is a fundamental underpinning of the alliance, despite the question of whether it would ever be implemented.[36] If the United States chose to alter its nuclear guarantee, it would be a serious disruption of the status quo and raise fundamental questions about the alliance and the U.S. commitment. Currently, the alliance is in good condition, and Japanese leaders are relatively confident of the U.S. security guarantee and the alliance. However, Japanese leaders and analysts watch closely to observe any potential changes in the nuclear umbrella, which they might perceive as a weakening of the broader U.S. commitment.[37] Important actions that have helped in this regard were the prompt U.S. assistance provided in the wake of the March 2011 tsunami and President Obama's pledge that Japanese administration of the Senkaku islands fell within the scope of Article V of the alliance. The April 2015 Japan-U.S. Defense Guidelines were another important indicator of the depth of the U.S. defense commitment. The document contained an early declaration of nuclear deterrence: "The United States will continue to extend deterrence to Japan through the full range of capabilities, including, U.S. nuclear forces."[38] The nuclear umbrella is an element of this multifaceted relationship that is as important for the political signal it sends to Japanese leaders and the public as it is for its military benefit.

STRENGTHENING THE U.S. NUCLEAR UMBRELLA

U.S. Credibility

For years, the United States provided the nuclear umbrella quietly and with little discussion about the details. As one Japanese official at the Ministry of Foreign Affairs described it, "when it comes to the nuclear umbrella, it is like a talisman from the United States. Japan is not sure how it works but they put their faith in it and believe it will protect them."[39] As the North Korean nuclear threat grew and concerns over China increased, worries and discussion within Japan about the nuclear umbrella and extended deterrence intensified. One U.S. scholar noted that "Japan hadn't really thought through the implications of deterrence, escalation ladders, and nuclear use."[40] During the 2000s, many Japanese worried about the growth of North Korea's capability and questioned U.S. resolve as North Korea appeared to be methodically crossing various redlines with few apparent consequences.[41] As a result, Japanese officials and the general public had significant questions about the details and credibility of the U.S. nuclear umbrella. Indeed, some conservatives even began raising the possibility that Japan should again consider acquiring its own nuclear weapons.

To address these concerns, in July 2009 U.S. and Japanese officials announced the start of a formal dialogue to focus on U.S. nuclear weapons and the defense of Japan. This type of formal planning group exists within NATO, called the Nuclear Planning Group, but no such organization existed for Japan or South Korea. The Extended Deterrence Dialogue (EDD), as it was called, was intended to "begin a deep discussion about the elements of nuclear deterrence"; Assistant Secretary of State Kurt Campbell stated that "our goal here is to make a very strong commitment to Japan about the fact that the nuclear deterrence of the United States is extended, the nuclear umbrella remains strong and stable, and our commitment to Japan is absolutely unshakable."[42] The EDD has continued meeting approximately twice each year but has received relatively little press coverage, at Japan's request.[43] The meetings have been well received and useful for both sides. Regarding the February 2015 meeting, the Japanese Ministry of Foreign Affairs stated this was an "opportunity for the two governments to frankly exchange views on how to secure alliance deterrence as part of their security and defense cooperation." In addition, Japan "can deepen understanding on its mechanisms and coordinate its security policy with the U.S. government."[44] The previous year, the U.S. State Department commented that the EDD "reinforces the credibility of the U.S. defense commitment to Japan, including thorough discussions about strategic and conventional capabilities, and helps to promote regional stability from a near- and long-term perspective."[45]

The EDD has enabled U.S. and Japanese officials to share ideas about nuclear weapons, extended deterrence, strategy, and planning to develop more of a shared understanding of these concepts. In addition, the meetings have provided an opening to have a broader discussion about nuclear issues and U.S. policy that in the past were taboo.[46] These meetings have also been occasions for conducting simulations and table-top exercises to facilitate testing and discussion of extended nuclear deterrence. U.S. officials and analysts note that the EDD has been critical in providing a bridge to understanding nuclear issues. Indeed, simply announcing and then holding the dialogue has gone a long way toward reassuring the Japanese public.[47]

In a number of respects, Japan has been easier to reassure than South Korea. Japan has been less in need of regular public declarations and actions to reaffirm the deterrence commitment and was often satisfied with quieter statements of assurance. One U.S. official noted that while Japan wants dialogue and insight into U.S. planning, they are content to "only see a little behind the curtain."[48] Japan has also been more willing to stay at the theoretical level, with less need for specific reassurances than South Korea. This is likely due in part to Japan's distance from the North Korean threat but also to greater certainty regarding its alliance with the United States. For years, Washington has referred to the U.S.-Japan alliance as the linchpin of its presence in Asia, providing critical forward basing for U.S. forces in the region. Thus, Japan has considerable confidence in its position with Washington. Meetings of the EDD are ongoing, however, and remain useful in maintaining dialogue regarding security and the nuclear umbrella.

Though Japan has needed fewer public reassurances of the nuclear umbrella, Japanese officials have been interested in specific weapons systems as a sign of the capability and credibility of the U.S. commitment. Washington has used the EDD as an opportunity to show Japanese officials the specific systems of the U.S. nuclear umbrella. In May 2012, the Japanese EDD delegation received a briefing at U.S. Strategic Command in Nebraska and was shown the control center for an ICBM at Malmstrom Air Force Base in Montana. The following year, Japanese officials visited Naval Base Kitsap in Washington State and boarded an *Ohio*-class submarine that carries the nuclear-tipped Trident II ballistic missile. In 2014, the EDD met in Albuquerque, New Mexico, and visited the Sandia laboratories.[49] In part, these measures were a response to some Japanese conservatives having raised the possibility of acquiring their own nuclear weapons. In addition, these demonstrations followed the retirement of the U.S. Navy's Tomahawk Land Attack Cruise Missile (TLAM/N), which many Japanese officials viewed as essential and whose elimination they believed damaged nuclear deterrence. Prior to the meeting, U.S. officials noted that the visit and dialogue would help Washington and Tokyo "to deepen their understanding of the strategic weapons systems that support U.S. extended deterrence guarantees, and how the United States ensures its strategic forces remain safe, secure and effective."[50] One U.S. analyst commented that "Japan loves to see the nuclear facilities; seeing the capability reassures them and makes the nuclear umbrella real."[51]

One particular system that was of great interest to Japan was the U.S. Navy's TLAM/N. The cruise missile, built in the 1970s, had the capability to launch from surface ships and submarines, carrying a conventional or nuclear warhead. The nuclear version of the missile, referred to as the TLAM/N, carried a W80 warhead with a yield of 200 KT. In 1991, under the Presidential Nuclear Initiatives, George H. W. Bush ordered the removal of a substantial number of tactical U.S. nuclear weapons from deployments abroad, hoping Moscow would do the same.[52] In 1994, the Clinton administration's Nuclear Posture Review (NPR) called for removing nuclear weapons from the entire surface fleet; attack submarines retained the capability to launch a TLAM/N, but they were not carried out to sea and remained in storage. In the early George W. Bush years, the navy argued for retiring the TLAM/N, but officials in the National Security Council and the Pentagon objected and were able to keep the system alive.[53]

The issue surfaced again during deliberations of the Congressional Strategic Posture Commission in 2009. Rumors had already surfaced that Washington was considering retiring the TLAM/N, and Japanese officials lobbied the commission to retain the system. A Japanese press account cited a "source close to Japan-U.S. diplomatic affairs" as saying, "Intercontinental ballistic missiles are devastating but inaccurate, and they inflict too many civilian casualties. A nuclear-powered submarine can gradually approach the target, allowing time for diplomatic negotiations while applying military pressure. If the submarine is close enough, it could have the option to launch highly accurate nuclear-tipped cruise missiles."[54] Indeed, the final report of the commission reflected these concerns.

> In Asia, extended deterrence relies heavily on the deployment of nuclear cruise missiles on some Los Angeles class attack submarines—the Tomahawk Land Attack Missile/Nuclear (TLAM/N). This capability will be retired in 2013 unless steps are taken to maintain it. U.S. allies in Asia are not integrated in the same way into nuclear planning and have not been asked to make commitments to delivery systems. In our work as a Commission it has become clear to us that some U.S. allies in Asia would be very concerned by TLAM/N retirement.[55]

Later, Japan's foreign affairs minister Katsuya Okada wrote a letter to Secretary of State Hillary Clinton that did not squarely confirm opposition to TLAM/N retirement but did appear to pass on the reservations of others in the government. Okada noted that Japan is dependent on the U.S. security commitment and the nuclear umbrella and that "it is necessary that trust in this deterrence be backed up by sufficient capability." However, Okada continued that while the Japanese government "has expressed no view" on the matter, if "hypothetically, such a view was expressed, it would clearly be at variance with my views, which are in favor of nuclear disarmament." Should the TLAM/N be retired, he requested "ongoing explanations of your government's extended deterrence policy, including any impact this might have on extended deterrence for Japan and how this could be supplemented."[56]

In many respects, the TLAM/N debate demonstrates the dichotomy of Japanese nuclear policy. While Tokyo has long been an advocate for denuclearization, the TLAM/N, according to one Japanese analyst, is an important capability that is a crucial symbol of U.S. credibility.[57] A U.S. analyst maintained that Japan saw the TLAM/N as "their weapon," providing a tangible capability below strategic nuclear weapons that could be used to retaliate in the event of a nuclear strike.[58] Despite Japanese concerns, the TLAM/N was formally retired in the Obama 2010 NPR, noting:

> This system serves a redundant purpose in the U.S. nuclear stockpile. It has been one of a number of means to forward-deploy nuclear weapons in time of crisis. Other means include forward-deployment of bombers with either bombs or cruise missiles, as well as forward-deployment of dual-capable fighters. In addition, U.S. ICBMs and SLBMs are capable of striking any potential adversary. The deterrence and assurance roles of TLAM-N can be adequately substituted by these other means, and the United States remains committed to providing a credible extended deterrence posture and capabilities.[59]

Or, as one former Obama administration official remarked, "it was a crappy system and the United States didn't need it."[60]

Though Japanese officials and analysts are relatively confident of the U.S. security commitment and the nuclear umbrella, concerns remain regarding its credibility. First, Japanese security is affected significantly by the state of U.S.-China relations. Should ties between Beijing and Washington warm while Japanese relations with China remain frosty, Japanese leaders fear the United States would be reluctant to confront China. Beijing would sense this and, in turn, would be less worried about U.S. retaliation, thereby reducing the credibility of the U.S. security guarantee for Japan.⁶¹ In particular, U.S. economic ties with China could make Washington reluctant to stand up for Japanese interests in the face of Chinese bullying, prompting a separate deal with China at Japan's expense.⁶² Given the current state and direction of U.S.-Sino relations, there is far less anxiety in Tokyo over this possibility.

Second, similar to concerns during the Cold War, Japan fears "decoupling" from the U.S. nuclear umbrella as Chinese and North Korean nuclear forces grow and the U.S. homeland becomes more vulnerable to their strategic nuclear forces.⁶³ Thus, the old adage of whether the United States would sacrifice Los Angeles or San Francisco for Tokyo remains in play. As North Korea's capabilities grow, particularly its ability to hit the continental United States with a nuclear-tipped missile, would Washington be reluctant to respond in kind or even with conventional weapons knowing it risks a North Korea nuclear strike? Indeed, if North Korea believed U.S. retaliation was a precursor to regime change, Pyongyang would be very willing to use nuclear weapons to defend the country.

China has long had the ability to reach the U.S. homeland with a nuclear-tipped missile. Moreover, Beijing is working hard to modernize and improve that capability through the expansion of its ICBM and SLBM force. Chinese leaders have maintained that their goal is to develop a minimum deterrence force that does not need to match the number of warheads in the U.S. and Russian arsenals. However, there is some skepticism that Beijing will stick with this nuclear posture in the years ahead, particular if relations with Washington were to deteriorate.

For a time, there was particular concern that if Washington and Moscow were to conclude further arms control reductions beyond the New START agreement that further reduced their arsenals, the Chinese might change their mind about minimum deterrence. The current state of U.S.-Russian relations make it very unlikely there will be further reductions, and indeed Vladimir Putin has indicated his determination to increase Russia's nuclear capability,⁶⁴ a sentiment that has been echoed by Donald Trump for the U.S. arsenal. Yet for a time, some Japanese analysts were concerned that either as a result of further arms control reductions that bring U.S. nuclear forces closer to the size of the Chinese arsenal or simply a decision to abandon minimum deterrence, Beijing might be tempted to match the U.S. stockpile and seek parity.⁶⁵ The result would be the same as during the Cold War, with a mutual assured destruction (MAD) standoff that would weaken the credibility of the U.S. nuclear umbrella and the overall U.S. defense commitment. As one Japanese official noted, once a condition of MAD existed between the United States and China, Beijing could deter Washington from intervening in the Senkakus or the South China Sea and become more aggressive if it is no longer vulnerable to a first strike.[66] Thus, one U.S. analyst noted, "the Japanese are very concerned with Chinese numbers and fear that China might one day seek parity with the United States; it is U.S. nuclear superiority that gives Japan peace at night."[67] There is particular worry should U.S. strategic forces drop below 1,000 warheads.[68] A Japanese analyst argued that "even if the United States and the Russians reduced their arsenals to 1,000 warheads each and the PRC remained at 250, Japan would remain worried and not sufficiently reassured. Washington should not find a solution for Europe at the expense of Asia because sometime in the future, Russia and China could be on the same side. Thus, the United States needs to maintain overwhelming nuclear superiority."[69]

Others also understand that while numbers are important, quality matters as well. When comparing the U.S. arsenal to that of China and Russia, one Japanese scholar argued that U.S. capabilities are far superior, and so long as this qualitative advantage is maintained, numerical reductions will have little effect on U.S. nuclear extended deterrence.[70] Modernization efforts by China and Russia are eroding the qualitative advantage, but Washington also has plans to upgrade its nuclear force over the next several decades.[71] Thus, with an expanded Chinese nuclear arsenal that can already reach the U.S. homeland, Japanese analysts fear Beijing could intimidate the United States and prevent Washington from coming to Japan's defense.[72] Japan has similar concerns as North Korea develops its ability to reach the U.S. homeland and possibly neutralize the U.S. commitment.

Circumstances for Using Nuclear Weapons

An element of Japanese concern regarding the U.S. nuclear umbrella is when Washington might consider the use of nuclear weapons. After President Obama's Prague speech and in the run-up to the release of the NPR, Japanese leaders feared these views echoed a reluctance to ever use nuclear weapons. In particular, there was concern that the United States would use the NPR review as an opportunity to issue a "no first use" guarantee so that nuclear retaliation would only follow the use of nuclear weapons. In addition, there were worries that the NPR would include a declaration that the "sole purpose" of nuclear weapons was to respond to nuclear use and that they would not be used in retaliation for a conventional strike or the use of chemical or biological weapons. Japan has historically expected that the United States would be willing to use nuclear weapons, and officials were unhappy with the U.S. declaration contained in the 1994 Agreed Framework agreement with North Korea stating that Washington would not threaten or use nuclear weapons against the DPRK. In 2003, Japan filed a formal request with the United States to refrain from making such a statement again. Japanese leaders understood the doubts about nuclear use but believed strategic ambiguity was important, so that absolutes such as "no first use" and "sole purpose" should not be part of stated doctrine.[73]

As the NPR took shape, the Obama administration reached out to allies for their input, and Japanese officials made their concerns known. In the end, the Obama administration opted for a nuanced declaration that pleased most Japanese defense analysts for not going too far but also received significant criticism by others in Japan and the United States for not going farther in renouncing nuclear weapons. Rather than "no first use," the NPR crafted a "negative security assurance" that pledged to refrain from threatening or using nuclear weapons against nonnuclear weapons states in compliance with their NPT obligations.

Doubts surfaced on this position as a result of events in Syria. In 2013, Syrian forces used sarin gas to kill hundreds in areas opposed to President Bashar al-Assad's rule. The year before, Obama had drawn a "redline" for Syrian use of chemical weapons, and many expected airstrikes or some other military action in retaliation. The administration asked Congress for authorization to use military force, but Secretary of State John Kerry indicated that the Assad regime could avoid airstrikes if it turned over all of its chemical weapons. Russia quickly stepped in to help broker a deal that forestalled U.S. retaliation. While the events in Syria are very different from a possible chemical weapons attack on Japan or South Korea, some wondered about the U.S. commitment to respond to chemical weapons use.[74]

While the NPR did not adopt "sole purpose" or "no first use" postures, the document contained the caveat that "the United States wishes to stress that it would only consider the use of nuclear weapons in extreme circumstances to defend the vital interests of the United States or its allies and partners."[75] It was not clear what was included under the extreme circumstances label.

The pronouncements of the NPR generated a great deal of discussion among Japanese leaders and analysts, and there was no consensus. For some, the "negative security assurance" was a good comprise and accommodation of Japan's concerns over the nuclear umbrella. Katsuya Okada, Japanese foreign minister at the time, noted that "through this NPR, the U.S. reassures its commitment to its allies, including Japan and partners to provide deterrence, including that by nuclear weapons."[76] However, others feared the posture weakened deterrence in regard to chemical and biological weapons. Ken Jimbo wrote, "Japan highly appreciates that the NPR did not adopt a universal policy that [the] 'sole purpose' of U.S. nuclear weapons is to deter nuclear attack on the U.S. and its allies. Given North Korea's potential capability to attack Japan with chemical and biological weapons, it is still crucial for Japan that the U.S. reserved the right to use nuclear weapons in response to a CBW attack."[77] One Japanese analyst noted simply that "we need nuclear weapons to deter North Korean chemical and biological weapons."[78]

Japanese assessments also raised concern about the reduced role of nuclear weapons and the overall credibility of the U.S. nuclear commitment. In the years since the release of the 2010 NPR, Japan's comfort level with U.S. extended deterrence has risen, requiring fewer public and direct pronouncements from Washington to reassure Japanese leaders and the public of its commitment. Continued dialogue in the EDD along with formal reassurances in the SCC, the 2015 Guidelines for Japan-U.S. Defense Cooperation, and the overall health of the alliance have buttressed Japanese confidence in the nuclear umbrella. Overall, there is greater assurance in Tokyo regarding the U.S. defense commitment, given the strong relationship and the large U.S. forward presence in Japan. Indeed, some have expressed an understanding that the likelihood of the United States using nuclear weapons was always very low, and as one Japanese analyst pointed out, if Washington hit North Korea with a nuclear weapon and fallout drifted over Japan, the Japanese public would be very unhappy.[79] Though the likelihood of nuclear use is small, as another Japanese analyst remarked, "it is the calculated ambiguity [of the nuclear umbrella] that is needed to counter the intimidation and military threat Japan faces."[80] As a result, as the NPR notes, Japan also sees the importance of conventional weapons in deterrence calculations and the need for continued U.S. conventional superiority in addition to the nuclear umbrella as crucial elements in overall strategic thinking and planning.

JAPANESE EFFORTS TO ENHANCE EXTENDED DETERRENCE

In the 2010 NDPG, Japan made an important addition to its previous position that it would rely on the U.S. nuclear deterrent against the threat of nuclear weapons. While reliance on the U.S. nuclear umbrella remained, Tokyo also declared that it would "implement its own efforts including ballistic missile defense and civil protection" to enhance the credibility of U.S. extended deterrence.[81]

In the 2010 NDPG, Japanese defense planners made a significant shift in their strategic thinking, adopting the idea of a "dynamic defense force": "Clear demonstration of national will and strong defense capabilities through such timely and tailored military operations as regular intelligence, surveillance, and reconnaissance activities (ISR), not just maintaining a certain level of defense force, is a critical element for ensuring credible deterrence and will contribute to stability in the region surrounding Japan."[82] In addition, as the security environment has become more complex, "Japan's future defense forces need to acquire dynamism to effectively deter and respond to various contingencies, and to proactively engage in activities to further stabilize the security environment in the Asia-Pacific and to improve the global security environment."[83] As a result, Japan began a process of expanding its own defense capabilities and hence the ability to assume a greater share of defense responsibilities. Sheila Smith noted, "Gone is the old idea that Japan should simply maintain a basic defense posture that could be ramped up if and when a threat should appear."[84] In addition, dynamic defense allows Japan to provide increased contributions to the U.S.-Japan alliance, a relationship that remains critical to Japanese security. Thus, Richard Samuels noted, "Japan is strengthening itself as an alliance partner while also hedging against the day when U.S. capabilities might slip below U.S. commitments."[85]

Ballistic Missile Defense

In 1998, North Korea launched a Taepodong missile that traveled over Japanese airspace. Japanese leaders were furious, and the public was shocked by this demonstration of their vulnerability to DPRK missiles. As a result, Japan committed itself to developing ballistic missile defense (BMD) and subsequently joined the United States in collaboration on a regional BMD system. One U.S. analyst noted that joint cooperation and planning are difficult for the U.S.-Japan alliance because it lacks the integrated command structure of the Combined Forces Command that is present in the U.S.-ROK alliance; for Washington and Tokyo, this comes together with BMD.[86]

Since North Korea's 1998 ballistic missile launch, Japan has poured billions into BMD. Japanese BMD is a multitier system that includes PAC-3 interceptors designed for shooting down incoming ballistic missiles in the terminal phase of their flight and Aegis-class destroyers equipped with SM-3 Block II missiles capable of shooting down high-altitude ballistic missiles in the middle one-third of their flight path. Japan currently has four *Kongō*-class destroyers equipped with BMD capability, has two more currently being outfitted, and plans to build two more with these capabilities in the next decade, for a total of eight.[87] Japan and the United States are currently working jointly on a more advanced SM-3 Block IIA interceptor that is expected to be ready by 2018.[88] Finally, Japan has a complex system of radars for detecting, tracking, and coordinating responses to a missile launch that are tied to U.S. radar systems, including two U.S. X-band (AN/TPY-2) radars located in Japan.

While Japanese and U.S. ballistic missile defense is directed largely toward North Korea, China has expressed strong concerns regarding these efforts. To this point, China has opted for a minimum nuclear deterrent that maintains a relatively small number of survivable systems. Chinese military leaders fear that BMD undercuts their strategic deterrent, an argument that may provide a rationale in the future for China to significantly increase its nuclear weapons force. Put more bluntly, in Beijing's mind, the North Korean threat provides Washington and Tokyo with a convenient excuse to undertake measures that are directed as much against China as against North Korea. Also, there are concerns in Beijing that Japan-U.S. cooperation on BMD and other defense matters encourages Japan to be more obstinate in its claims to the Senkaku/Diaoyu islands. According to one Chinese academic, "the joint missile defense system objectively encourages Japan to keep an aggressive position in the Diaoyu Islands dispute, which sends China a very negative message. Japan would not have been so aggressive without the support and actions of the U.S."[89] Despite Chinese objections, Japan will continue its enthusiastic pursuit of BMD.

Conventional Strike

From time to time, some Japanese leaders and analysts have also raised the possibility of acquiring a conventional strike capability to allow for preempting an imminent threat, typically a ballistic missile strike, before the launch occurs. Most attention here has been focused on North Korea's growing ballistic missile capability. Though China remains a serious concern for Japanese defense planners, there is little likelihood Tokyo would direct a preemptive strike against Chinese forces.

International law does allow for states to preempt an imminent attack without first having to absorb the assault. In addition, several Japanese administrations have stated that Article 9 of the constitution does not prohibit this option. In 1956, Prime Minister Ichiro Hatoyama provided the first explication:

> If Japan were in imminent danger of an illegal invasion, and the method of invasion were a missile attack against Japan's national territory, I simply cannot believe that the spirit of the Constitution requires that we merely sit and wait to die. In such a case, I believe that we should take the absolute minimum measures that are unavoidably necessary to defend against such an attack, so that in defending against a missile attack, for example, if no other suitable means are available, striking the missile base should be legally acceptable and falls within the range of self-defense.[90]

The intent of this statement has been reaffirmed by subsequent administrations in 1959 and 1999. While there is some disagreement over whether these interpretations mesh with Japan's defense strategy of "exclusive defense-oriented policy" (EDOP),[91] the legal basis for possessing a conventional strike capability to preempt an imminent attack has been fairly well established. Despite the legal grounding and occasional proposals to pursue this capability, Japanese leaders have refrained from doing so for several reasons. First, despite the size and advanced technology of the JSDF, EDOP has meant eschewing weapons that are offensive strike systems and confining acquisition to defensive capabilities. As a result, Japan has no ballistic missiles or cruise missiles to use for a conventional strike. Instead, the JSDF would have to rely on its fleet of F-15J Eagles.[92] However, if trying to penetrate North Korean airspace, Japanese pilots would face a formidable challenge in the DPRK's air defense system consisting of more than 10,000 surface-to-air missiles. In part to address this deficiency, Japan has indicated plans to purchase more than forty of the stealthy F-35 Joint Strike Fighter.

However, Japan will need more than aircraft. An effective conventional strike capability requires a network of ISR assets, which Japan does not possess. To acquire these capabilities would be very expensive and burden its defense budget, which already finds it difficult to meet a growing list of requirements. Moreover, much of the North Korean missile force the JSADF would need to target are on mobile launchers that are notoriously difficult to track and hit even with extensive ISR assets. In addition, Japanese fighters would not have the range to reach North Korean targets and return safely without aerial refueling, assets that Japan does not have. In the past, as well as under the current Guidelines for U.S.-Japan Defense Cooperation, the division of roles and missions within the alliance confined Japan to purely defensive responses, particularly BMD, while the United States would "conduct operations to support and supplement the Self-Defense Forces' operations," presumably any strike operations away from the home islands.[93] However, the 2013 NDPG also notes that "Japan will study a potential form of response capability to address the means of ballistic missile launches and related facilities, and take means as necessary."[94] Though Japanese officials continue to explore the possibility of acquiring the necessary assets,[95] it would be a difficult and costly endeavor that would likely stir up regional anxieties as well as provoke a contentious debate within Japan. Indeed, some Japanese analysts have raised concerns that if Japan should acquire a conventional strike capability, it would actually lead to a decoupling of the U.S. nuclear umbrella because Japan would be able to assume a greater share of deterrence on its own without the need for the umbrella.[96]

In the end, Japan will continue to study the acquisition of conventional strike capabilities and has established the legal basis to do so, but operational and budgetary challenges will make this a long-term project. Instead, Japan will continue to rely on U.S. forces for this mission. Pinkston and Sakurai may be most prescient in their analysis: "Tokyo is so constrained that Japan's domestic debate on preemption against North Korea is mostly for domestic consumption as Japanese politicians and policy makers seek to establish their credentials as tough leaders in the face of a rising North Korean threat."[97]

Civil Defense

Finally, Japan has undertaken several efforts to enhance its civil defense response should a WMD attack ever occur. In 2004, in response to the North Korea threat and the possibility of terrorist attacks, the government began to take steps to protect the public by providing a better system of civil defense. The first measure was the Civil Protection Law, which provided guidance for national and local government response to an attack through evacuation and relief operations. In subsequent years, Tokyo passed follow-on legislation that set up civil protection plans. These actions were followed with planning measures by prefectural governments and other institutions. Finally, the national government set up a communications system to issue warnings and evacuation orders.[98] Implementation of these measures remains an ongoing process.

WOULD JAPAN EVER DEVELOP ITS OWN
NUCLEAR WEAPONS?

The short answer to this question is "not likely," though scholars disagree over the reasons.[99] For years, analysts have spoken of a "nuclear allergy" in Japan resulting from World War II that prevented Japanese leaders from discussing nuclear weapons, much less consider acquiring them. Though constrained from discussing the issue publicly, Japan's conservative leaders often discussed the issue privately, believing Japan must keep the option open.[100] Yet for Japan to make the decision to go nuclear would require a drastic deterioration of its security environment accompanied by a collapse of the Japan-U.S. alliance. In many respects, a Japanese decision to head in this direction is what Campbell and Sunohara call "the ultimate contradiction." Japan's "standing as a non-nuclear nation is a virtual bedrock of the nonproliferation regime" yet "at the same time, suspicion and speculation have persisted that, given the right set (really the wrong set) of international and domestic conditions, Japan might seriously consider the nuclear option."[101] Japan clearly possesses the technology and infrastructure for a breakout through its extensive civil nuclear energy program should it desire to do so.[102] Estimates of Japan's necessary breakout time range from a few months to a year or two.

The disaster that followed the March 2011 tsunami and nuclear catastrophe at Fukushima-Daiichi nuclear power plant raised the possibility that Japan might permanently shut down its nuclear reactors and scrap its nuclear energy industry entirely, removing its breakout capability. Yet in the end, Japan remains committed to its nuclear energy program and in August 2015 restarted its first nuclear power plant since shutting them all down in 2011. A few months after the disaster, former Defense Minister Shigeru Ishiba stated, "I don't think Japan needs to possess nuclear weapons, but it's important to maintain our commercial reactors because it would allow us to produce a nuclear warhead in a short amount of time. It's a tacit nuclear deterrent."[103] Maintaining a civilian nuclear program even after the tragedy at Fukushima has a clear connection to maintaining some level of nuclear breakout capability and nuclear deterrent. Referring to the LDP's determination to maintain a nuclear energy program, Narushige Michishita argued, "What they are saying in a tacit manner is that 98 percent of our program is peaceful, but we have the potential for something else."[104]

Japan would face some serious operational and political obstacles should it seek nuclear weapons. Japan's people are concentrated in several densely populated urban areas that makes them very vulnerable to a nuclear exchange. To have an effective deterrent, Japan would need many weapons, and given Japan's lack of geographical depth, there are few places to deploy these systems, making them vulnerable to a first strike. Acquisition of the necessary weapons systems, especially strategic bombers and ballistic missiles, would violate the constitution and the EDOP.[105] Some disagree that nuclear weapons are acceptable as a defensive system used only for retaliation, and there would likely be a highly divisive debate in Japan should any government head in this direction under any but the most dire circumstances. Even in the wake of what many would argue is an increasingly aggressive China, Prime Minister Abe had a difficult time obtaining public support for a constitutional reinterpretation of collective self-defense. Finally, "going nuclear" would also entail leaving the NPT and damaging Tokyo's reputation as a nonproliferation stalwart. Economic sanctions would likely follow, as well as restrictions on Japan's nuclear industry.[106]

For all these reasons, Japan would incur a heavy cost, domestically and internationally, should it move to acquire nuclear weapons. Every time Japanese leaders have examined this possibility, they have acknowledged this reality and chosen instead to rely on the U.S. defense commitment. As one study notes, "In the context of the gulf between Japanese public opinion, which is largely ill-disposed toward nuclear weapons and security hawks at the elite level eager to push back against this 'nuclear allergy,' the END [extended nuclear deterrent] offered and continues to offer a neat and practical solution."[107] Thus, Japan will continue to rely on the U.S. alliance and the nuclear umbrella while also slowly increasing its own conventional capabilities and leaving the door open for nuclear acquisition. In the end, Samuels and Schoff provide the most pointed analysis: "Although Japan's nuclear hedging strategy is likely to continue in the near future, U.S. policy makers (and those throughout the region) should not be sanguine about this strategy continuing indefinitely. Japan's choices will be determined ultimately by how well potential threats can be managed and by the strength of the U.S. commitment to extended deterrence."[108]

CONCLUSION

Japan's position with regard to nuclear weapons is unusual. While the "nuclear allergy" remains a potent force in Japanese society and Japan has been a staunch advocate of the elimination of nuclear weapons,[109] it has relied on the U.S. nuclear umbrella and has been concerned about the credibility of the U.S. commitment to use nuclear weapons to defend Japan. In addition, despite a strong aversion to nuclear weapons among the public, Japanese leaders have been far less "allergic" and have periodically examined the possibility of acquiring nuclear weapons, with some advocating strongly for moving in this direction. In the end, these studies concluded it was not in Japan's interests to go nuclear at this time and that Japan should continue to rely on the U.S. umbrella while retaining the ability to go nuclear should circumstances warrant.

Despite Japanese reliance on the U.S. nuclear umbrella, periodically the commitment has been questioned amid fears that U.S. resolve to use nuclear weapons was slipping. Yet Washington has worked hard to reassure Japan of its commitment, not only the nuclear umbrella but the overall security commitment under the alliance. The Japan-U.S. alliance remains on solid ground, and U.S. bases in Japan along with the broader defense commitment are central to Washington's ability to maintain a forward presence and "rebalance" to the Asia-Pacific region. The U.S. nuclear umbrella remains only one part of a much larger relationship that helps to reassure Japan of the U.S. commitment. Even with a relatively small chance the United States would ever use nuclear weapons (a reality that some Japanese analysts acknowledge), when combined with a robust alliance, the nuclear umbrella provides a significant degree of reassurance while also furnishing enough strategic ambiguity to contribute to deterrence. The political dimensions of the alliance are strong, in part because of the nuclear umbrella, and in turn Japan sees the nuclear umbrella as reasonably credible because it is part of a healthy alliance relationship. At the same time, the nuclear umbrella helps to reassure Japan so that it does not feel the need to acquire its own nuclear weapons.

CHAPTER FIVE

South Korea and the U.S. Nuclear Umbrella

Like Japan, South Korea has relied on the U.S. nuclear umbrella as a crucial component of the alliance. Throughout the Cold War, the nuclear umbrella was focused largely on deterring or defeating another North Korean conventional assault across the DMZ. Washington and Seoul had few discussions about the nuclear umbrella;[1] South Korea took comfort in its existence but left the specifics of strategy and planning to Washington. As North Korea's nuclear ambitions grew, however, ROK defense planners became increasingly interested in the details of the nuclear umbrella and began to ask tough questions about the credibility of that part of the ROK-U.S. alliance.

On October 9, 2006, North Korea conducted its first nuclear test, crossing a redline that forever altered the regional security environment. Though the test produced a relatively small yield, leading most observers to deem it unsuccessful, North Korea had now joined the ranks of states with nuclear weapons. Pyongyang conducted its second test in May 2009 and the following year further rattled the security environment by sinking the ROK corvette *Cheonan* and shelling the island of Yeonpyeong off South Korea's west coast. North Korea's capabilities were increasing, as was its aggressive behavior. Fears rose that North Korea would use its nuclear capability to pressure South Korea and the United States in new ways. The nuclear umbrella during the Cold War against Moscow and Beijing had been part of a hostile though stable relationship in which all the players understood the rules of the game, but a nuclear North Korea might be an entirely different matter. This dramatic change in the security environment required greater attention to the dynamics of deterrence, new thinking on how to adapt deterrence and defense to the new situation, and ROK-U.S. discussion regarding the nuclear umbrella. In addition, some people were calling for South Korea to develop its own nuclear weapons.

The U.S. nuclear umbrella provides reassurance to South Korea and a certainty to North Korea that it would face a devastating response if it were ever to use nuclear, chemical, or biological weapons against the South. The umbrella is also viewed as an important piece of the overall alliance commitment, furnishing a political signal of the value of the relationship that has become part of the overall security architecture for South Korea and the region. Finally, the nuclear umbrella has played a crucial role in convincing South Korea that it does not need to acquire its own nuclear weapons.

This chapter will begin with a brief review of the nuclear umbrella for South Korea, followed by the role it plays in ROK security planning and the concerns of South Korean leaders and analysts over the nuclear commitment. In addition, this chapter will examine South Korean actions, such as missile defense and increasing its own conventional strike options, that complement the U.S. nuclear umbrella.

UNDER THE U.S. NUCLEAR UMBRELLA

In 1958, the United States deployed its first tactical nuclear weapons to the peninsula. U.S. policy was to "neither confirm nor deny" the presence of nuclear weapons, but in 1975 Secretary of Defense James Schlesinger formally acknowledged the presence of U.S. nuclear weapons to make the umbrella more explicit. This public admission was done in large part to address South Korean concerns that the alliance was slowly weakening and to forestall ROK efforts to build its own nuclear weapons. In 1969, Nixon had announced what became known as the Nixon Doctrine, which reaffirmed U.S. commitments, including the nuclear umbrella, to its allies in Asia and pledged to provide economic and military assistance when needed. In the future, however, U.S. allies would be expected to provide a greater share of manpower for their own defense.² For South Korea, the result was the withdrawal of the Seventh Infantry Division, approximately 20,000 U.S. troops, a move made with little consultation with the ROK government. In 1970, Vice President Spiro Agnew stated that more withdrawals would follow, with all of USFK removed over the next five years.³ Soon after, Park Chung-hee discovered U.S. efforts to reach out to China, again with little consultation or advance warning. When he learned of Kissinger's secret visit to Beijing in 1971, Park lamented, "How long can we trust the United States?"[4] As a result of what appeared to be serious shifts in the security environment and the alliance, Park began a clandestine effort to acquire nuclear weapons.[5] When Washington found out, it put great pressure on Seoul to abandon its nuclear program, including threats to make drastic changes to the alliance. In addition, the Ford administration decided to formally acknowledge the presence of U.S. nuclear weapons to reassure Seoul of its commitment and convince South Korea to remain nuclear free. In a 1975 interview with Don Oberdorfer at the *Washington Post*, Park stated that he had no plan to develop nuclear weapons but that "South Korea would do everything in its power to defend its own security—including development of nuclear weapons if necessary—if the U.S. nuclear umbrella were withdrawn," though he considered that unlikely.[6]

In addition to the formal acknowledgment of U.S. tactical nuclear weapons in Korea, in 1978 the Pentagon began to provide an annual, on-the-record declaration of the nuclear umbrella in the joint communique that accompanied the fall Security Consultative Meeting (SCM). Since the late 1960s, the U.S. secretary of defense and the ROK minister of defense had met to assess the overall state of the ROK-U.S. alliance and plan for future actions. The meeting produces a joint communique that provides a threat assessment, a summary of defense cooperation and joint capabilities, and reaffirmation of the critical nature of the alliance. In 1978, the communique began to include a succinct but specific reference that "Korea is and will continue to be under the U.S. nuclear umbrella."[7] For the next twenty-five-plus years, the phrasing stayed relatively similar, though its position in the joint communique changed depending on the events of the year and the prioritization of communique items that leaders wished to emphasize.

In 2006, the SCM followed North Korea's October nuclear test, and the communique contained a slight change in wording concerning the nuclear umbrella: "Secretary Rumsfeld offered assurances of firm U.S. commitment and immediate support to the ROK, including continuation of the extended deterrence offered by the U.S. nuclear umbrella, consistent with the Mutual Defense Treaty."[8] The key change was the addition of the "extended deterrence" reference, one the South Korean government had lobbied hard to include, believing it was a crucial declaration of the U.S. commitment.[9] U.S. officials were reluctant, believing the commitment had always been firm and that no further emphasis was necessary.[10] The paragraph contained a strong condemnation of North Korea's test, but the umbrella remained similar to past statements. Most significant was that the statement, which normally appeared further down the list of numbered paragraphs, had now jumped to number three, making it one of the focal points of the communique. A U.S. press report indicated that ROK officials had also lobbied for a more specific statement of the nuclear umbrella, including the types of tactical nuclear weapons the United States could use for a nuclear strike. In response, a U.S. official stated anonymously that the nuclear umbrella "simply is a fact. It's a component of our mutual defense treaty. And we're happy to let the statements stand for themselves as they have for the past 30 odd years."[11]

Following North Korea's second test in 2009, the nuclear umbrella statement in the SCM was altered once more. While again reaffirming the extended deterrence commitment, the language was more detailed, adding the use of "the full range of military capabilities, to include the U.S. nuclear umbrella, conventional strike, and missile defense capabilities."[12] Thus, South Korea received its reassurance of the extended deterrence commitment, and the United States clarified that its commitment to defend South Korea against the DPRK nuclear threat was more than the nuclear umbrella. From that point on, the SCM communique has used similar language to emphasize that the U.S. security guarantee to South Korea is multifaceted, including nuclear weapons, conventional assets, and ballistic missile defense.

Finally, in the October 2016 SCM joint communique, the usual affirmation of the U.S. defense commitment of "the full range of military capabilities" was followed by a reiteration of "the long-standing U.S.

policy that any attack on the United States or its allies will be defeated, and any use of nuclear weapons will be met with an effective and overwhelming response."[13] Again, this statement indicates that a nuclear attack would not necessarily be followed by a nuclear strike but rather by "an effective and overwhelming response," which could be achieved without the use of nuclear weapons.

THE ROLE OF THE U.S. NUCLEAR UMBRELLA IN SOUTH KOREA'S DEFENSE PLANNING

As a result of North Korea's growing nuclear and ballistic missile capability, ROK scholars and analysts have done considerable thinking over the past decade or so about extended deterrence and the role the U.S. nuclear umbrella plays in South Korean security. Many ROK analysts argue that the security environment is far different now than it was during the Cold War, requiring new thinking about the nuclear umbrella and extended deterrence. At the same time, they offer several reasons for the continued importance of the nuclear umbrella.

First, the destructive power of nuclear weapons is deemed essential to deter a nuclear North Korea. The current security environment differs from the Cold War in that Washington, Moscow, and Beijing were rational actors who understood the stakes and logic of deterrence. There is far less confidence in the rationality of the Kim Jong-un regime and concern that he may be inexperienced and far more tolerant of risk.[14] In June 2016, ROK defense minister Han Min-koo remarked, "Kim Jong-un was just 27 when he came to power with very little time to prepare. Add to that, he is very young, he lacks experience, and he has a rash, impulsive character. We are very concerned."[15] Nuclear weapons and the U.S. umbrella present a certainty that North Korean aggression would result in tremendous costs to the North Korean regime. As Chang Kwoun Park, senior research fellow at the Korea Institute for Defense Analysis, notes, "In order to deter North Korea's nuclear threat, North Korea must be made to accurately understand that any North Korean provocation will be promptly followed by punishment that will overwhelm them."[16] South Korea does not have sufficient conventional strength to impose the costs necessary to punish and hence deter Pyongyang; nuclear weapons and the U.S. nuclear umbrella are required for this purpose.[17] Indeed, North Korean use of nuclear weapons must be deterred because the South is too small a landmass to absorb an attack and the potential destruction of Seoul, located a short distance from the DMZ, is unthinkable. According to one study, detonation of a twenty-kiloton bomb in Seoul would result in 900,000 killed and 1.36 million wounded in the first twenty-four hours.[18] Thus, nuclear retaliation on North Korea is essential for successful deterrence.

Second, North Korea must know that it cannot escalate a conflict to nuclear weapons and get away with it without a nuclear response. Phrased another way, North Korea must not be allowed to have escalation dominance in a conflict with the South. In addition, the nuclear umbrella allows South Korea to respond, even escalate, with conventional weapons without fear that North Korea will escalate to nuclear weapons, given the likelihood of nuclear retaliation under the umbrella.[19]

Third, some ROK analysts add that the nuclear umbrella is less about military operations and more about countering any perceived political leverage Pyongyang thinks it may gain with nuclear weapons. North Korea is likely to use its nuclear capability to intimidate the South to obtain political concessions or perhaps to achieve domestic political goals.[20] The nuclear umbrella is necessary to offset any political power that possession of nuclear weapons generates for North Korea.[21] In addition, the nuclear umbrella against North Korea gets China's attention, reminding Beijing of the dangers of nuclear escalation should Pyongyang act in a provocative manner.[22] As a result, Beijing may work harder to restrain the DPRK than it would if there were no nuclear umbrella.

Fourth, the U.S. nuclear umbrella has important implications for ROK domestic politics. When North Korea conducts tests of nuclear weapons and ballistic missiles, the ROK government comes under great pressure to "do something" to address the threat. The umbrella provides reassurance to the ROK public and provides its leaders with the cover to show they are addressing the threat while avoiding what could be a contentious decision to consider acquiring its own nuclear weapons.[23] Each time North Korea has tested a nuclear weapon, calls for building the South's own nuclear weapons resurfaces. After the January 2016 test, one ROK lawmaker argued, "We cannot borrow an umbrella from a

South Korea and the U.S. Nuclear Umbrella   129

neighbor every time it rains. We need to have a raincoat and wear it ourselves."[24] The U.S. nuclear umbrella provides the needed reassurance in the face of these pressures.

Finally, while many recognize the limited military utility of nuclear weapons in responding to North Korean actions, the political importance of the nuclear umbrella is critical. At a ROK think tank gathering, several scholars indicated that the nuclear umbrella was an important signal of the strength of the alliance and a crucial sign of assurance.[25] At another ROK think tank, participants talked about how the nuclear umbrella provides confidence to South Korea and demonstrates a level of commitment to ROK security that goes beyond any that could be provided by conventional forces. The U.S. nuclear umbrella is a valuable part of the defense architecture, and although the United States is unlikely to use nuclear weapons, the umbrella is more important as a political weapon providing reassurance.[26] As one ROK defense analyst noted, the overall extended deterrence commitment is a series of connected parts that include military, political, and economic dimensions. The nuclear umbrella, according to this analyst, is an important component of extended deterrence, and without it there would be a gap.[27] Thus, the nuclear umbrella is one important part of the overall alliance that sends a clear political signal of the U.S. commitment to ROK leaders and the public. The nuclear umbrella helps to strengthen the alliance, and in turn, a healthy alliance helps to make the nuclear commitment more credible in the eyes of the ally.

STRENGTHENING THE U.S. NUCLEAR UMBRELLA

South Korean leaders and analysts have been relatively satisfied with the U.S. nuclear umbrella and U.S. nuclear policy as expressed in the Nuclear Posture Review.[28] Yet concerns remain, and many people have offered ways to bolster the U.S. commitment. Their worries generally fall into three categories: concerns about U.S. resolve, the need for consultation and planning, and the overall decline of U.S. power and influence. Many of these concerns have surfaced in earnest in the past five to ten years, and although actions have been taken to address them, reassuring allies is an ongoing task in an extended deterrence relationship.

Credibility of the Nuclear Umbrella

One of the central challenges in extended deterrence is reassuring an ally of the certainty of the defender's commitment. During peacetime, a promise to defend is easy, but allies worry that in a crisis, the defender will not follow through on its guarantee. Concerning the nuclear umbrella, there are doubts that the United States would actually follow through with its pledge to use nuclear weapons, particularly as the Obama administration sought to downplay their role. Though the 2010 Nuclear Posture Review (NPR) provides a strong statement of the U.S. deterrence commitment to its allies, it also indicates that nuclear weapons would only be used under "extreme circumstances."[29] Will Washington and Seoul have the same interpretation of this phrase, or will it provide an escape clause from using nuclear weapons when South Korea expects nuclear retaliation?[30] Though many understand that the United States would likely not use nuclear weapons first, if North Korea used them first, there are strong expectations for a U.S. response in kind.[31]

Some ROK analysts have also raised concerns about the distance and decision-making process for using nuclear weapons. The authority to use nuclear weapons resides with the U.S. president in Washington, not with the U.S. military in Korea, and it could potentially take a considerable amount of time to deploy the necessary weapons, thereby weakening deterrence. The solution, from this point of view, is the redeployment of U.S. tactical nuclear weapons.[32]

Finally, regarding the size of the U.S. arsenal needed for an effective nuclear umbrella, one U.S. official noted that South Korean officials are very concerned about the numbers and policy related to the nuclear umbrella. They do not typically express specific concerns regarding minimum numbers but watch very closely for any changes in U.S. force posture or policy.[33]

A particular concern is the fear of decoupling.[34] As North Korea's nuclear capabilities continue to grow, it is certain to have an ICBM capable of reaching the United States with a nuclear warhead one day, if it does not already. Would North Korea's ability to hit the U.S. homeland cause Washington to hesitate or not respond at all to a North Korean nuclear strike? Some analysts worry that North Korea would be emboldened to use its nuclear capability to intimidate the South while holding a U.S. response at bay with threats to strike the U.S. homeland or U.S. bases in the Pacific. South Korea understands this dilemma but also fears North Korea's possible exploitation of it and calls on the United States to strengthen its capability and resolve despite the dangers.

Requests for the United States to reinforce its deterrence posture were particularly strong in spring 2013. North Korea conducted another satellite launch in December 2012 and its third nuclear weapon test in February 2013. The UN Security Council followed with another resolution in March that condemned North Korea and tightened sanctions. Annual spring ROK-U.S. military exercises provoked a rhetorical barrage from North Korean leaders that included threats to use nuclear weapons. Though they did not have the capability to carry out many of these threats, tension levels in the region rose dramatically. As a result, many South Koreans were pleased when the Pentagon sent B-52 and B-2 bombers to participate in the exercises as a visible sign, particularly for the ROK public, of U.S. resolve with nuclear assets. One group of ROK analysts noted that its government was under a great deal of pressure to do something in response to the increased tension levels, and the 2013 flyovers did much to calm nerves in the South and build trust.[35] Several ROK analysts also noted the need to repeat the demonstration should tensions rise again to that level; if North Korea tests again, the United States must be ready to show its strength and resolve.[36]

In 2016, another confluence of events similar to 2013—January nuclear weapons test, February satellite launch, UN Security Council resolution, more sanctions, ROK-U.S. military exercises, and North Korean threats—again raised tensions above normal levels. Shortly after North Korea's 2016 test, the United States sent a B-52 from Guam to fly over Korea as a sign of reassurance.[37] The U.S. military followed up by sending the *John S. Stennis* carrier strike group, the *Virginia*-class attack submarine *North Carolina*, F-22 fighters, and B-2s to the region at various times during the spring to provide a visible show of reassurance.

After the October 2016 SCM and the "two plus two" alliance meetings between the U.S. secretaries of state and defense and their ROK counterparts, press reports indicated that ROK officials had approached the U.S. delegation about the possibility of permanently deploying some of these strategic assets to the Korean peninsula. South Korean officials were pleased with the 2013 and 2016 demonstrations of U.S. resolve with aircraft and other strategic assets but argued that these "one-off" actions were no longer sufficient to deter the North.[38] The United States agreed to review the possibility of rotational deployments of strategic military assets, and although Seoul was disappointed at not receiving an affirmative decision, it was content that Washington had expressed a willingness to discuss the matter further.[39]

In December 2016, the possibility of permanent deployments was revisited during the first meeting of the Extended Deterrence Strategy and Consultation Group, a newly formed high-level U.S.-ROK planning group. In the joint statement that followed the meeting, Washington "reaffirmed the commitment of the United States to regularly deploy U.S. strategic assets for the defense of the ROK, as well as to enhance such measures and identify new or additional steps to strengthen deterrence."[40] The statement also highlighted missile defense and demonstrations of the U.S. nuclear triad, including B-52 flights and visits by ROK officials to observe an ICBM test launch at Vandenberg Air Force Base and a U.S. ballistic missile submarine during a port visit in Guam, as further steps to reinforce deterrence. However, the key issue was the meaning of the word "regular"; some South Korean critics maintained that the government had failed to achieve its goal because regular deployment could mean periodic visits of strategic assets rather than their "permanent deployment."[41] It is also important to note that deploying B-52s or other strategic platforms to South Korea does not mean they would be carrying nuclear weapons.

At the same time, there were also concerns about these actions to demonstrate a more credible nuclear umbrella. While the flyovers were signals of reassurance for some, others were concerned that these measures were highly provocative and stoked the possibility of war on the peninsula. Some, particularly on the ROK left, fear that actions to make the nuclear umbrella more credible provide North Korea with continued justification for its own nuclear program and make denuclearization an even more distant goal. Moreover, explicit nuclear threats ratchet up tensions and generate greater hostility from North Korea.

U.S. officials recognize the difficulty of reassuring South Korea of the credibility of the nuclear umbrella. A U.S. official indicated that although South Korea wants a credible U.S. nuclear umbrella, it would probably be upset if the United States ever used nuclear weapons in Korea.[42]

A former U.S. official noted that many South Koreans would recoil at the United States using nuclear weapons on the North, which could lead to a serious backlash against Washington.[43] Thus, answering the call for increased credibility is difficult. As one U.S. analyst noted, "providing positive security assurances to allies must be a continuous process because the recipient will always doubt the extended deterrence commitment."[44] As a result, according to one U.S. official, South Koreans tend to be fairly insecure about the U.S. defense commitment and analyze every word related to the alliance.[45]

Need for Increased Consultation and Planning

After North Korea began testing nuclear weapons, South Korea had a renewed interest in the U.S. nuclear umbrella. Though South Korea often let nuclear matters during the Cold War reside with U.S. planners, there was also a sense that U.S. officials were reluctant to talk about nuclear weapons and the umbrella. Consequently, after 2010, calls increased for more ROK-U.S. direct dialogue and joint planning concerning the nuclear umbrella, including release of some of the details to help reassure the ROK public and give leaders confidence in addressing the North Korean threat.[46] One ROK defense scholar noted that "joint planning is reassuring and helps to address public frustration because they really don't know much about the nuclear umbrella and what the U.S. is thinking about."[47]

Several important initiatives have been undertaken over the past several years to address these concerns. First, in 2010, South Korea and the United States began the Extended Deterrence Policy Committee (EDPC). Now named the Deterrence Strategy Committee, the body was formally announced in the October 2010 SCM Joint Communique, but several meetings had already taken place prior to the public announcement. Similar to the EDD with Japan, the EDPC helps to fill the gap that in Europe is covered by the NATO Nuclear Planning Group. One U.S. official noted that even the announcement of the EDPC helped to ease ROK anxiety.[48] The EDPC is a forum to share ideas, conduct planning on nuclear issues, and let South Korea see how the U.S. thinks about using nuclear weapons in Korea. The dialogue helps both sides understand how the other thinks about deterrence and helps to reassure ROK officials through greater awareness of the details of nuclear planning. The meetings also help to address the problems of escalation control and conduct tabletop exercises to explore the thinking of both sides in crisis situations.[49]

To bolster strategic deterrence, Seoul and Washington developed a "tailored deterrence strategy" (TDS) to focus on North Korea's nuclear, chemical, and biological weapons programs.[50] The TDS, which grew out of meetings of the EDPC, was announced in 2013 at the conclusion of that year's SCM. Details of the plan are classified, but press reports indicate that the strategy includes options for preemptive strikes if North Korea prepares to use nuclear weapons.[51] In addition, the TDS shifts the U.S. nuclear umbrella into the formal alliance planning process.[52] South Korea and the United States also developed a new operations plan, OPLAN 5015. The specifics are classified, but according to press reports, OPLAN 5015 includes the possibility of rapid precision strikes on North Korean nuclear and missile targets along with the use of decapitation strikes on DPRK leadership following an attack.[53] The spring 2016 joint exercises included simulated plans for preemptive strikes against North Korea's nuclear weapons, including its mobile missile launchers as well as its underground and hardened storage facilities.[54] The exercises also implemented a preemptive strike plan called 4D (detect, disrupt, destroy, and defend) designed to destroy and secure North Korean nuclear and chemical weapons facilities and materials so that they do not disappear and fall in the hands of terrorist groups or show up in other countries.

ROK and U.S. defense planners have also been concerned that North Korea's nuclear capability might embolden it to undertake more lower-level provocations, believing it will be safe from retaliation. To address this concern, in March 2013, ROK and U.S. officials announced a Combined Counter-Provocation Plan (CCP). According to press reports, the plan places South Korea in the lead to respond to any North Korean provocations but allows it to request assistance from the United States if needed. The plan outlines a set of options for a joint response; it "defines action down to the tactical level and locks in alliance political consultations at the highest level," according to a U.S. official.[55]

Washington had an additional motive for the CCP. After the shelling of Yeonpyeong Island in November 2010, South Korean officials were ready to retaliate and possibly escalate in response. Defense Minister Kim Kwan-jin said at that time, regarding any future attack, "Do not hesitate whether to shoot or not. Report after taking action first,"[56] and U.S. officials were very concerned where this might lead. Regarding the artillery exchange, U.S. secretary of defense Robert Gates recalled in his memoirs: "We were worried the exchanges could escalate dangerously. The president, Clinton, Mullen, and I were all on the phone often with our South Korean counterparts over a period of days, and ultimately South Korea simply returned artillery fire on the location of the North Korean's batteries that had started the whole affair."[57] Concluding the CCP involved the United States in the planning and implementation of any future ROK response, making the United States a participant rather than an observer and providing some degree of influence and control over ROK actions. In addition, planning for a joint response would convey a strong deterrence signal to North Korea that could help prevent a repeat of Yeonpyeong Island in the first place.

All three of these initiatives—EDPC, TDS, and CCP—helped to further solidify various levels of the ROK-U.S. alliance and deterrence. In addition, they helped to improve coordination and collaboration throughout the alliance while further enmeshing the United States in ROK security. These formal mechanisms help to make defense cooperation more seamless and reassure South Korea of the staying power of the U.S. defense commitment.

Sustaining the "Rebalance"

For the past few years, a central tenet of U.S. foreign policy has been the "rebalance" to Asia. With the U.S. involvement in Iraq and Afghanistan decreasing, the Obama administration announced it would be refocusing and giving greater attention and resources to the Asia-Pacific area. While many analysts have focused on the military portion of the rebalance, the policy also increased diplomatic and economic dimensions, including regular attendance at regional meetings and promotion of greater economic integration through trade and investment, with the Trans-Pacific Partnership (TPP) as its centerpiece. Many applauded the announcement of the "rebalance," but as the years have passed, concerns have appeared in South Korea and throughout Asia regarding the U.S. ability to sustain the initiative.[58] U.S. economic woes, congressional gridlock, budget deficits, sequestration, and an overall sense that the United States is in decline has raised questions about the U.S. commitment to the region along with its ability to remain a player in Asia.

The 2016 U.S. presidential election raised further questions as the candidates from both parties challenged the benefits of free trade and the TPP. Eventually, the Trump administration pulled out of the TPP. In addition, Donald Trump questioned the value of the ROK and Japan alliances, particularly given what he has characterized as insufficient burden sharing by U.S. allies. Though many South Koreans were able to dismiss some of Trump's language as campaign rhetoric, they wondered if fundamental doubts in the U.S. public and the Congress about the value of these alliances might have underlied Trump's remarks.[59] Upon taking office, the Trump administration has affirmed its commitment to the alliances but continues to call for a more equitable sharing of the costs. The future of U.S. strength and its commitment to Asia, particularly in relation to China's rise, will be closely watched by South Korea, Japan, and others in Asia, a concern that U.S. leaders will need to continue addressing in the years ahead.

SOUTH KOREAN NIGHTMARE SCENARIOS

The job of defense planners is to develop ways to secure the goals established by leadership, using whatever resources are available. This process often entails devising a variety of scenarios, including worst-case versions in which a state and its military might be tested to defend the national interest. North Korea's growing nuclear weapons capabilities have prompted ROK planners to consider new possibilities, all of which raise concerns for extended deterrence and the U.S. nuclear umbrella. During the course of researching this book, ROK officials and analysts commonly mentioned several scenarios as concerns for security and nuclear deterrence. These scenarios are also tied to assessments of how North Korea may view the utility of its nuclear capability, along with its strategy and doctrine.[60] While the plausibility of some of these scenarios is open to debate, they are nonetheless on the minds of ROK defense planners and influence their assessments.

First, emboldened by its nuclear capability or a need to bolster domestic political support, the Kim regime might consider a conventional assault across the DMZ, seizing ROK territory, including possibly Seoul, and then holding its ground. Pyongyang declares that if retaliation occurs, against either its forces in the South or the DPRK proper, it will respond with nuclear weapons. Thus, North Korea would be in control of the escalation ladder. Another variant of this scenario is a North Korean launch of a single nuclear weapon on South Korea, Japan, or possibly some remote location for a demonstration effect. Should the United States or others respond, North Korea would launch several more nuclear weapons on these targets or, more significantly, once its long-range missile capability improves, on the U.S. homeland. North Korea would exacerbate the decoupling problem, deterring Washington from responding for fear of nuclear destruction raining down on U.S. cities.

A second scenario involves the possibility of Chinese intervention. Suppose North Korea conducted a very serious conventional operation or used nuclear weapons on South Korea or Japan. With impending U.S. and ROK retaliation, might Beijing step in and draw a redline against actions to respond to North Korea, including the possibility of nuclear retaliation for a strike against Pyongyang? A 2011 editorial in the conservative *Chosun Ilbo* put it this way:

> The chances are nil that Washington, which trembled at the artillery attack on Yeonpyeong Island, would risk a war with China by deploying its nuclear umbrella when the North launches a nuclear attack. That is the limitation of the nuclear umbrella, and there lies the reason why Pyongyang will not give up its nuclear weapons. Nuclear weapons can be subject to negotiations, but a nuclear umbrella cannot.[61]

Some ROK analysts believe that this possibility would certainly make Washington pause before intervening. In addition, some of North Korea's nuclear and missile facilities are relatively close to North Korea's border with China, increasing the chance of drawing in Beijing and making U.S. retaliation even riskier.[62]

A third concern is the danger of an escalating conventional confrontation. If North Korea conducts another military provocation like the shelling of Yeonpyeong Island, ROK leaders have vowed to retaliate and possibly escalate. Moreover, the CCP poses the prospect of a joint ROK-U.S. response to any North Korean actions. How would North Korea react? Is there a danger it would escalate to nuclear weapons and, similar to the first scenario, launch one in retaliation with threats to lob more if South Korea or the United States responded again? If the survival of the Kim regime was believed to be at stake, there is little doubt it would resort to nuclear weapons. In a crisis, North Korea would have a relatively short period of time to determine if a ROK-U.S. military strike was a one-time retaliation for a DPRK action or the opening round of regime change. If its nuclear forces were on a high-alert launch-on-warning status, events could quickly spiral into a nuclear conflagration.

Finally, one former government official raised the possibility of North Korea using one of its nuclear weapons to create an electromagnetic pulse (EMP).[63] An EMP blast could take out the ROK's electrical grid, disabling computers, communications networks, and transportation. The burst could be detonated high above South Korea or out at sea so that there would be no casualties. The economic and physical consequences would be catastrophic, but without the loss of life. What would be considered a proportional response? Would U.S. and ROK leaders be less determined to retaliate with nuclear weapons or to mount a massive conventional strike in response to an attack of this nature? If it is difficult to determine proportional retaliation in this case, how does one go about deterring the act in the first place?

These scenarios raise some dangerous possibilities and difficult questions for analysts and planners. The stakes and risks are high, and compelling answers are few. However, this type of scenario planning assumes that North Korea is so tolerant of risk that it might be willing to try almost anything. In many of these scenarios, North Korea would be risking its survival, betting it could control the escalation ladder. While Pyongyang has certainly demonstrated that it is willing to "push the envelope," there are limits because it raises the specter of the regime being brought to an end if it were to push Seoul and Washington too hard and too far.

Patrick Morgan raises a crucial question here.⁶⁴ North Korean use of nuclear weapons would likely lead to the end of the Kim regime. Therefore, are North Korean threats to use a nuclear weapon really credible for anything less than an existential threat to the regime? Credibility questions cut both ways.

If there is one thing Korean analysts agree on, it is that regime survival is the most important goal of the Kim family, and traveling down the road of one of these scenarios jeopardizes that goal. While many analysts speculate on the gains North Korea could make through an aggressive posture facilitated by nuclear weapons, Pyongyang has even more to lose should it miscalculate and overplay its hand. Though the regime has long been willing to take risks, it is not so irrational as to undertake actions that are likely to bring its downfall. A large-scale combat operation by North Korea, including anything that resembled an invasion of the South, would start a chain of events that could easily lead to the end of the regime, and North Korean leaders know it. The more probable and dangerous event is a small-scale confrontation in which North Korean leaders believe they can successfully control the escalation ladder or one that unexpectedly gets out of hand. However, should they fail to prevent ROK-U.S. escalation, so long as it does not portend the end of the regime, it does not mean they would escalate to using nuclear weapons.

SOUTH KOREA'S RESPONSE TO THE NUCLEAR UMBRELLA

Despite U.S. assurances, there remain concerns in South Korea about the credibility of the U.S. nuclear umbrella. To address these concerns and to ensure it has greater control over its own security, South Korea has increased its military capabilities to make a greater contribution to the alliance but also to buttress deterrence independent of U.S. assistance. Deterrence theory tells us there will always be questions regarding the credibility of an extended deterrence commitment, but few doubt the resolve of threats to respond when it is primary deterrence. Consequently, South Korea has undertaken several measures to improve its conventional strike capability to hit North Korean targets, in addition to building a BMD system. Some ROK voices have also called for the return of U.S. tactical nuclear weapons to the peninsula or the development of South Korea's own nuclear weapons capability.

Conventional Strike

During the Cold War, U.S.-Soviet deterrence was based on mutually assured destruction, with both sides maintaining sufficient second strike capability to ride out an attack and have plenty of firepower remaining to retaliate. For South Korea, absorbing a nuclear strike from the North is not an option; Seoul is too close and the country is too small. As a result, ROK defense planners have been determined to acquire the capabilities to preempt an impending North Korean WMD attack through what the Ministry of Defense calls the "Kill Chain."[65] It envisions an array of sensors, including satellites and UAVs, to detect imminent North Korean threats and "to promptly strike fixed and mobile facilities related to nuclear weapons and missiles throughout all domains of North Korea from the ground, sea and air."[66] Assets available for these missions include extended range ballistic missiles, air-to-surface missiles, and precision-guided munitions. In September 2016, the Ministry of Defense released details of the Korea Massive Punishment and Retaliation operational concept, that outlined plans for a massive bombing and missile strike campaign on Pyongyang should North Korea show signs of a nuclear strike.[67]

An important element of South Korea's conventional strike effort is development of an indigenous ballistic missile program. For years, these efforts were limited to short-range missiles. In 1979, Seoul and Washington signed an agreement that gave South Korea access to U.S. missile technology in return for limiting the range of its ballistic missiles to 180 kilometers, a range sufficient to reach Pyongyang (approximately 150 kilometers from the DMZ). U.S. leaders were insistent on the limits, fearing a regional arms race and destabilizing regional security should South Korea increase the range of these assets. The ROK government was never happy with these constraints and requested revisions from the United States on many occasions, but to no avail. Finally, in 2001, Washington relented, but only as part of a deal in which South Korea also joined the Missile Technology Control Regime (MTCR). Upon joining the MTCR, the range limit was increased to 300 kilometers with a payload restriction of 500 kilograms.[68]

After the sinking of the *Cheonan* and the shelling of Yeonpyeong Island, ROK leaders began rethinking deterrence and concluded that to deter North Korea from future provocations, it needed to have its own capability to strike targets throughout the DPRK. Consequently, South Korea began pushing for a revision of the ballistic missile limits, and in April 2012 it announced a new "corresponding target strike plan" to respond to North Korean provocations by hitting the source of the provocation and possibly other targets of similar value.[69] After numerous rounds of difficult negotiations, Washington finally relented and agreed to Seoul's demands. The new guidelines allowed South Korea to produce missiles with a maximum range of 800 kilometers and a payload of 500 kilograms. For payloads of 1,000 kilograms, the range would be limited to 550 kilometers.[70] The agreement also included extended limits on ROK unmanned aerial vehicles (UAVs), allowing payloads of 500 to 2,500 kilograms. The extended range allows South Korea to target all of North Korea without being a threat to China or Japan. With the ability to hit all North Korean targets, ROK defense planners believe they have available more credible responses to DPRK actions, improving their deterrence posture. Minister of National Defense Kim Kwan-jin proclaimed in 2013: "Many of North Korea's missile bases are located in the rear (northern region). To be able to destroy the origin of provocations, ballistic missiles with an 800-kilometer range should be promptly put in place."[71] In April 2014, South Korea test fired a new version of the Hyunmu-2 ballistic missile with a range of 500 kilometers.[72] By 2017, South Korea is expected to have 1,700 ballistic missiles in service.[73]

In part to work around the earlier restrictions on its ballistic missiles, South Korea also developed a robust cruise missile program. Since these weapons did not fall under the MTCR, Seoul had far more latitude to expand these systems. The ROK cruise missile, the Hyunmu-3, has three variations, with ranges from 500 to 1,500 kilometers, capable of carrying a payload of 500 kilograms and accurate to three meters. The Hyunmu-3 was first presented to the public during a parade in April 2012, and a Defense Ministry spokesman at the time remarked, "The cruise missile being unveiled today is a precision-guided weapon that can identify and strike the window of the office of North Korea's leadership."[74] Few countries have long-range cruise missiles, and this system allows South Korea to strike targets throughout the North with pinpoint accuracy using conventional munitions. As a result, South Korea is not reliant solely on U.S. conventional strike or the nuclear umbrella to preempt or retaliate. In addition to ground launchers, South Korea also has plans to deploy the Hyunmu-3 on its *King Sejong the Great* destroyers and its new KSS-III submarines.

Ballistic Missile Defense

One of the most serious North Korean threats is its large ballistic missile force. Pyongyang has hundreds of short- and medium-range missiles that can cover all of Korea and Japan and is continuing work on intermediate- and long-range missiles that will eventually be capable of hitting a variety of regional targets as well as the continental United States. To deal with this threat, the United States has worked to construct a regional BMD architecture with the help of Asian allies. U.S. assets for the BMD effort include Aegis-class destroyers outfitted with AN/SPY radar capable of tracking and detecting multiple targets simultaneously and SM-3 Block II surface-to-air missiles that can hit ballistic missiles at high altitudes. Japan has been an enthusiastic participant in U.S. BMD efforts, but South Korea has not.

Instead, South Korea has constructed an independent capability called Korean Air and Missile Defense (KAMD). KAMD consists of three Aegis-class destroyers, with plans to build three more during the next decade. While U.S. and Japanese Aegis destroyers are equipped with the SM-3, ROK destroyers carry the SM-2 missile, which is largely an air defense interceptor designed to shoot down airplanes but has insufficient range to shoot down ballistic missiles. ROK officials have been reluctant to buy the SM-3 because of the cost, but with the North Korean threat growing, in May 2016 South Korea announced plans to outfit its existing Aegis destroyers and future ships of this class with the more capable SM-3.[75]

South Korea also has 300 PAC-2 interceptors for terminal phase BMD. The PAC-2 uses fragmentation warheads to shoot down aircraft and has some ability to hit short-range ballistic missiles.[76] South Korea also intends to purchase the more capable PAC-3 interceptor.[77] PAC-3s are equipped with onboard radar and guidance systems and designed for all-weather operations with "hit-to-kill" technology that can target ballistic and cruise missiles as well as aircraft.[78] In addition to the PAC-3, South Korea has plans to build its own long-range surface-to-air missile (L-SAM) interceptor, with production slated for 2023.[79]

South Korea has been hesitant to join the U.S. BMD system in part because of cost but more importantly because of the strenuous objections raised by Beijing over regional BMD. Trilateral BMD cooperation between Washington, Seoul, and Tokyo is worrisome to China, and though the United States has sought to convince Beijing that BMD efforts are intended for North Korea, Chinese officials believe Pyongyang is a convenient excuse for actions that are actually directed at them. The Chinese Foreign Ministry protested that "the deployment of anti-missile systems in the Asia-Pacific and seeking unilateral security are not beneficial to strategic stability and mutual trust in the region. It is not beneficial to peace and stability in Northeast Asia."[80] These objections are complicated by the fact that China is South Korea's number one trade partner, accounting for more trade volume than Japan and the United States combined.

The BMD issue was stirred further by the U.S. deployment of the Terminal High Altitude Area Defense (THAAD) system to South Korea. THAAD has the capability to shoot down ballistic missiles at higher altitudes and is equipped with a powerful AN/TPY X-band radar. In many respects, Beijing was more concerned about the capabilities of the radar than of the THAAD interceptors. In addition, while U.S. officials briefed Chinese leaders on the limited impact THAAD would have on China's deterrent, Beijing was possibly more concerned about THAAD as a signal of an incremental step by South Korea to join the U.S. BMD system and its future effect on China's strategic deterrent.

USFK commander General Curtis Scaparrotti first recommended the United States deploy THAAD in June 2014, but despite press reports to the contrary, the South Korean government showed little interest, fearing this would be viewed negatively in Beijing. However, when North Korea conducted its fourth nuclear test, followed shortly after by another ballistic missile launch, the thinking on THAAD began to change. Up to this point, President Park had been cultivating a close relationship with Chinese president Xi in hopes that closer ties would mean greater effort on China's part to rein in North Korea. Following the January 2016 nuclear test and China's initial tepid response, Seoul announced that it was reopening the THAAD issue. Soon after, there appeared to be indications that THAAD might be shelved again in exchange for Chinese support for a tougher UN Security Council resolution in the wake of the tests.[81] Chinese leaders continued to keep the heat on South Korea regarding THAAD. In February, the Chinese ambassador to South Korea, Qiu Guohong, cautioned that Sino–South Korean relations could be "destroyed in an instant" if THAAD were deployed, but a spokesman for the Park administration shot back: "This is a matter we will decide upon according to our own security and national interests. The Chinese had better recognize this point."[82] An anonymous senior official at the ROK Foreign Ministry went further, instructing China to "look into the root of the problem [North Korea's nuclear weapon and ballistic programs] if it really wants to raise an issue with it."[83] It was not long before talks between Washington and Seoul resumed on implementing a THAAD deployment, and on July 8, 2016, the decision to deploy the battery was announced.

Return of U.S. Tactical Nuclear Weapons to South Korea

Over the past decade, ROK analysts have had probing discussions over the credibility of the U.S. nuclear umbrella. Would the United States truly use nuclear weapons to defend the South? During the Cold War, the presence of nuclear weapons on the peninsula was designed to be a tangible link to that commitment and a signal that a conventional assault could quickly escalate into a nuclear conflict. The presence of nuclear weapons ensured there would be less likelihood of "decoupling," in which Washington would refrain from using nuclear weapons for fear of nuclear retaliation. A warfighting measure intended to blunt a North Korean invasion, the deployment of U.S. tactical nuclear weapons to Korea was also intended to bolster deterrence.

U.S. nuclear weapons have been absent from the peninsula since 1991, but over the past decade some Korean politicians and analysts have called for their return. A prominent and vocal proponent of redeploying tactical nuclear weapons is Chung Mong-joon, a member of the ROK

National Assembly and principal shareholder of Hyundai Heavy Industries. In a 2011 parliamentary session, Representative Chung argued:

> Because a nuclear umbrella is not enough to make the North give up its nuclear weapons, we must consider redeployment of (U.S.) tactical nuclear weapons. It is impossible to peacefully coexist with a nuclear armed North Korea. North Korea's nuclear program is a political weapon that wields massive power just by possessing nuclear arms and shakes up the military balance between the South and the North. The North will resort to a "nuclear shadow" strategy of repeating conventional provocations with nuclear weapons on its back.[84]

Another politician from the conservative Saenuri Party declared in 2016, "Against the North, which claims it will develop intercontinental ballistic missiles (ICBMs) on top of a hydrogen bomb, redeployment of U.S. tactical nuclear weapons to [the] Korean Peninsula is necessary."[85]

One plan to redeploy U.S. nuclear weapons proposes beginning negotiations with North Korea on denuclearization while setting a deadline for completion of this process.[86] Should Pyongyang fail to provide credible signs that it will begin to denuclearize, Washington would redeploy twenty to thirty tactical nuclear weapons to the peninsula. Negotiations could continue after deployment but now would focus on joint denuclearization. In addition to applying pressure on North Korea, this proposal would also turn up the heat on China and Russia to pressure Pyongyang to give up its nuclear ambitions, because neither Beijing nor Moscow would relish the return of U.S. tactical nuclear weapons to the region.

The possibility of reintroducing U.S. nuclear weapons was first broached in November 2010 by then ROK defense minister Kim Tae-young when he indicated in testimony to a parliamentary committee that the issue might be "reviewed" by U.S. and ROK officials.[87] However, Lee Myung-bak administration officials quickly backtracked from any consideration of the suggestion. In 2011, Gary Samore, the Obama administration's coordinator for arms control and WMD, remarked at a conference that although discussion of the issue had not occurred, if South Korea made a formal request to reintroduce nuclear weapons, the Obama administration would likely agree to do so, given the close alliance relationship.[88] Soon after, however, NSC spokesman Robert Jensen responded, "Our policy remains in support of a non-nuclear Korean peninsula. There is no plan to change that policy. Tactical nuclear weapons are unnecessary for the defense of South Korea and we have no plan or intention to return them."[89]

In May 2012, the U.S. House Armed Services Committee inserted an amendment into the FY 2013 Defense Authorization Bill that called for reviewing the decision to remove tactical nuclear weapons from South Korea.[90] The White House was again quick to state that nuclear weapons were unnecessary and there was no plan to return them to South Korea. Since then, there have been no formal discussions to implement a return, and the ROK government has shown little interest in moving in this direction, though the issue resurfaces from time to time.

Returning U.S. nuclear weapons to the peninsula would be a bad idea for several reasons. As U.S. defense officials recognized in the 1970s and 1980s, forward deployed nuclear weapons raise serious problems concerning possible North Korean preemption or a dangerous "use or lose" situation.[91] These concerns were the main reasons for removing nuclear weapons then and remain important reasons today for not returning them. Moreover, U.S. military leaders were convinced that nuclear weapons were not necessary to defend South Korea, and that has not changed. The return of U.S. nuclear weapons would do little to improve strategic stability and would stir a contentious debate in South Korea that would likely fuel anti-American sentiment. Thus, the reintroduction of tactical nuclear weapons would reassure some but be a disturbing move for others. China and Russia would be very unsettled by this alteration of the strategic environment, and Beijing in particular would argue again that North Korea was an excuse for deploying nuclear weapons that could be targeted against China. Finally, it has been more than two decades since U.S. troops in Korea have been prepared for a nuclear mission. Resuscitating the expertise, training, and infrastructure to perform a nuclear mission takes time and money. Though the U.S. military could conduct the mission if ordered, the cost and political fallout would not be worth the benefits. Finally, the strategic signal to others of encouraging the spread of tactical nuclear weapons would not be in the U.S. interest.

Building a South Korean Nuclear Weapon

Another proposal bandied about by some ROK politicians and analysts has been that South Korea acquire its own nuclear weapons. If the nuclear umbrella has credibility problems and Washington is reluctant to redeploy nuclear weapons, some South Koreans have argued that this is a necessary alternative. The idea received further attention during the 2016 U.S. presidential campaign when Donald Trump suggested that it might not be such a bad outcome if South Korea and Japan had their own nuclear weapons. Indeed, this was not a new option considered by ROK leaders.

In the early 1970s, South Korea, worried about its own military capabilities and the certainty of the U.S. defense commitment in the wake of Vietnam, the Nixon Doctrine, and U.S.-China rapprochement, turned to the French to begin a nuclear weapons program.[92] Once India surprised Washington with a nuclear weapon test in 1974, U.S. intelligence agencies were on the lookout for other would-be proliferators. U.S. officials examined import requests for critical materials and, according to one assessment, "when they got to Korea, everything snapped into place."[93]

After putting all the pieces together, the Ford administration exerted intense pressure on France to stop its nuclear dealings with South Korea, but the French refused. Washington next applied pressure on Seoul, including threats to restrict export licenses and Export-Import Bank financing while implying that failure to desist would cause a fundamental rethinking of the alliance. Eventually, the pressure led to South Korea's ratifying the NPT in 1975 and abandoning its nuclear weapons ambitions.[94] Secretary of Defense James Schlesinger publically acknowledged the presence of nuclear weapons in Korea during his trip to Seoul in 1975 to provide some degree of assurance to compensate for U.S. pressure. Washington also remained vigilant that South Korea might restart its program, especially in the wake of Jimmy Carter's call for withdrawing all U.S. combat troops from the peninsula. South Korea has a world-class nuclear energy industry that provides the foundation and breakout capability for a nuclear weapons program, but since then it has decided not to move in that direction.[95]

In the wake of North Korea's nuclear tests, calls for South Korea to acquire its own nuclear weapons increased, particularly after the last two tests. Again, one of its most vocal advocates was conservative politician Chung Mong-joon, who argued, "We, the Korean people, have been duped by North Korea for the last 20 to 30 years and it is now time for South Koreans to face the reality and do something that we need to do. The nuclear deterrence can be the only answer. We have to have nuclear capability."[96] Other conservative politicians followed suit in calling for a South Korean bomb, and ROK public opinion provided further support for going nuclear. For example, a poll conducted by the Asan Institute in February 2013, prior to North Korea's third nuclear weapons test, found that 66 percent of South Korean respondents supported a ROK nuclear weapons capability with only 31 percent opposed. These numbers included 58 percent support from Progressives, South Korea's left, and showed a significant increase in those who "strongly support" a nuclear South Korea.[97] Other surveys reported similar results.

After the January 2016 nuclear test, several politicians again spoke out for South Korean nuclear weapons. Conservative party floor leader Won Yoo-chul remarked, "It's time for us to peacefully arm ourselves with nuclear weapons from the perspective of self-defense to fight against North Korea's terror and destruction."[98] Surveys that followed the test also continued to show majority support for acquiring nuclear weapons. However, a study by the Carnegie Endowment compared political elite sentiment, media attention, and polling data from 2013 and 2016 and found that while elite support was relatively consistent and media attention had increased, public support for acquiring nuclear weapons had decreased by as much as 10 percentage points. Although the study points to the difficulty of interpreting the data and the complexity of these views, it concludes that "public opinion is malleable, but support for nuclear options has declined."[99]

Despite these pressures, the ROK government has remained committed to a nuclear-free South Korea. At the 2014 Nuclear Security Summit held at The Hague, President Park reaffirmed her support for a nuclear-free Korean peninsula, asserting that "the journey toward a world without nuclear weapons should start from the Korean Peninsula."[100] According to a former U.S. official, the nuclear umbrella makes an important contribution here in helping to support South Korea's nonnuclear position and relieving pressure on ROK leaders to consider acquiring their own nuclear weapons.[101] Choi and Park maintain,

"A strong U.S. security commitment and the provision of its nuclear umbrella play the role of a 'bottle cap' that keeps South Korea from thinking it needs to develop nuclear weapons. Thus the current nonnuclear posture of South Korea is a direct result of the strength and credibility of the U.S. commitment."[102]

The ROK public has been very frustrated with North Korea's efforts to develop nuclear weapons and looks to the government for a solution. Politicians feel they need to do something.[103] Yet, as one U.S. analyst argued, "provocative statements by some Korean commentators, and instinctive public support in favor of nuclear weapons registered by pollsters, express anxiety and vulnerability to North Korea's threat, not a strategy."[104] Others, such as Moon Chung-in, have argued that South Korean nuclear weapons would be a "curse," not a "blessing."[105] As one ROK scholar told me, the South Korean public doesn't really want nuclear weapons; it is more that they are frustrated and doubt the credibility of the U.S. nuclear umbrella.[106]

Should South Korea develop its own nuclear weapons, it would face several serious consequences.[107] First, South Korea has been a member in good standing of the NPT since ratifying the agreement in 1975. Developing nuclear weapons would entail withdrawing from the NPT, the most important international endeavor to stop the proliferation of nuclear weapons, while joining North Korea as one of two states leaving the NPT to acquire this capability. South Korea's withdrawal would have devastating implications for nonproliferation efforts in Korea and the world. Seoul would likely receive international censure for leaving the NPT, accompanied by economic sanctions that would rock its export-driven economy. South Korea's world-class civilian nuclear energy sector would likely face numerous penalties, including restricted access to nuclear fuel and technology, in addition to the loss of sales opportunities abroad. Moreover, South Korea has long hoped to obtain revisions to the 123 Nuclear Cooperation Agreement with the United States that would let South Korea enrich and reprocess fuel for its civilian nuclear industry. Developing nuclear weapons would kill any possibility of the United States relenting on this demand.

Second, South Korea's goal of denuclearizing the peninsula would be dealt a mortal blow. Pyongyang would have another argument for retaining its nuclear program, and Seoul would lose the moral high ground along with any international support for its efforts. Despite North Korea's voiding of the 1992 Denuclearization Agreement and the 2005 Joint Statement of the Six Party Talks, both of which commit the Koreas to denuclearization, Seoul's acquisition of nuclear weapons would end its leadership in global nonproliferation that was exemplified in its hosting of the 2012 Nuclear Security Summit. South Korea's quest for nuclear weapons would jeopardize the credibility of the NPT and weaken the constraints on others, such as Saudi Arabia, Iran, and Japan, to acquire nuclear weapons, leading to further weakening of nonproliferation norms. Likewise, any calls by Seoul for other countries, especially China and Russia, to increase pressure on North Korea to denuclearize would now fall on deaf ears.

Finally, there would be serious consequences for the ROK-U.S. alliance. For years, the United States has provided a credible security commitment that included the nuclear umbrella in return for Seoul's forgoing nuclear weapons. ROK acquisition of them would remove the argument for maintaining U.S. extended nuclear deterrence and undermine the overall U.S. defense commitment for South Korea.

More important, nuclear weapons would do little to improve South Korean security. Strategic deterrence in Korea has long been robust, and the chances of North Korea mounting another Korean War–type invasion or other large-scale military action are very small. A DPRK assault of this sort would provoke an overwhelming military response from Seoul and Washington that would bring about the end of the regime. ROK acquisition of nuclear weapons would do little to improve the strategic stability that has been present in Korea for decades. On the contrary, ROK security would be damaged by weakening the ROK-U.S. alliance, undermining Chinese and Russian support for continuing sanctions on the North, and providing Pyongyang with greater justification for expanding its own nuclear weapons program. Deterring lower-level provocations such as the sinking of the *Cheonan*, the shelling of Yeonpyeong Island, and cyberattacks are far greater challenges for ROK security, and nuclear weapons would do little to remedy these problems. For example, Israel's nuclear weapons have not deterred rocket attacks from Gaza or Lebanon. Thus, "going nuclear" would entail significant costs for South Korea while providing only minimal security benefits. The feelings of vulnerability and frustration are understandable, but acquiring its own nuclear deterrent is not the solution and would cause more harm than good.

CONCLUSION

For decades, the U.S. nuclear umbrella has been part of ROK security calculations and planning. Lingering doubts remain about its credibility and the circumstances under which the United States would use nuclear weapons to defend South Korea. ROK leaders and analysts watch closely for any changes to U.S. nuclear capability or policy shifts that might indicate a weakening of the nuclear umbrella and call for greater assurances of the nuclear security guarantee. For ROK defense planners and the public, the nuclear umbrella counters a growing North Korean capability by promising overwhelming destruction should Pyongyang challenge strategic deterrence. The umbrella also negates any perceived political leverage and ability to intimidate the South that the North might believe it gains with nuclear weapons. As with Japan, the nuclear umbrella provides a crucial political signal that conveys the depth of the U.S. commitment to defend South Korea in the context of a strong alliance while helping to ensure that South Korea will not go nuclear.

Alliance planning and preparations remain robust to address a growing set of North Korean asymmetric capabilities, as demonstrated by a new OPLAN, the Tailored Deterrence Strategy, and the Combined Counter-Provocation Plan. However, South Korea is also expanding its own capabilities such as BMD and conventional strike, enabling it to contribute to alliance efforts while also retaining an independent capability to hedge for future changes to the alliance. Indeed, South Koreans have similar concerns as others in Asia regarding the staying power of U.S. strength and its commitment to the region in the years ahead, and it should not be a surprise that South Korea is engaging in some degree of hedging.

South Korea's civilian nuclear energy industry provides the base for South Korea to go nuclear, and periodically voices in the South call for moving in this direction. Although public support for a ROK nuclear option has declined, several surveys continue to show that a majority of South Koreans believe developing their own nuclear weapons is a necessary response to North Korea's nuclear weapons. So far, the ROK government has continued to reject this option, recognizing the serious difficulties that would accompany the possession of nuclear weapons, and it is not clear if survey data reflect a genuine desire for these weapons or simply frustration and a felt need to take some type of action following North Korea's testing. So long as the ROK-U.S. alliance remains strong, South Korea will likely continue its "nuclear restraint." Many ROK analysts acknowledge that the U.S. nuclear umbrella is essential in keeping South Korea from pursuing its own nuclear weapons.

CHAPTER SIX

The U.S. Nuclear Umbrella

Planning, Capabilities, and Credibility

The United States has provided an extended deterrence commitment to both Japan and South Korea, including placing both countries under the U.S. nuclear umbrella. For South Korea, that commitment included the deployment of tactical nuclear weapons to the peninsula from 1958 until their withdrawal in 1991. In Japan, the United States maintained a secret nuclear arsenal on Okinawa until 1972. When the weapons were removed upon the return of Okinawa to Japan, Washington and Tokyo maintained a secret agreement allowing for their return in a crisis. Though the weapons were removed, the United States continued its commitment under the nuclear umbrella. For years, there was relatively little change to the details of the nuclear commitment.

Under the Obama administration, the United States made some important changes to U.S. nuclear policy and doctrine. In 2002, George W. Bush and Vladimir Putin had signed the Strategic Offensive Reductions Treaty, establishing new limits on the number of deployed strategic warheads. Obama sought to further reduce the number of nuclear weapons in the U.S. arsenal and lessen the role of these weapons in security planning, at the same time acknowledging that so long as nuclear weapons exist, the United States will maintain a credible nuclear deterrent. In an address at the Shangri-La Dialogue in June 2010, U.S. Secretary of Defense Robert Gates stated:

> We are renewing our commitment to a strong and effective extended deterrence that guarantees the safety of the American people and the defence of our allies and partners. As President Obama has stated, this administration is committed to reducing the role of nuclear weapons as we work toward a world without such weapons but, as long as these weapons exist, we will maintain a safe, secure, and effective nuclear arsenal.[1]

Six years later, in May 2016, Obama traveled to Hiroshima and reaffirmed his position on nuclear weapons:

> But among those nations like my own that hold nuclear stockpiles, we must have the courage to escape the logic of fear, and pursue a world without them. We may not realize this goal in my lifetime. But persistent effort can roll back the possibility of catastrophe. We can chart a course that leads to the destruction of these stockpiles. We can stop the spread to new nations, and secure deadly materials from fanatics.[2]

While the Obama administration made some progress on moving in this direction, the United States maintains a large nuclear arsenal and a commitment to nuclear deterrence as part of its national security strategy.[3] In addition, Trump has said he would like to see a world without nuclear weapons, but that the United States should never fall behind other countries with nuclear weapons.

The U.S. military has the capability to carry out an order from the president to use nuclear weapons in defense of one of its allies. U.S.-Russian arms control measures have reduced nuclear stockpiles, but Washington retains thousands of strategic and tactical nuclear weapons, either deployed or in storage, along with the necessary delivery vehicles for a nuclear umbrella. Moreover, U.S. forces train to conduct these missions and would certainly execute them if ordered to do so. Thus, the United States unquestionably has the capability to support its commitment of a nuclear umbrella.

The more difficult question is resolve. Despite having the capability, would a U.S. president ever order the use of nuclear weapons to defend

Japan or South Korea? What circumstances would generate such a decision? This study argues it is highly unlikely that a U.S. president would ever be willing to use nuclear weapons, for a variety of strategic, tactical, and moral reasons. That is not to say the United States would shirk its defense commitments. The U.S. guarantee to defend Japan and South Korea is highly credible, and there is little doubt the United States would come to their aid, but it likely would not and should not be with nuclear weapons. Instead, the United States has numerous, potent conventional options that would have similar strategic effects on an adversary and would be highly credible, because the United States would have far less hesitation to use these weapons.

Despite the significant credibility problems of nuclear weapons in extended deterrence, problems that have been around for much of the Cold War, the nuclear umbrella is an important political signal that reflects and helps buttress the overall health of the alliances. These commitments are part of a regional security architecture that helps support deterrence but are only one component of that structure. Despite the inherent credibility problem, so long as the United States has nuclear weapons, an adversary can never be quite sure they would not be used. Thus, as Thomas Schelling once wrote, even if there is a small chance a nuclear weapon might be used, its destructive power may still have deterrent value.

This chapter examines the role that nuclear weapons play in U.S. extended deterrence commitments, the U.S. nuclear arsenal that constitutes the nuclear umbrella, the reasons why using nuclear weapons is very unlikely and indeed unwise, and the links between U.S. nonproliferation goals and the nuclear umbrella.

THE ROLE OF NUCLEAR WEAPONS IN U.S. EXTENDED DETERRENCE

After World War II, the United States' monopoly on nuclear weapons allowed it to adopt an extended deterrence strategy based on the concept of massive retaliation. Facing the challenge of Soviet conventional strength around the globe that could be matched only at huge cost, Washington opted to use its nuclear card to deter Soviet aggression in Europe and around the world. As articulated by John Foster Dulles soon after the Korean War, the United States could not afford to commit troops to protect all areas of importance to its interests. As a result,

> there is no local defense which alone will contain the mighty landpower of the Communist world. Local defense must be reinforced by the further deterrent of massive retaliation. A potential aggressor must know that he cannot always prescribe battle conditions that suit him. Otherwise, for example, a potential aggressor, who is glutted with manpower, might be tempted to attack in confidence that resistance would be confined to manpower. He might be tempted to attack in places where his superiority was decisive.[4]

Instead, the United States would "depend primarily upon a great capacity to retaliate, instantly by means and at places of our choosing."[5] Thus, any Soviet assault held out the possibility of U.S. escalation to nuclear weapons, hopefully convincing Moscow to refrain from attacking in the first place. Since the Soviets could not respond in a similar manner, there was some degree of credibility to U.S. massive retaliation.

As the Soviet arsenal grew in size and capability, massive retaliation became exceedingly less credible. If the United States responded to a Soviet conventional attack with nuclear weapons, Moscow could retaliate on the U.S. homeland with nuclear weapons to devastating effect. Increasingly, massive retaliation was no longer credible, especially for extended deterrence and the nuclear umbrella.[6]

Washington sought to remedy this situation by altering its strategy. In the 1960s, defense planners began to think about providing the president with a broader range of options that spanned conventional and nuclear weapons. Labeled "flexible response," these alternatives were laid out across an escalation ladder that provided a list of graduated alternatives, increasing the level of response as circumstances dictated.[7] In Europe, the United States forward deployed nuclear weapons so that if the Red Army invaded, Washington would be forced to move up the ladder, likely to nuclear weapons, to counter Soviet conventional strength. Because a Soviet attack would be the trigger for escalation to nuclear weapons, the responsibility was on the Soviets, and the belief was that this would make them hesitate and be more cautious in the first place.[8] Thus, regarding Europe and elsewhere, Secretary of Defense Melvin Laird stated in 1972:

> Our theater nuclear forces add to the deterrence of theater conventional wars in Europe and Asia; potential opponents cannot be sure that major conventional aggression would not be met with the use of nuclear weapons. The threat of escalation to strategic nuclear war remains a part of successful deterrence at this level. Our planning reflects a continued requirement to relate our nuclear weapons posture in the theater to our conventional posture in such a way that we have realistic options in the theater which do not require sole reliance on strategic nuclear weapons.[9]

This strategy applied to Korea and Japan as well, including in Korea an emphasis on nuclear weapons as warfighting tools. Tactical nuclear weapons in Korea could be used early to blunt a North Korean advance, strike rear echelon targets, and block invasion corridors. However, U.S. leaders eventually decided that forward deployed, tactical nuclear weapons in Korea were too dangerous because they were vulnerable to preemption or being overrun in the early hours of an invasion. Moreover, U.S. military leaders began to question the need for nuclear weapons to successfully defend South Korea.[10]

With the end of the Cold War, thinking about nuclear weapons strategy waned. When the Soviet Union fell, deterrence and nuclear weapons seemed less important, and despite the existence of thousands of nuclear warheads worldwide, relatively little thought was given to U.S. nuclear strategy in this new security environment. In the wake of the terrorist attacks of September 11, many people continued to challenge the utility of deterrence, particularly as it related to the challenges of terrorist groups and so-called rogue states such as Iran, Iraq, and North Korea. The 2002 Bush National Security Strategy described this concern by suggesting that "deterrence based only upon the threat of retaliation is less likely to work against leaders of rogue states more willing to take risks, gambling with the lives of their people and the wealth of their nations."[11]

In response, the Bush administration began developing a strategy of tailored deterrence. Articulated in the 2006 Quadrennial Defense Review (QDR), tailored deterrence meant that the United States would no longer use a "one size fits all" approach as it had during the Cold War.[12] The idea of tailoring deterrence is not new; adjusting deterrence to circumstances based on what an adversary values and how to best manipulate costs and benefits have long been a part of deterrence theory. Yet this was the first time an administration had conceived of deterrence in such a manner. Consistent with the concept of a "New Triad" spelled out in the 2001 Nuclear Posture Review (NPR), under tailored deterrence, "the force will include a wider range of non-kinetic and conventional strike capabilities, while maintaining a robust nuclear deterrent, which remains a keystone of U.S. national power."[13] In contrast to the usual conception of the nuclear triad—land, sea, and air-delivered nuclear weapons—the 2001 NPR described a new triad of offensive strike (nuclear and conventional), defense systems, and a revitalized defense infrastructure.[14] The 2006 QDR also spoke of new, conventional precision-guided munitions "which can hold at risk targets that might have required nuclear forces in the past."[15] Finally, the QDR stressed the importance of missile defense in broadening U.S efforts to bolster extended deterrence.

In Korea, a subtle but important shift followed this apparent broadening of deterrence. The restatement of the U.S. nuclear umbrella that was part of the SCM joint communique was typically a fairly straightforward declaration. For example, in 2008, the communique provided assurance of the U.S. commitment as "including continuation of the extended deterrence offered by the U.S. nuclear umbrella."[16] Recall that the line had been changed in 2006 with the addition of the phrase "extended deterrence." In 2009, in a further broadening of the language, Secretary of Defense Robert Gates "reaffirmed the U.S. commitment to provide extended deterrence for the ROK, using the full range of military capabilities, to include the U.S. nuclear umbrella, conventional strike, and missile defense capabilities."[17] U.S. extended deterrence had never been a guarantee to use nuclear weapons, only that they were one of a broad array of tools available to protect U.S. allies. The SCM now began to state that formally.

Early in the Obama administration, it became clear that some policy shifts were in the works regarding nuclear weapons. In April 2009, Obama declared at Prague that he intended to reduce the role of nuclear weapons in U.S. security strategy and decrease the number of weapons in the arsenal, with the eventual goal of eliminating them. However, he affirmed that as long as these weapons existed, the United States would continue to maintain a robust nuclear deterrent.

These declarations were followed by more formal pronouncements, outlined in the 2010 Nuclear Posture Review that reaffirmed the intentions expressed at Prague. Concerning extended deterrence, the NPR maintained that "U.S. nuclear weapons have played an essential role in extending deterrence to U.S. allies and partners against nuclear attacks or nuclear-backed coercion by states in their region that possess or are seeking nuclear weapons."[18] But the NPR also noted, "The United States will continue to strengthen conventional capabilities and reduce the role of nuclear weapons in deterring non-nuclear attacks, with the objective of making deterrence of nuclear attack on the United States or our allies and partners the sole purpose of U.S. nuclear weapons."[19] Thus, the NPR expressed an aspiration for a "sole purpose" declaration, but it stopped short of making one at that time.

The NPR also refrained from providing a "no first use" declaration for nuclear weapons, but it did craft a "negative security assurance," stating that the United States would not use or threaten to use nuclear weapons against any nonnuclear state that was a member of the Nuclear Nonproliferation Treaty and in full compliance with its NPT obligations. For those not covered by the negative security assurance, there was a small range of contingencies in which the United States would use nuclear weapons to deter an attack with conventional, chemical, or biological weapons. Citing Ronald Reagan's dictum that "a nuclear war cannot be won and must never be fought," the NPR maintained that "the United States wishes to stress that it would only consider the use of nuclear weapons in extreme circumstances to defend the vital interests of the United States or its allies and partners."[20]

Analysts and leaders in Japan and South Korea followed the progress of the NPR and Obama administration nuclear strategy very carefully. The Obama administration reached out to Tokyo and Seoul for input on these issues, and both allies were pleased that the document did not go further regarding "no first use" or "sole purpose," though there was some concern over what might constitute "extreme circumstances." Throughout the Bush and Obama years, there was significant effort to remind everyone that extended deterrence did not, and never did, rely solely on nuclear weapons—that while the United States maintained its nuclear umbrella, there were a host of other, more usable options it could and would use to defend Japan and South Korea. Subsequent statements by U.S. officials confirmed these positions.

In 2012, U.S. Air Force General and Commander of Strategic Command (STRATCOM) Robert Kehler pointed out that many assets are part of an extended deterrence relationship:

> It is about what the U.S. and our allies as a whole can bring to bear in both military and a nonmilitary sense. Its practice encompasses a wider range of complementary tools today, both nuclear and strong conventional forces, nonkinetic force perhaps, limited missile defenses, unfettered access and use of space and cyberspace, and in all warfare areas, modern capabilities that are both resilient and sustained.[21]

In a 2014 interview, Under Secretary for Arms Control and International Security Rose Gottemoeller emphasized that

> extended deterrence is not only about nuclear weapons. Extended deterrence has to do with our complete alliance relationship and that, of course, contains within it a full panoply of weapons systems and everything that goes with weapons systems to make them effective—such as effective command, control, communications, and reconnaissance capabilities. Conventional weapons—and very effective conventional weapons at that—are a core, inherent part of extended deterrence. And, along with that, when we get to where the President wants to go, which is—as he mentioned in his Prague speech in 2009—the security of a world without nuclear weapons, our extended deterrence relationship with our allies will still be very much intact, and very coherent in the array of conventional defense that we will have to offer them.[22]

Thus, the nuclear umbrella was one tool, but not the sole or preferred tool, to use if deterrence should fail. U.S. leaders often say that "all options are on the table"; nuclear weapons are one of many options, but one that is very unlikely to be used.

COMMAND AND CONTROL OF U.S. NUCLEAR WEAPONS: NATIONAL COMMAND AUTHORITY

Should the need ever arise, the national command authority (NCA) to order the launch of U.S. nuclear weapons rests with the president as commander-in-chief, as outlined in the 1986 Goldwater-Nichols Act. An order to launch nuclear weapons requires secondary confirmation from the secretary of defense (SECDEF) as the deputy commander-in-chief. Should the SECDEF refuse to concur with the launch order, the president may replace the current officeholder with the deputy SECDEF as acting secretary. Should nonconcurrence continue with this appointee, the president may continue the process until finding a deputy who agrees to the launch. However, the vice president and a majority of the executive department heads could invoke section 4 of the Twenty-Fifth Amendment and declare the president incapacitated, at which point the vice president would assume the position of president. Should the president and the defense secretary be killed, NCA would follow the guidelines in the Constitution and the 1947 Presidential Succession Act. This process presents a serious hurdle for using nuclear weapons and demonstrates how differently they are viewed than conventional weapons, requiring extra layers of safeguards to ensure the wisdom of their use.

Though the structure of the NCA is public, the specific procedures for ordering a nuclear launch remain classified. Indeed, it is not clear how a request for nuclear weapons would flow up the chain of command. For example, in a Korea scenario, could USFK initiate a request for nuclear weapons, and would that request go directly to the president, or would it go to some other entity in between, such as PACOM or STRATCOM, before being sent to the White House? Planning between USFK and STRATCOM continues to improve, especially as a result of the tailored deterrence strategy.[23]

THE U.S. NUCLEAR UMBRELLA: CAPABILITIES AND OPTIONS

The United States possesses a large nuclear arsenal, and in spite of significant cuts from Cold War force levels, it remains more than capable of imposing unacceptable costs on any adversary should Washington choose to do so. U.S. nuclear forces fall broadly into two categories: strategic and nonstrategic, or tactical, nuclear weapons. Analysts have not agreed on a precise definition to distinguish the two, and many would argue that the distinction is irrelevant, given the destructive power of even a "small" nuclear weapon and the reality that the use of any size weapon would mean crossing the nuclear firebreak.[24] Yet the distinction is relevant when assessing the nuclear umbrella.

Strategic Nuclear Weapons

The U.S. strategic arsenal is often described as the "triad," consisting of land-based intercontinental ballistic missiles (ICBM), submarines equipped with ballistic missiles (SLBM), and gravity bombs or cruise missiles carried by aircraft. The ICBM leg of the triad is made up of 440 Minuteman III missiles divided into three wings deployed in underground silos at Malmstrom Air Force Base (Montana), Minot AFB (South Dakota), and F. E. Warren AFB (Wyoming).[25] Each missile carries a single warhead with a yield of 300 to 500 kilotons. The sea-based portion of the triad is furnished by fourteen *Ohio*-class submarines (SSBN) or "boomers" that each carry twenty-four Trident II D-5 missiles in vertical launch tubes. To meet New START limits, the SSBNs will be modified to carry twenty Trident missiles. The D-5 SLBM is a MIRVed missile capable of carrying twelve warheads with a yield of 300 to 475 kilotons each. The last leg of the triad consists of ten B-2A Stealth bombers and seventy-seven B-52H bombers, both of which are configured for nuclear missions and capable of dropping nuclear gravity bombs or launching nuclear-tipped cruise missiles.[26]

The size of the U.S. nuclear force is shaped in large part by the parameters of the New START agreement that was signed in 2010 and entered into force on February 5, 2011. The treaty limits U.S. and Russian forces to 700 total deployed and 800 deployed and nondeployed launch vehicles, including ICBMs, SLBMs, and heavy bombers. Each side is also limited to 1,550 deployed warheads, but there are no limits to the number that can remain in storage in nondeployed status. The ICBMs will all be armed with a single warhead, but the SLBMs will remain MIRVed. Each bomber will be counted as carrying one warhead.[27] To meet these numbers, the United States is expected to reduce its Minuteman III force to 400 deployed missiles while retaining 240 deployed SLBMs and 60 deployed bombers. Washington and Moscow must meet these limits by 2018, and the treaty will expire in 2021 unless extended.

Regarding the nuclear umbrella, though U.S. leaders often indicate that "all options are on the table," Washington is very unlikely to use any of its strategic nuclear force in defense of Japan or South Korea. First, the destructive power of strategic forces, particularly the ICBMs and SLBMs, is excessive and likely to be viewed as disproportionate overkill. Given the size of these weapons—300 to 500 kilotons—a U.S. president is likely to avoid their use in any retaliatory strike. Thus, when commenting on the Air Force's proposed new cruise missile, one Pentagon official noted concerning ICBMs and SLBMs, "they're all brute weapons with high-yield warheads. We need the targeting flexibility and lower-yield options" of the new cruise missile.[28]

Second, the launch of a strategic nuclear weapon raises some dangerous possibilities for jangling the nerves of others in the region. For example, the telemetry of an ICBM or SLBM launch toward North Korea, at least during the initial and midcourse portions of the flight, would make it difficult to determine if the intended target was Pyongyang or some other location in Asia. As a result, there could be considerable consternation in Beijing or Moscow over the intended target. Some of these concerns could be diminished through communication and coordination with Chinese and Russian leaders. Yet, depending on the level of involvement of Beijing or Moscow in whatever events precipitated the crisis, there could be serious room for misunderstanding and tremendous risk over these uncertainties. If the launch were intended for China, that would raise a host of even more serious concerns. For all these reasons, the United States would be far more likely to use nonstrategic nuclear weapons when implementing the nuclear umbrella, if it ever chose to do so.

Nonstrategic/Tactical Nuclear Weapons

During the Cold War, the United States had thousands of tactical nuclear weapons, with some deployed in Europe and Asia and others at sea on U.S. Navy vessels. As the Cold War wound down, Washington began to pull some of these weapons back from their forward deployed locations and reduce the overall number. In 1987, Washington and Moscow concluded the Intermediate-range Nuclear Forces (INF) Treaty banning ground-launched ballistic and cruise missiles with ranges of 500 to 5,500 kilometers. Although the agreement required that the missiles be destroyed, the warheads were retained. In 1991, the United States completed a process of removing all of its nuclear weapons from Korea, and the following year the U.S. Navy removed all nuclear weapons from its surface ships, attack submarines, and forward bases, retaining only the strategic weapons on its ballistic missile submarines. Though not deploying the system, the Navy kept the nuclear-tipped Tomahawk cruise missile (TLAM-N), but the 2010 NPR announced its retirement, noting that the deterrence mission of this system "can be adequately substituted by other means."[29] Since 1991, the U.S. has destroyed approximately 90 percent of its nonstrategic/tactical nuclear stockpile, but the remaining 10 percent would furnish sizable destructive power.[30]

The U.S. arsenal contains two general types of nonstrategic weapons relevant to the nuclear umbrella: gravity bombs and nuclear-tipped cruise missiles. It is estimated the United States has approximately 760 nonstrategic bombs and warheads, including 160 to 200 B-61 gravity bombs deployed in five NATO countries: Belgium, Italy, Turkey, Germany, and the Netherlands.[31] Another 300 B-61s are in storage in the United States.[32] The B-61 bomb is an adjustable-yield weapon with two versions: the B61-3, which can be set for yields ranging from 0.3 to 170 kilotons, and the B61-4, with yields from 0.3 to 50 kilotons.

The remainder of the nonstrategic arsenal consists of 260 W80-1 warheads for deployment on cruise missiles. These warheads are also adjustable, with yields estimated to range from 5 to 150 kilotons. Though some of these warheads were previously mounted on the retired TLAM-N, most were designed for use on the Air Force AGM-86B air-launched cruise missile (ALCM). With a range of 1,500 kilometers, the AGM-86B is configured for deployment on B-52 bombers. Each plane can carry twenty ALCMs, with twelve under the wings and eight in a rotary dispenser in the bomb bay. In 2010, the Air Force reported having 1,142 AGM-86Bs designated for a nuclear mission and 528 AGM-86 C/D models configured to carry conventional warheads.[33] The Air Force has plans to replace the current ALCM with a new

Long-Range Standoff (LRSO) cruise missile by 2027 to 2030. The LRSO will use a modified version of the W80-1 warhead. The Air Force also has plans to build a new long-range strike bomber.[34]

Dropping bombs for a nuclear strike requires planes to travel long distances and pierce air defense systems that may make it very difficult to reach the intended target and risk having nuclear-armed planes shot down. Stealth aircraft have made the task easier, but adversaries will chip away at this technology through countermeasures.[35] In contrast, cruise missiles are highly accurate weapons that are difficult to shoot down, allowing aircraft to fire at a considerable distance from the target without fear of confronting an opponent's air defense system.[36] As noted previously, cruise missiles also provide decision makers with lower-yield options compared to strategic nuclear weapons.

Aircraft have one other advantage over ICBMs and SLBMs in that, once launched, they can still be recalled. Moreover, for extended deterrence, planes can be flown in ways that are visible and obvious, especially to public audiences, displaying the potential reach of the nuclear umbrella for both allies and adversaries. A land-based ICBM does not have any "demonstration" capability, except perhaps with a test launch, and although a submarine could be used in this way, its primary role is to remain survivable by staying underwater and hidden. In spring 2013, the Pentagon used B-52 and B-2 bombers during exercises in Korea to reinforce deterrence during tense times and to provide a visible signal of reassurance to South Korea. USFK emphasized that "the United States is steadfast in its alliance commitment to the defense of the Republic of Korea, to deterring aggression, and to ensuring peace and stability in the region. The B-2 bomber is an important element of America's enduring and robust extended deterrence capability in the Asia-Pacific region."[37] The action was most definitely noticed by ROK leaders, who had asked for such a gesture, as well as by the ROK public. No doubt Japanese leaders and citizens were paying attention as well.

So long as the United States maintains an operational nuclear capability, there is always a possibility that Washington might use it. As a result, the U.S. nuclear umbrella is credible in part simply because these weapons exist. Given the costs that nuclear weapons can impose, adversaries, who often assess security from a "worst case" perspective, will need to account for the possibility of nuclear use in their calculations. The other part of credibility, resolve, is another matter; having the capability does not guarantee that a defender will actually use these weapons to defend an ally.

RESOLVE AND THE U.S. NUCLEAR UMBRELLA

Defenders undertake numerous efforts to ensure that both its allies and its adversaries are convinced it will not retreat should deterrence fail. For Japan and South Korea, the United States has concluded security treaties, stationed military forces on their soil, conducted regular military exercises, poured in large amounts of military and economic aid, and provided regular declarations of their inclusion under the U.S. nuclear umbrella. The combination of these measures provides a robust demonstration of the U.S. commitment to its alliances. Though relations have not always been smooth and there remain ongoing issues of alliance management that accompany any long-term relationship, the U.S. alliances with Tokyo and Seoul have been relatively strong and credible. Should either one be attacked, there is little doubt the United States would come to their assistance and uphold these decades-long defense commitments.

Despite the overall credibility of these alliances, however, the defense of either one is very unlikely to include the use of nuclear weapons. Even with overwhelming nuclear capability, nuclear forces that train to conduct these missions, and regular statements of inclusion under the nuclear umbrella, serious questions remain about the overall credibility of the U.S. nuclear umbrella. What circumstance would prompt a U.S. president to use nuclear weapons for the first time since 1945? Unless there was an existential threat to the United States that required a nuclear response, there would be immense pressure on the president to avoid using nuclear weapons. A U.S. president would think long and hard about escalating to nuclear weapons in a nonnuclear fight and even if North Korea or China were to use nuclear weapons first, would likely refrain from doing so, for several reasons. The discussion that follows will focus first on a North Korean scenario and then address China. North Korea is by far the more immediate challenge.

North Korea

First, if a crisis with North Korea were at a point where the United States was considering using nuclear weapons, Pyongyang would have crossed a very serious redline. Perhaps North Korea had launched a major conventional attack on the South or had sent a ballistic missile armed with a conventional, nuclear, or chemical warhead to South Korea, Japan, U.S. bases in the region, or the U.S. homeland. The likelihood of some of these scenarios is highly questionable short of the Kim regime believing that its rule was coming to an end. Yet if North Korea had done something sufficiently serious to prompt consideration of nuclear retaliation, it is likely that the United States and its allies, accompanied by far-reaching international support, would move to eliminate this troublesome security problem once and for all. According to two U.S. government analysts, "once North Korea uses nuclear weapons, all options are on the table. The regime will come to an end but it is not clear what that would mean or look like"; subsequent dialogue would flesh out the response, with a decision made by the president.[38] Thus, Quester suggests, "If the perpetrator of nuclear escalation was a dictatorial regime, this transgression might be viewed internationally as a reason to impose democracy on that country, to liberate the people from being governed without their consent, while presumably reducing the risk for other countries that such nuclear attacks would be repeated in the future."[39]

Consequently, a ROK-U.S.-led coalition would move North across the DMZ to take out the DPRK regime. Seoul and Washington would need to send ground forces to subdue the North Korean military, and contaminating the battlespace with nuclear strikes would be highly problematic for these operations. U.S. and ROK troops train to fight in a nuclear environment, but these types of operations are difficult and would slow any advance up the peninsula. Follow-on operations and occupation would be further complicated by the residual effects of U.S. nuclear weapons. Thus, there are important military reasons to avoid the use of nuclear weapons against North Korea, regardless of the scenario that might prompt their consideration in the first place.

Second, the U.S. military's use of nuclear weapons in Korea could have devastating effects throughout the region, in both the short and long term. Possible targets for a U.S. nuclear strike on the DPRK include leadership, command and control, nuclear weapon and ballistic missile facilities, and hardened bunkers, either underground or in mountainsides. How many nuclear weapons would be needed? One or two might be used to send a message and demonstrate U.S. credibility, or multiple launches might be deemed necessary to hit all the relevant targets. When analyzing the First Gulf War and the possible use of nuclear weapons, General Charles Horner, who commanded the bombing campaign in Iraq, noted that "you could use nuclear weapons but for what targets? The nuclear weapon's only good against cities, it's not any good against troops in the desert, I mean it takes too many of 'em, so the problem you have is, you have a war where if you kill a lot of people, particularly women and children, you lose the war no matter what happens on the battlefield."[40] Colin Powell also remarked, when looking at nuclear options for the First Gulf War, "The results unnerved me. To do serious damage to just one armored division dispersed in the desert would require a considerable number of small tactical nuclear weapons. . . . If I had had any doubts before about the practicality of nukes on the field of battle, this report clinched them."[41]

The geography of the Korean peninsula is vastly different from Iraq, but many of these concerns would also apply. Korea's mountainous landscape would divide the battlespace into various sectors, requiring multiple nuclear strikes to hit the necessary targets in each area. Despite the accuracy of today's nuclear weapons, even low-yield devices remain incredibly blunt and destructive. Using these weapons in a relatively confined space such as the Korean peninsula would kill thousands of North Korean civilians in addition to destroying any military targets. South Korea would face many challenges and great expense in unifying Korea after these events. South Korea will inherit this mess and cleaning up the nuclear devastation of even a few nuclear strikes in the North would be an unnecessary cost for Seoul.

In addition, the effects of a nuclear detonation would not be confined to the immediate area; radioactive fallout, depending on wind patterns, could blow these materials over South Korea and Japan or to China and Russia. Seoul's proximity to possible targets of forward deployed North Korean forces, which would likely be early targets, makes nuclear use a risky proposition for this metropolitan area of 25 million. Some analysts maintain that, given the accuracy of U.S. delivery systems and the use of earth-penetrating nuclear weapons, the effects of a nuclear blast could be contained. Yet, depending on the number of nuclear weapons used and the uncertainty of weather patterns, there would be great risk to civilian populations of the DPRK as well as surrounding states. The dangers to allies, possible Chinese and Russian reactions, and potential international condemnation in making such a decision would weigh heavily on any U.S. president's mind.

Third, whether calling it a taboo or a tradition of nonuse, scholars point to a strong international norm against the use of nuclear weapons. Tannenwald notes, "Despite cases where nuclear weapons were perceived to have military utility, U.S. leaders have ruled out their use for political and normative reasons. . . . States are not free to resort to nuclear weapons without incurring moral opprobrium or political costs. National leaders are forced to seek alternatives for use in war or defense or else risk being classified as outside the bounds of 'civilized' international society."[42] T. V. Paul argues that these restraints are an important normative and intermediate prohibition against the use of nuclear weapons but are not yet a formal, legal norm, especially since several nuclear weapon states retain the right to the first use of nuclear weapons.[43] Nonetheless, according to Paul, the United States would face high reputational costs.[44] Despite these differences in characterizing the norm, there remain significant moral and strategic reasons why a president would refrain from using nuclear weapons in all but the most dire circumstances. Referencing his time as secretary of defense, Robert McNamara recalled that "in long private conversations with successive Presidents—Kennedy and Johnson—I recommended, without qualification, that they never initiate, under any circumstances, the use of nuclear weapons. I believe they accepted my recommendation."[45] U.S. leaders would be under tremendous pressure to avoid crossing the nuclear firebreak that has existed since 1945 by escalating to the use of nuclear weapons, especially if the United States were to go nuclear first. The potential for death and destruction, imposed on another country in Asia, would be a strong barrier against Washington's use of nuclear weapons.

Even if responding to North Korean first use of nuclear weapons or to an attack with chemical or biological weapons, the president would face the same moral considerations. Survey evidence in a study by Press,

Sagan, and Valentino found that U.S. respondents were not averse to using nuclear weapons "if they promise even modest benefits in effectiveness over conventional strikes."[46] Yet U.S. leaders have hesitated to use nuclear weapons, even when retaliation was not a factor. For example, during the First Gulf War (1991–92), Brent Scowcroft notes in his memoir with George H. W. Bush, "no one advanced the notion of using nuclear weapons, and the President rejected it even in retaliation for chemical or biological attacks. We deliberately avoided spoken or unspoken threats to use them on the grounds that it is bad practice to threaten something you have no intention of carrying out. Publicly, we left the matter ambiguous. There was no point in undermining the deterrence it might be offering."[47] Thus, while leaders recognized the deterrent benefit from an ambiguous, possible use of nuclear weapons, there was little willingness to ever use them.

From a strategic standpoint, there would be equally important motivations for not responding with nuclear weapons. As the dominant global military power, U.S. leaders should be very concerned about setting a dangerous precedent. U.S. use, especially first use but also in retaliation, would lower the firewall and make it more difficult to begin rebuilding nuclear norms so that others did not resort to nuclear weapons too quickly in the future against either the United States or another country. Any use is problematic for the United States; as Quester argued, "the difficulty with accepting a 'good' use of nuclear weapons, however, is that it may set a precedent for a host of 'bad' uses."[48] In addition, notes Sagan, U.S. use of nuclear weapons would complicate nonproliferation efforts because it "would encourage many other states to abandon their ethical inhibitions against developing nuclear weapons and thus would eventually increase the likelihood of future nuclear wars."[49] Thus, Washington would be setting a precedent for the utility and acceptability of using nuclear weapons. This would be a mistake because upholding these nonuse norms are clearly in U.S. interests.

U.S. interests are best served by others' refraining from the use of nuclear weapons. T. V. Paul argues that the nonuse of nuclear weapons "is in the national interest of the United States as the hegemonic power, as nuclear weapons can constitute a 'great equalizer' in the hands of weaker challengers, who may increasingly seek these weapons to thwart U.S. intervention. By propagating the virtues of the [nonuse] tradition to others, the United States can help legitimize its leadership role in the international system and exert considerable pressure on revisionist states that may plan to use WMD to advance their politico-military objectives."[50] Consequently, writes Paul, "the tradition of non-use is one norm that Washington would be well advised to preserve, for once it is broken, it may not be easy to resurrect it even if future leaders wished to do so."[51] Thomas Nichols further argues that "if the nuclear taboo is violated, however, it makes no sense to try to reestablish it by violating it *again*. The argument for engaging in nuclear retaliation as punishment for breaking the nuclear taboo is short-term thinking that makes little sense as a long-term strategy for the restoration of peace and the future protection of the United States."[52] In the end, the goal is not to ensure a U.S. nuclear response but to deter the use of nuclear weapons in the first place. All have an interest in the norms against using nuclear weapons, and further use will not help to achieve that goal.

Finally, although the use of nuclear weapons is highly unlikely, raising significant questions about the credibility of the U.S. nuclear umbrella, Washington has numerous precise and lethal conventional options available that it would not hesitate to use against North Korea. This list of conventional assets includes only those within the region, not other resources outside East Asia that could also be brought to bear in a North Korean contingency. The Seventh Air Force units in South Korea consist of two fighter squadrons, for a total of forty F-16 C/D aircraft, and a squadron of twenty-four A-10C close support aircraft. Both are capable of carrying a variety of precision weapons, including laser-guided bombs and air-to-surface missiles. Washington could also quickly deploy aircraft based in Japan or from its carrier strike group based in Japan. In addition to airplanes, the United States could launch a barrage of highly accurate Tomahawk land attack cruise missiles (TLAM). The U.S. Navy has seven destroyers and two cruisers based in Japan, and all are capable of launching TLAMs. Finally, the Air Force has the B-2 stealth bomber, which can evade DPRK air defenses to drop conventional ordnance, and the B-52 bomber, which can launch conventionally armed cruise missiles at North Korean targets. Use of these weapons is highly credible, avoids the problems of a nuclear response, and could have similar strategic effects for North Korea, depending on the targets. Indeed, one U.S. planner noted that North Korea would be annihilated if it crossed the nuclear threshold, with little distinction between a nuclear and conventional response; the goal is to inhibit North Korea's use of all WMD.[53]

China

A North Korean first use of nuclear weapons is difficult to imagine, because doing so would be tantamount to regime suicide. Still, it is possible to devise scenarios in which Pyongyang might feel its security is so seriously threatened that it believes it has no choice but to use nuclear weapons first. It is far more difficult to conceive of a plausible scenario in which the United States would be likely to use nuclear weapons in a conflict with Beijing. China has nuclear weapons that can reach the U.S. mainland, and the Pentagon has targeting plans for China that are part of U.S. general deterrence preparedness. Each side has sufficient nuclear capability to deter the other from escalating to nuclear weapons.

There are certainly potential flashpoint issues between the United States, Japan, and China that could lead to conflict. The disputes in the South China Sea over sovereignty and freedom of navigation are worrisome, with serious potential for violence. The likelihood of a major power war is difficult to imagine, but the possibility of an accident or an action sparked by an overzealous local commander that could escalate is of greater concern. A report by CNA noted that the Chinese People's Liberation Army (PLA) has shown a good deal of concern for these types of crises and the dangers of escalation. The report also raises fears that PLA actions during a crisis, while viewed by China as a way of controlling the situation, might actually be viewed as escalatory by others.[54]

The ongoing dispute between Japan and China over the Senkaku/Diaoyu islands is another potential flashpoint with particular implications for extended deterrence. Though Washington does not take a position on the sovereignty of this or any other islands under dispute in Asia, the United States has stated firmly that Japan's administrative control of the Senkakus falls under Article V of the U.S.-Japan Mutual Security Treaty, committing the United States to the defense of these islands should China seek to seize them.[55] That this dispute would escalate to the use of nuclear weapons, however, is hard to imagine. Washington would go to considerable lengths to support Japan in maintaining its administrative control of the islands, but not with nuclear weapons.

A dangerous possibility in any of these situations would be if U.S. forces were to implement a plan or operational concept originally labeled Air-Sea Battle but now called Joint Concept for Access and Maneuver in the Global Commons, or JAM-GC.[56] As a response to China's A2/AD efforts, JAM-GC calls for early, preemptive strikes on PLA targets, including strikes on the Chinese homeland to take out communications and surveillance facilities along with disrupting its ability to retaliate. Even if done with conventional weapons, Beijing might view this as an attempt to take out its nuclear deterrent.[57] As a result, China might feel it has no choice but to escalate. Conflicts that include such dangerous possibilities for escalation are unlikely because any U.S.-China clash is expected to involve limited objectives, such as an incident in the South China Sea, and not threaten the existence of either state.[58] Thus, a RAND report noted that any future conflict between China and the United States is likely to remain regional. "It is unlikely that nuclear weapons would be used: Even in an intensely violent conventional conflict, neither side would regard its losses as so serious, its prospects so dire, or the stakes so vital that it would run the risk of devastating nuclear retaliation by using nuclear weapons first. We also assume that China would not attack the U.S. homeland, except via cyberspace, given its minimal capability to do so with conventional weapons."[59]

Though it is difficult to determine the circumstances that might trigger a U.S. nuclear response in a China scenario, it would likely require something akin to a large-scale Chinese conventional assault or nuclear strike on the Japanese home islands or the United States. The chances of either of these occurring are almost nil. Certainly, there remains the possibility that incidents and clashes between Japan and China could cause a larger conflict, but the likelihood of escalation to nuclear war is remote. Thus, as one former U.S. official noted, "the nuclear umbrella is an easy guarantee to give because it is so unlikely to ever be implemented."[60]

A number of the same restraints on using nuclear weapons against North Korea would also be present in a China scenario. A U.S. president would face the same moral considerations of the nuclear taboo or non-use tradition, especially if contemplating first use, and should be loath to set a precedent for escalating a conflict to nuclear use. Given China's vast landmass, there may be less concern for using nuclear weapons than would be the case in the more compressed geographic space of Korea, but a U.S. nuclear strike, even if directed at military targets, would cause thousands of Chinese civilian casualties and, depending on wind patterns and ocean currents, would endanger surrounding populations in Russia, South Korea, Japan, and Southeast Asia.

Finally, the same conventional options available for a Korean conflict could be used in a conflict with China, avoiding escalation to nuclear weapons or the likely retaliation that might follow. U.S. first use would breach the nuclear firewall, and even retaliation for Chinese first use would set off a horrendous chain of events that no one could be certain of controlling. Setting a precedent that makes it easier for states to use nuclear weapons is not in the U.S. interest, whether done first or in retaliation.

The U.S. nuclear umbrella vis-à-vis China is better characterized as general deterrence, as opposed to the more immediate deterrence problem posed by North Korea.[61] There is no imminent threat of war between the U.S. and China or China and Japan. To be sure, tensions exist on a number of issues, and there are serious concerns for the future of these relationships. However, the nuclear umbrella is part of the military preparation of general deterrence that helps to prevent relations from reaching the crisis of an immediate deterrence problem and, for Japanese leaders, provides a counterweight to any political leverage Beijing may feel it has to intimidate Japan. The concern, of course, is whether general deterrence might shift to a crisis of immediate deterrence. However, the likelihood of ever using nuclear weapons against China is very remote, but so is the possibility of China's ever using nuclear weapons. Thus, the nuclear umbrella is part of a broad effort to deter the use of nuclear weapons, provide reassurance to Japan and South Korea of the U.S. defense commitment, contribute to the overall credibility of the alliance, and convince Tokyo and Seoul that they do not need their own nuclear weapons.

THE NUCLEAR UMBRELLA AND U.S. NONPROLIFERATION GOALS

Preventing the spread of nuclear weapons has long been part of U.S. foreign policy. Policy makers became particularly concerned in 1964 when China detonated its first nuclear weapon and Mao Zedong's rhetoric indicated a relative willingness to use nuclear weapons and an acceptance of the death and destruction that would follow.[62] In response, the Johnson administration formed the Gilpatric Committee to study the dangers of nuclear proliferation and provide recommendations for U.S. policy. The committee's report, completed in January 1965, concluded that "the spread of nuclear weapons poses an increasingly grave threat to the security of the United States" and noted that the threat emanated not only from adversaries but also from states "friendly to the United States" because they "will add complexity and instability to the deterrent balance between the United States and the Soviet Union, aggravate suspicions and hostility among states neighboring new nuclear powers."[63] Committee members expressed particular concern for the dangers of a nuclear domino effect. Should India or Japan acquire nuclear weapons, "we do not believe the spread of nuclear weapons would or could be stopped there."[64] The report recommended that Washington exert greater effort to conclude a nonproliferation treaty and work harder to convince nonnuclear states not to acquire nuclear weapons. One tool to accomplish this regarding India and Japan was to reinforce the U.S. defense commitment to these states should they forgo nuclear weapons.[65]

Though debate remains over U.S. nonproliferation policy and whether dominoes would truly follow,[66] recent studies have shown that the United States exerted significant pressure on its allies to refrain from acquiring nuclear weapons.[67] Miller notes that "the United States has played an important role in rolling back active nuclear programs through sponsoring the NPT, sanctions, security guarantees, technology denial, and military force."[68] Regarding Germany, Gerzhoy and Gavin both present convincing evidence that U.S. efforts were decisive in Germany's decision to forgo nuclear weapons.[69]

Concerning Japan, chapter 2 demonstrated how U.S. security guarantees, especially the assurance of the nuclear umbrella given by Johnson to Satō in 1965 and reaffirmed in 1967, were critical to Japan's signing the NPT and not acquiring nuclear weapons. However, Japanese leaders insisted on maintaining their civilian nuclear program and the right to reprocess as a hedge to enable rapid breakout later should the security situation change.

Despite the nuclear umbrella, during the early 1970s, South Korea, fearing the growing North Korean threat and worried about a lessened U.S. commitment after Vietnam and the Nixon Doctrine, embarked on its own nuclear weapons program. When the pieces began to fall into place concerning ROK efforts, the Ford administration pressured Park to give up his nuclear ambitions.[70] Eventually, Seoul relented. It was clear that Washington was willing to exert serious effort to prevent even one of its allies from going nuclear in support of its overall nonproliferation goals.

In subsequent years, U.S. concerns for the proliferation of nuclear weapons increased. The 1987 Reagan administration National Security Strategy (NSS) listed as one of its major objectives "to prevent the spread of nuclear weapons,"[71] and the goal has remained firm in every administration since. The 2015 Obama administration NSS maintained that "no threat poses as grave a danger to our security and well-being as the potential use of nuclear weapons and materials by irresponsible states or terrorists." As a result, "vigilance is required to stop countries and non-state actors from developing or acquiring nuclear, chemical, or biological weapons or the materials to build them."[72] Though unstated, preventing anyone, including allies, from acquiring nuclear weapons is equally important. Though candidate Trump indicated that he might be comfortable with Japan and South Korea acquiring their own nuclear weapons, his administration is likely to remain consistent with past U.S. nonproliferation goals.

Preventing the spread of nuclear weapons to foes and allies remains a crucial U.S. goal for several reasons. First, proliferation can be a direct threat to U.S. security, especially if adversaries or nonstate actors acquire these weapons. The threat could emanate from direct use against the United States or from these entities' further spreading nuclear materials, know-how, or a complete bomb to others. Although this is an important goal for the United States, it is less so for its allies. One ROK scholar noted that the vision of nonproliferation was the "ultimate disconnect" between Washington and Seoul; while the United States was largely concerned about the spread of nuclear weapons to nonstate actors, South Korea was concerned about the North.[73]

Second, acquisition of nuclear weapons, whether by an adversary or an ally, upsets regional stability and may create a domino effect, causing others in the region to respond in a variety of ways that may include acquiring their own nuclear weapons. Many people are concerned that if Iran goes nuclear, then others in the Middle East, especially the Saudis, might follow, disrupting the status quo in the region as well as globally. From time to time in South Korea, prominent advocates have called for the pursuit of nuclear weapons, and polling data in the ROK have indicated public support. If Seoul went nuclear, that would place even greater pressure on Tokyo to follow suit. Indeed, one ROK scholar argued that a credible U.S. nuclear umbrella for South Korea has the second-order effect of enhancing deterrence for Japan, in turn helping to keep Tokyo from acquiring nuclear weapons.[74] The dynamics would be similar if Japan went nuclear first; South Korea would likely follow. While dominoes may or may not fall as states acquire nuclear weapons, the danger remains. With each addition to the list of nuclear weapons states, even if the entry is a U.S. ally, the NPT is weakened, making it easier for others to follow.

As a result, while the nuclear umbrella has been an important signal of U.S. assurance and the commitment to defend its allies, it has also been an important nonproliferation tool to contain the spread of nuclear weapons. The 2010 NPR notes that security relationships with allies "can also serve our non-proliferation goals . . . by reassuring nonnuclear allies and partners that their security interests can be protected without their own nuclear deterrent capabilities."[75] Van Jackson, former Asia hand at the Pentagon, argues that "in my conversations with experts from Australia, Japan and South Korea over the years, . . . I've concluded that these states are signatories of the Nuclear Nonproliferation Treaty and have not gone nuclear mostly because of the U.S. nuclear umbrella extended to them."[76] In some respects, the alliances with Japan and South Korea are an arrangement in which the United States provides a security commitment, including the nuclear umbrella, in return for these allies refraining from going nuclear. When North Korea first tested nuclear weapons in 2006, the Bush administration was quick to reassure Seoul and Tokyo of the U.S. guarantee that included the "full range of capabilities." Subsequent debate, particularly in South Korea but also in Japan, raised the possibility that these allies, under the right circumstances, might feel compelled to acquire nuclear weapons. The likelihood that South Korea or especially Japan would go nuclear is remote, but both clearly have the technical capability. Thus, while security considerations have been central to U.S. assurances of the nuclear umbrella, nonproliferation concerns have also been important. The U.S. nuclear umbrella is a crucial tool to convince allies that they need not acquire their own nuclear weapons.

NEVER SAY NEVER

I have argued here that despite U.S. capabilities and strong declaratory statements, it is highly unlikely the United States would ever use nuclear weapons to defend its allies in Asia. Once, when presenting an earlier version of this argument at an academic conference, I was accused of being a "chicken" for not categorically declaring that the United States would never use nuclear weapons. While I believe it would be a mistake for the United States to use nuclear weapons and that the chances of its doing so are very small, there are some factors that might prompt their use regardless.

The first factor is the role of emotion in decision making.[77] If North Korea launched a first strike on Seoul or Tokyo that killed thousands, or a strike on the U.S. homeland, despite all of the cerebral reasons for not using nuclear weapons, the resulting emotion might be overpowering. The outrage and demands to "do something," similar to the feelings that followed the September 11 attacks, might place tremendous pressure on a U.S. president to respond in kind by striking targets in the DPRK with nuclear weapons. Thus, the logic and important reasons for refraining from a nuclear response might be overwhelmed by the emotions and domestic political pressure of the moment.

Second, critics of this book are likely to argue that the United States must respond to a nuclear strike with nuclear weapons, or the U.S. nuclear umbrella and U.S. security guarantees would become meaningless. One ROK scholar asked me, "If the United States does not retaliate with nuclear weapons after North Korean first use, how can Washington ever reconstruct the nuclear umbrella afterward?"[78] A U.S. defense analyst asked me rhetorically, "If the United States won't use nuclear weapons in Korea, what does this say to Japan? What impact will it have on assurances even for Saudi Arabia?"[79]

Again, there is little doubt the United States would respond to a nuclear attack on Japan or South Korea, a horrendous event that would drastically alter regional and global security. Yet, as U.S. policy makers have argued regularly, given the range of available options, the response need not be nuclear. One U.S. official noted that while "the U.S. must continue saying the nuclear umbrella is in place, its credibility is restrained. In responding with conventional weapons, we can say we did not blink, just that we chose not to use nuclear weapons."[80] A vigorous U.S. conventional response to a North Korean attack, which might also lead to regime change in North Korea, would not necessarily damage U.S. credibility. There is no iron law that a nuclear attack must be met with another nuclear attack, especially given all of the reasons, noted previously, why this is a bad idea. U.S. policy is not that a nuclear strike must be matched by nuclear retaliation, but rather that there will be a strong, appropriate U.S. response. Indeed, an overwhelming conventional response that has the same strategic effect would soon put to rest any perception, within the United States or among U.S. allies and potential adversaries, that its security guarantee is not credible. However, it is possible that U.S. leaders might believe that the country's reputation was at stake and that they could not afford to jeopardize it by not responding in kind with nuclear weapons.

Finally, should any state become involved in a conflict that threatens its existence, it will not hesitate to use any means at its disposal to avoid its demise. It is highly unlikely that a conflict with North Korea would produce an existential threat for the United States or its allies, though this certainly might be the case for North Korea. A conflict with China is a different matter, as Beijing has a far larger nuclear force capable of causing horrendous damage to the United States or Japan. However, the chances of a conflict escalating to the level that threatens the existence of the United States, Japan, or China is remote, despite the current competition among these three. Yet if U.S. leaders believed that the threat to the United States and its people, or those of its allies, was sufficiently great to threaten their existence, they would consider using nuclear weapons, though it is still not at all certain they would be used.

CONCLUSION

Though some people have questioned its existence, the nuclear umbrella is real. The United States has a sizable nuclear force with sufficient options and firepower to defend Japan and South Korea with nuclear weapons. Consequently, the capability portion of the nuclear umbrella is very credible. Resolve remains the part of credibility that is problematic, as it was throughout the Cold War and will likely be in the future. The U.S. commitment to defend Japan and South Korea is highly credible; there is little doubt that the United States would be there to defend these two valued allies. However, the U.S. response would almost certainly be with conventional weapons. Given the power and precision of U.S. conventional weapons, their use can have strategic effects similar to nuclear weapons, and threats to use them are far more credible. As argued in this chapter, U.S. use of nuclear weapons, even in response to a nuclear attack, is not in anyone's interest. Using nuclear weapons in defense of Japan and South Korea is unlikely and unwise for a number of strategic, operational, and moral reasons. Yet the nuclear umbrella continues to have an important political impact in reassuring allies and supporting U.S. nonproliferation goals and is likely to remain in place.

CHAPTER SEVEN

Implications for Security and Extended Deterrence in Northeast Asia

The nuclear umbrella has been one element of the U.S. security commitment to Japan and South Korea. It is embedded in alliances that are multidimensional, using a variety of tools to demonstrate that commitment and to prepare for a response should deterrence fail. The nuclear umbrella itself is a complex mix of a security commitment, a form of political signaling, and a nonproliferation tool that has become a part of the regional security architecture. Attention to the nuclear umbrella by leaders and renewed study of its function and dynamics by scholars have both increased as a result of North Korea's growing nuclear and missile capabilities, along with concerns for China's increasing military power, aggressive behavior, and uncertain strategic direction. The nuclear umbrella for each U.S. ally is, in many respects, an interconnected commitment, with U.S. allies maintaining a careful watch on U.S. statements and actions for one that might have an impact on them. However, the nuclear umbrella also means very different things for different allies. Thus, pronouncements that an ally is "under the nuclear umbrella" or, more ambiguously, that "all options are on the table" raise different questions, answers, and perceptions depending on where one sits. As a result, the complexities of tailored deterrence, eschewing a "one size fits all" model, are a prominent part of the U.S. nuclear umbrella. These dynamics and complexities have numerous implications for security and extended deterrence. To conclude, this chapter turns to an examination of the key implications and to some final thoughts on the questions raised at the start of this book.

WHAT DOES THE NUCLEAR UMBRELLA DETER?

A fundamental question regarding the nuclear umbrella is, what exactly does it deter? Is a precise answer to this question even desirable, given the argument that "strategic ambiguity" improves the deterrent effect because adversaries are never quite sure when nuclear retaliation is a possible response? As noted earlier by a Japanese analyst, Tokyo understands that the likelihood of using nuclear weapons is very small, but to make a formal pronouncement of when and how nuclear weapons might be used detracts from the benefits of strategic ambiguity. Indeed, U.S. policy has long been grounded in ambiguity, maximizing the deterrence effect by raising the possibility that any number of adversary actions could trigger a nuclear response—Schelling's "threat that leaves something to chance." In addition, ambiguity does not tie the hands of U.S. leaders in a crisis, leaving room for discretion and flexibility in determining appropriate responses.

The 2010 Nuclear Posture Review (NPR) sought to narrow the answer, reaffirming the role of nuclear weapons in deterring a nuclear strike on the United States or its allies but reducing their role in deterring nonnuclear attacks by continuing to strengthen U.S. conventional options, thereby moving toward deterrence of nuclear weapons as their "sole purpose." At the same time, the 2010 NPR acknowledged that "U.S. nuclear weapons may still play a role in deterring a conventional or CBW (chemical or biological weapons) attack against the United States or its allies and partners."[1] Japan and South Korea have been concerned with this narrowing and any further reduction in the role of nuclear weapons, particularly with regard to North Korea's possible use of chemical, biological, and conventional-tipped missiles and artillery. This effort to narrow the role of nuclear weapons and broaden the likelihood of a nonnuclear response had begun under the Bush administration with the 2001 NPR's "New Triad," ballistic missile defense (BMD), tailored deterrence, and the 2006 Quadrennial Defense Review (QDR), which noted the ability of conventional precision-guided munitions (PGMs) to hold at risk targets that in the past required nuclear weapons.

The likelihood of a nuclear exchange between China and the United States over a bilateral issue or one between China and a U.S. ally is very remote at this time. There are numerous points of friction, particularly in the maritime domain, but these do not involve existential interests that are likely to lead to the use of nuclear weapons. While both Washington and Beijing have plans and targeting options for nuclear strikes against each other, these are the preparations of a general deterrence situation in which there is no immediate danger of attack. However, concerns about potential Chinese political leverage and intimidation based on its nuclear capabilities make the U.S. nuclear umbrella important for Japan in the face of growing Sino-Japanese rivalry.

Sino-ROK ties are not nearly as contentious, and the nuclear umbrella is not a significant consideration in their relationship. However, ROK-U.S. efforts to deter North Korea and to counter DPRK ballistic missiles through BMD are a source of friction in Sino–South Korean relations. Chinese leaders and analysts often express the view that actions taken against North Korea have serious strategic effects on China. This concern has been particularly prominent concerning BMD and the decision to deploy Terminal High Altitude Area Defense (THAAD) to Korea. China would no doubt protest even more over any U.S. plan to redeploy nuclear weapons to South Korea. As a result, U.S. actions to reassure allies through the nuclear umbrella and BMD also carry some risk that these efforts could drive adversaries to respond in ways that actually worsen the security situation. For example, U.S. activities to bolster deterrence against North Korea may prompt Pyongyang to take more provocative actions or to expand its nuclear arsenal further. Regarding China, it is possible that U.S. efforts to reassure its allies and develop regional BMD could prod Beijing into abandoning its minimum deterrence posture and expanding its nuclear arsenal to match the United States. Thus, the U.S. extended deterrence commitment to Japan and South Korea concerning China and North Korea presents a complex mix of deterrence and reassurance messaging between adversaries and allies.

The more serious and immediate concern for regional security is North Korea. Pyongyang's nuclear weapon and ballistic missile capabilities continue to grow along with periodic testing and provocative rhetoric that in recent years has grown worse, even by North Korean standards. What does the nuclear umbrella deter regarding North Korean behavior?

At the strategic level, the security situation on the Korean peninsula has long been stable, and there is little likelihood that North Korea will come rolling across the DMZ. The conventional balance is not in North Korea's favor. Although the Korean People's Army (KPA) could do serious damage in the early weeks of a conflict, it could not sustain large-scale combat operations for very long or hold onto any gains it might achieve as a result of surprise. Some analysts have suggested that with nuclear weapons, North Korea might be emboldened to strike across the DMZ, possibly seizing Seoul and issuing threats of follow-on nuclear attacks on other parts of South Korea, Japan, or the United States should Seoul and Washington retaliate or attempt to drive them back across the DMZ.

There are serious questions whether North Korea could successfully pull off such a thrust into the south, given logistics challenges and the extensive defensive preparations the alliance has in place to stop such an assault. In contrast to June 1950, the United States and South Korea have far better intelligence and surveillance, making it difficult to launch a large-scale assault without prior warning, and extensive defensive preparations are in place along the likely North Korean invasion routes. Finally, for North Korea to wager that Seoul and Washington would be held at bay by nuclear threats following such an egregious violation of the status quo would be foolish in the extreme. Certainly, North Korea has long displayed behavior that is tolerant of risk, but these types of scenarios suggest that Pyongyang has almost no limits to the risks it is willing take. To be sure, North Korea would not hesitate to lash out with nuclear weapons if it believed its survival was at stake. However, the first use of nuclear weapons in anything but the direst of circumstances also risks the survival of the regime, and it is very unlikely Kim Jong-un would be willing to take such a risk. North Korea has been successfully deterred at the strategic level for the past six decades, and its acquisition of nuclear weapons is unlikely to change that.

The nuclear umbrella adds another layer of punishment to inflict on North Korea should it cross these lines, but it is not clear that the DPRK is any more deterred by the threat of nuclear weapons than it is by the likelihood of an overwhelming conventional response that would have the same strategic effect. Though no one can be certain, the nuclear umbrella may enhance deterrence based on the possibility of overwhelming nuclear destruction, even with a small chance of its actually being used. However, strategic deterrence would likely hold either way, as it has for decades. To ask the counterfactual question, would North Korean behavior have been, or would it now be, different without a formal nuclear umbrella? It is not at all clear that the answer would be yes. In a number of respects, the nuclear umbrella vis-à-vis North Korea is more important as a message of reassurance for U.S. allies than a tool that adds further to an already stable strategic situation. As North Korean nuclear capabilities grow, this will bear watching, but it is difficult to envision strategic deterrence weakening appreciably as a result of North Korea's possessing a small nuclear weapons force.

While strategic stability is solid in Korea, the greater danger is lower-level conflict. Increasingly, many analysts are examining the North Korean threat through the Cold War lens of the stability/instability paradox in which nuclear weapons give North Korea a shield to conduct lower-level provocations with less fear of retaliation and escalation to a nuclear conflict. The role of the nuclear umbrella in these types of lower-level scenarios is tenuous at best and simply is not credible as a response. From 1958 to 1991, the United States had tactical nuclear weapons in South Korea along with the nuclear umbrella. Nonetheless, North Korea was willing on numerous occasions to undertake very risky actions, including several assassination attempts on ROK leaders, the seizing of the USS *Pueblo*, infiltration of North Korean commandos by land and submarine, the blowing up of Korean Air flight 858, and in 2010, the sinking of the ROK *Cheonan* and the shelling of Yeonpyeong Island. North Korean leaders were apparently not deterred from these low-level operations by U.S. nuclear weapons.

Van Jackson notes, "extended deterrence [read nuclear weapons] is a blunt instrument: good for some things, like deterring nuclear attack, but not for others, like deterring provocations or low-intensity conflict."[2] Thus, the U.S. nuclear umbrella did little to deter North Korean provocations. Instead, the United States and South Korea have undertaken specific measures such as the Combined Counter-Provocation Plan to better deter lower-level provocations. South Korean demonstrations since 2010 of its determination to respond to North Korean military action has also likely had a significant deterrent effect.

Regarding China, strategic deterrence is also stable, and though Sino-U.S. and Sino-Japan tensions continue to grow, major power war remains unlikely in the near future. The greater challenge is restraining Beijing's behavior in the South and East China Seas, in the so-called gray zones where there is neither peace nor war. Despite the Obama administration's declaration that Japan's administrative control of the Senkakus falls under Article 5 of the mutual security treaty, the nuclear umbrella has little impact and is not credible in restraining Chinese behavior in these areas. Deterring gray zone actions require a different set of tools that demonstrate U.S. resolve to respond to these lower-level provocations.[3] Sometimes the solutions can be relatively simple, such as calling for U.S.-Japan Coast Guard exchanges that position U.S. officers on Japanese vessels in the East China Sea to provide "a symbolic demonstration of American support that could also subtly but distinctly increase the potential cost for Chinese harassment of Japanese ships and their crews."[4] U.S. nuclear weapons will not be part of this mix.

The United States continues to maintain some degree of ambiguity over what the nuclear umbrella deters, and Japan and South Korea support this position, particularly as it relates to possible chemical and biological weapons use by North Korea. Yet, in the end, the nuclear umbrella likely does little to deter anything other than nuclear war, because threats to use nuclear weapons against conventional, chemical, and biological attacks are simply not very credible.

CREDIBILITY AND THE NUCLEAR UMBRELLA

Throughout this book, I have argued that the United States is unlikely to ever use nuclear weapons to defend Japan or South Korea. While Sino-Japanese relations are poor, it is very difficult to conceive of a scenario in which China would undertake an action against Japan that would warrant U.S. use of nuclear weapons. Both the United States and China have nuclear arsenals capable of reaching most of the East Asian region and each other's homeland, making it very difficult for either side to escalate to nuclear weapons without paying a severe cost. Limited conventional conflict is possible, and clashes that might be spawned by miscalculation or inadvertent small-scale actions in the South China Sea are very plausible. However, a scenario in which these skirmishes would escalate to a nuclear exchange or that Chinese aggression against Japan would reach a level requiring a U.S. nuclear response is difficult to imagine.

It is far easier to conceive of a nuclear scenario involving North Korea, yet in the end, even the DPRK's first use of nuclear weapons would be unlikely to prompt the United States to use nuclear weapons to defend South Korea or Japan. These arguments also apply to any possible situation for using nuclear weapons against China.

Although North Korea has been provocative and willing to take risks, it is questionable whether it is willing to take an action that might prompt nuclear retaliation from the United States. To be sure, Pyongyang has taken countless lower-level actions that might bring some type of retaliation, but it is unlikely that North Korea would attempt an action that could bring a U.S. nuclear response. Indeed, a U.S.-ROK conventional response would leave it up to North Korea to escalate to nuclear weapons, a decision that would produce dreadful consequences for the regime. Given that North Korean first use of nuclear weapons would lead to the end of the Kim regime, North Korean threats to use nuclear weapons, except where its existence is at stake, lack credibility.[5] Thus, it is difficult to conceive of a situation in which the DPRK, or China for that matter, would cross a threshold that might generate a nuclear response.

Even if North Korea took some type of action against Japan or South Korea that was sufficiently serious for the United States to contemplate responding with nuclear weapons, Washington would likely not do so, and indeed should not do so for several reasons. First, for the United States to be contemplating the use of nuclear weapons, North Korea would have to have taken some highly contemptible action. If that occurred, Washington and Seoul would likely be moving toward regime change and reunification, ending this security problem once and for all. International support for such an operation would be high, and it would be difficult for China to intervene to stop such a move. To irradiate the North prior to sending ROK and U.S. ground forces across the DMZ would make the operating environment very difficult for follow-on forces and severely complicate these efforts. Moreover, South Korea would be stuck with the cleanup in the reunified Korea that would follow.

Second, though few would have much sympathy for the North Korean leadership, nuclear strikes on the DPRK would kill countless civilians, and the fallout might drift south over Seoul or into China, Japan, or Russia. Nuclear weapons are unforgiving instruments of military power, and their effects would be difficult to control or anticipate. This problem would grow significantly, depending on the number and type of nuclear weapons used.

Third, the norm of nonuse of nuclear weapons creates a number of obstacles. The president would likely have grave moral misgivings to be the first to order a nuclear strike since 1945 if responding to a conventional or chemical attack, but also if retaliating for North Korean nuclear use. Taken together, the destructive power of nuclear weapons, their questionable utility, the uncertain potential for catastrophe, the reputational costs, and international condemnation, particularly if using nuclear weapons first in a conflict, would strongly inhibit their use.

From a strategic perspective, the United States gains little from crossing a nuclear firewall that has existed for more than seven decades. Using nuclear weapons, whether first or in retaliation, sets a dangerous precedent that makes their use by others easier and reconstruction of the nuclear firewall more difficult. Critics will argue that the failure to demonstrate a willingness to use nuclear weapons will damage U.S. credibility. Given that the United States would act with a massive conventional response to protect its allies, it is not clear that perceptions of reduced credibility would result. However, multiple uses of nuclear weapons would certainly lower the threshold for nuclear use in future conflicts, a result that is in no one's interest, especially the United States. For all these reasons, the U.S. use of nuclear weapons is not in its strategic interests and should be avoided at all costs.

While a U.S. nuclear response is highly unlikely, and indeed counter to U.S. interests, the U.S. military has many precise, lethal conventional options that would achieve similar strategic effects against North Korea as well as China. Thus, despite the credibility problems of a nuclear strike, a U.S. conventional response is highly credible. The U.S. alliances with Japan and South Korea are healthy and strong. There is little doubt the United States would defend these two allies if attacked, but that response would almost certainly not include nuclear weapons.

The questions raised in this study and others have prompted calls for the United States to develop smaller, more usable nuclear weapons to provide more options to U.S. leaders and make nuclear use more acceptable and credible.[6] However, the use of smaller nuclear weapons would still constitute nuclear use and would face the same obstacles that have been laid out in this book. Building more and different types of nuclear weapons would be a further strain on the U.S. defense budget, which has many more pressing priorities. A great deal of money would be sunk into weapons systems that would never be used and would do little to improve an already stable strategic security situation in the region. Others have called for the return of U.S. tactical nuclear weapons to the region so that they are forward deployed for more prompt use against adversaries.[7] This argument has been most vigorously promoted by some in South Korea who believe that returning U.S. tactical nuclear weapons is essential to deter the DPRK and its growing nuclear program. Yet the reasons tactical nuclear weapons were removed in the first place remain, and returning them would raise a host of unnecessary problems. The return of tactical nuclear weapons would do little to improve strategic deterrence while actually making crisis stability more fragile.

IMPORTANCE OF CONVENTIONAL SUPERIORITY AND BALLISTIC MISSILE DEFENSE

In conjunction with forgoing the use of nuclear weapons, it is important to consider conventional firepower and other options for responding to an attack on an ally, along with the increasing role of BMD.[8] By the late 2000s, the United States had begun to frame the extended deterrence commitment in terms of three components: the nuclear umbrella, conventional strike, and ballistic missile defense. Central to the argument of this book is that the United States would respond to an attack on Japan or South Korea with conventional weapons in the context of a credible alliance. Thus, maintaining an array of precision conventional capabilities with strategic effects similar to nuclear weapons will be essential. Indeed, while allied leaders and analysts watch for signs of a credible nuclear umbrella, they also give considerable attention to the conventional balance of forces. Forgoing a nuclear response depends on the maintenance of credible conventional options.

The conventional force balance also points to another aspect of the nuclear umbrella in Asia, and that is the power differential between the players involved. China is not yet a peer competitor of the United States, but it is moving ever more in that direction. Chinese military capabilities have grown considerably, and within the next two decades they may begin to change the deterrence situation to one that is more symmetric. Even if China maintains its nuclear posture of minimum deterrence, Sino-U.S. nuclear forces will be at a relative standoff and attention will be focused on conventional forces. Both sides will have ample motivation to keep any conflict limited and avoid escalation. Yet, so long as the United States maintains a strong conventional capability, it will be able to support credible security assurances for Japan and other U.S. interests in the region.

How would these dynamics change if, or more likely when, China reaches conventional parity, which might inhibit the United States from defending its allies with conventional assets? Would this circumstance force the United States to rely on nuclear weapons? In a number of respects, China has already achieved some of this capability in its A2/AD efforts. These circumstances would certainly complicate a U.S. response, making it more difficult and costly for Washington to defend its allies and interests in the region. Despite growing Chinese conventional capabilities, however, the United States could still bring to bear considerable conventional military power. For example, U.S. submarines and TLAMs could cause considerable damage to Chinese forces. Moreover, though carrier strike groups would likely need to operate at greater distances from China, the airpower from these ships would remain a potent response. Thus, even with increasing Chinese conventional capabilities, the United States would not need to escalate to nuclear weapons but would have credible conventional options to respond to Chinese aggression.

Concerning North Korea, the situation will remain one of asymmetric deterrence. While North Korea has a formidable conventional military and a growing nuclear arsenal, it will never be able to match U.S. conventional power along with a modern, well-equipped ROK military. As a result, Washington and Seoul will have a number of ways to respond with conventional options should North Korea choose to challenge the U.S. deterrence commitment. Given the continued asymmetry of this deterrence situation, the conventional military power of the ROK-U.S. alliance will be more than sufficient to maintain a robust deterrent posture to prevent war on the Korean peninsula.

BMD has also become a part of the U.S. defense commitment, but the role it plays is different for each ally. Japan has been an enthusiastic partner with the United States in building a BMD architecture in East Asia to protect against North Korean missile launches. Washington and Tokyo maintain that the system is directed at North Korea, but Chinese leaders are convinced that North Korea is a convenient excuse for a system of which they are the likely targets. The primary focus is clearly North Korea, but any benefits BMD might provide in countering Chinese capabilities is no doubt appreciated by U.S. and Japanese defense planners as well.

South Korea has been more reluctant to join U.S. regional BMD because of strong opposition from China. The decision to allow the United States to deploy THAAD notwithstanding, South Korea continues down the path of building its own, independent BMD system. Seoul's position may change in the years ahead, but it is incumbent on Washington to avoid placing pressure on the ROK government to join the U.S. BMD system. To do so will risk alliance cohesion by forcing a contentious domestic debate that will stir up any latent anti-Americanism. This is a decision that South Korea must arrive at of its own accord. It is also important to have a clear view of what BMD can do. The technology has improved markedly over the years, but it remains limited in the number of missiles it can shoot down at any one time and can be overwhelmed by a barrage of missiles and countermeasures. BMD is an important and increasingly capable system that supports the U.S. defense commitment to its allies, but it is not a panacea to solve the region's security problems, and it is costly.

THE NUCLEAR UMBRELLA AS A POLITICAL SIGNAL

Scholars and analysts have long recognized the credibility problems in extended deterrence, not only for the nuclear umbrella but as a broader commitment to defend an ally. Despite military preparations, security treaties, and regular statements of resolve, there is always a chance that in a crisis, the defender will choose to back away from its commitment. Even when the overall alliance is highly credible, as is the case with Japan and South Korea, the nuclear umbrella has lingering questions of resolve that were present during the Cold War and are likely to continue in the future. Would the United States ever use nuclear weapons to defend an ally? The answer is likely to remain "no."

In the face of these credibility problems, does the nuclear umbrella have any value, or should it be withdrawn? Indeed, does the nuclear umbrella even exist? The United States does possess the necessary capability, and the military trains to carry out an order for a nuclear strike. Thus, regarding capability, there is no doubt the United States possesses a credible nuclear umbrella. The questions arise with the other part of credibility, namely resolve and the likelihood the United States would ever be willing to carry out a nuclear strike in defense of an ally.

Though significant credibility questions persist, the nuclear umbrella will remain in place because of the political and symbolic benefits it provides. The affirmation of the nuclear umbrella plays a central role in reassuring allies. Japan and South Korea have not always been involved in nuclear planning or been certain how it might work, but the nuclear umbrella furnishes a strong pronouncement of the U.S. commitment to defend those allies. To withdraw the nuclear umbrella would be to change the regional security architecture in a way that would be difficult for Tokyo or Seoul to understand and accept, and would likely lead to a reassessment regarding acquisition of their own nuclear weapons. Thus, Patrick Morgan argues, "American extended nuclear deterrence *is woven into East Asian international politics and US relations with East Asia* [italics in the original]. In the eyes of various governments, it is one of the salient characteristics of a satisfactory status quo."[9] The 2010 NPR notes that "enhancing regional security architectures is a key part of U.S. strategy for strengthening regional deterrence." Moreover, "these regional security architectures include effective missile defense, counter-WMD capabilities, conventional power-projection, and integrated command and control—all underwritten by strong political commitments."[10] Thus, the nuclear umbrella sends an important political signal of support that reinforces the overall credibility of the alliance.

Despite questions of credibility, given the overwhelming power of nuclear weapons, an uncertain umbrella retains value as a deterrent. As Robert Jervis notes, "the argument that the American threat to use nuclear weapons is not very credible glosses over the point that only a little credibility may be required."[11] As former British secretary of state for defence Denis Healey remarked, regarding deterrence in Europe, "it takes only 5 percent credibility of American retaliation to deter the Russians, but 95 percent credibility to reassure the Europeans."[12] Given the devastation and risks involved with nuclear weapons, even small amounts of credibility may be useful to deter adversaries. In addition, no one knows how a crisis that escalates to nuclear use would play out, raising a host of unnerving possibilities that are likely to evoke caution, even with leaders who are judged to be minimally rational.

Washington and Pyongyang have so little trust in each other that the nuclear umbrella, even with its credibility questions, likely has an impact on the North Koreans because they can never be certain the United States might not use nuclear weapons. No doubt, one of the chief motivations behind the DPRK's nuclear program is to counter any perceived vulnerabilities Pyongyang believes it has in the face of the U.S. nuclear umbrella. Thus, while allies may see a lack of credibility and reassurance, enemies will see it differently. Adversaries conducting threat analyses tend to view security challenges from a worst case perspective, and the possibility that the defender might use nuclear weapons makes credibility stronger in their eyes.

Do nonnuclear states recognize the existence of the norms that constrain nuclear-armed states and discount the chance of nuclear use in a crisis? Phrased another way, have leaders like Kim Jong-un read Tannenwald and Paul and come to believe the United States will never use nuclear weapons? In a study on the impact of nuclear weapons on decision makers in nonnuclear states, Paul Avey found that when involved in confrontations with nuclear-armed adversaries, "non-nuclear state leaders took their opponents' nuclear arsenals very seriously and sought to reduce the risks of nuclear war."[13] Thus, despite low levels of credibility, there is evidence that nuclear deterrence may still be effective.

These credibility questions are also tied to the Obama administration's reluctance to provide a "no first use" guarantee and its willingness to go only so far as a negative security assurance. There is merit in providing a "no first use" guarantee, particularly in regard to China. While these guarantees are suspect, they can contribute to overall strategic stability, particularly in a crisis. However, in the case of North Korea,

Pyongyang is unlikely to believe it regardless. Even if the United States rescinded the nuclear umbrella in a formal declaration, North Korea and other adversaries could never be certain whether Washington would use nuclear weapons. As long as the United States possesses a nuclear arsenal, the DPRK will likely have little trust in a U.S. commitment not to use nuclear weapons first or a declaration that removes the nuclear umbrella from Japan and South Korea.[14] U.S. skeptics place little faith in the "no first use" statements of North Korea and China, and the reverse would also likely be the case.

Given widespread doubts about the credibility of the nuclear umbrella, why do U.S. allies continue to call for this commitment? Surely, officials and analysts in Japan and South Korea have read the same literature that raises these credibility questions? Despite the long-standing credibility questions, Japan and South Korea continue to place a high value on the U.S. nuclear umbrella as a sign of the U.S. security commitment to defend them and an important statement of reassurance. The credibility of the nuclear umbrella is tied to the overall credibility of the individual alliance. Again, Healey maintained, "Europe's concern with the credibility of American deterrence is a function of its general confidence in the wisdom and consistency of American leadership rather than changes in the relative military power of the United States and the Soviet Union."[15] A strong alliance buttresses the nuclear umbrella, and vice versa. Thus, the political aspects of the nuclear umbrella are as important as the security dimensions. Moreover, though Japan and South Korea have separate bilateral alliances with the United States, their security has always been linked; both Tokyo and Seoul watch closely their counterpart's alliance with the United States and the impact it may have on their own security. The U.S. nuclear umbrella helps Japanese and South Korean leaders demonstrate that they are doing something to respond to rising threat levels and helps them avoid contentious domestic debates over acquiring their own nuclear weapons. Though the credibility questions linger and resurface periodically, the symbolic and political value of the nuclear umbrella, accompanied by an assessment that the credibility of the U.S. commitment is sufficient, motivates leaders in Japan and South Korea to continue their calls for reasserting the nuclear umbrella and to rely on the commitment for their security.

Implications for Security and Extended Deterrence in Northeast Asia

NONPROLIFERATION GOALS

The U.S. nuclear umbrella plays an important security role for Japan, South Korea, and other U.S. allies, but it has an equally important function for U.S. efforts to stem the proliferation of nuclear weapons. Whenever nuclear threats have arisen in Asia, the United States has been quick to reassert that its allies are under the nuclear umbrella while continuing to provide regular pronouncements of this commitment in a variety of venues, both formal and informal. The 2010 Nuclear Posture Review states squarely that strong security ties with U.S. allies "can also serve our non-proliferation goals . . . by reassuring non-nuclear allies and partners that their security interests can be protected without their own nuclear capabilities."[16]

Calls have been particularly strong in South Korea for the acquisition of nuclear weapons, with surveys indicating as much as 60 percent support after North Korea's 2013 nuclear test. The ROK government has been steadfast in maintaining its nonnuclear status, but the issue will resurface, particularly when North Korea succeeds in disrupting the security environment again, as it certainly will. Though Japanese leaders have long considered the nuclear option privately, public sentiment continues to be far more restrained than in South Korea. Japanese politicians are a bit freer to raise the subject now than in the past, but while Japan will continue to keep the option open by maintaining a civilian nuclear energy program, it will refrain for the time being from developing nuclear weapons. Thus, in the wake of the March 2011 tsunami and the disaster at the Fukushima Daiichi nuclear power plant, former Japanese defense minister Ishiba Shigeru remarked, "I don't think Japan needs to possess nuclear weapons, but it's important to maintain our commercial reactors because it would allow us to produce a nuclear warhead in a short amount of time. It's a tacit nuclear deterrent."[17]

To the surprise of many, the nonproliferation issued surfaced in the 2016 U.S. presidential primary season. Republican nominee Donald Trump stated in a *New York Times* interview,[18] and later in a *CNN*-sponsored town hall meeting,[19] that he believed nuclear proliferation was inevitable and suggested it would not be such a bad idea if Japan and South Korea, among others, acquired their own nuclear weapons.

These views were accompanied by assertions that Japan and South Korea were not contributing sufficiently to support the alliance and U.S. troops in their respective countries. Should they balk at increasing their contributions, Trump suggested, the United States could withdraw its forces, and possessing their own nuclear weapons could fill the gap left by the departure of the U.S. military. Ben Rhodes, deputy national security adviser, responded emphatically:

> The entire premise of American foreign policy as it relates to nuclear weapons for the last 70 years is to prevent the proliferation of nuclear weapons to additional states. That's the position . . . of everybody who has occupied the Oval Office. It would be catastrophic were the United States to shift its position and indicate that we support somehow the proliferation of nuclear weapons to additional countries.[20]

Despite the headlines generated by Trump's campaign comments, U.S. nonproliferation policy and the role of the nuclear umbrella in that policy are likely to remain the same.

So long as Tokyo and Seoul view the nuclear umbrella as sufficiently reliable, they are unlikely to acquire their own nuclear weapons. Yet herein lies the conundrum of the nuclear umbrella. Extended nuclear deterrence is a central part of alliance relations that helps reassure allies of the U.S. defense commitment. The nuclear umbrella bolsters allied confidence, and as a result, they do not seek their own nuclear weapons. Yet despite these dynamics, serious questions remain regarding the credibility of the nuclear commitment. The U.S. alliances with Japan and South Korea are strong, and there is little doubt the United States would defend these two allies if attacked, but it is unlikely to do so with nuclear weapons, regardless of the circumstances. In the final analysis, there will always be credibility questions regarding extended deterrence and the nuclear umbrella. But despite these concerns, the nuclear umbrella will be "good enough" when it is part of a strong, credible alliance. Moreover, from an adversary's perspective, even if U.S. credibility is low, it will never be zero, providing a tangible degree of deterrence that will make challengers hesitate. So long as both allies retain confidence in the overall U.S. defense commitment and the costs of going nuclear are sufficiently high, Japan and South Korea will continue their nonnuclear status.

※ ※ ※

Despite the hopes and work of those who seek to rid the planet of nuclear weapons, these horrendous weapons are here to stay. The genie is out of the bottle, and it cannot be put back in. Though reaching this goal would be a godsend to humankind, these weapons will never be eliminated. Short of this goal, it is important to continue work on reducing the numbers of nuclear weapons in the world and limiting as far as possible their role in maintaining security, but achieving even these goals will be daunting. The world has gone more than seven decades without the use of another nuclear weapon in wartime. World leaders need to increase efforts to ensure that more states do not acquire nuclear weapons and that nuclear material remains secure and in the hands of responsible state authorities. Nuclear material and technology that stray into the hands of terrorist groups who would not hesitate to use them is one of the most serious challenges facing the world. Nuclear weapons will not be eliminated, but as far as possible, they must be managed by reducing nuclear arsenals, and never used again. No one knows what would happen once a nuclear exchange began, and we must never find out.

Notes

INTRODUCTION

1. See B. H. Liddell Hart, *Deterrent or Defense: A Fresh Look at the West's Military Position* (New York: Praeger, 1960), 23; and Glenn Snyder, *Deterrence and Defense: Toward a Theory of National Security* (Princeton, NJ: Princeton University Press, 1961), 226.
2. For assessments of these early years of the North Korean nuclear problem, see Michael J. Mazarr, *North Korea and the Bomb* (New York: St. Martin's Press, 1995); Joel S. Wit, Daniel B. Poneman, and Robert L. Gallucci, *Going Critical: The First North Korean Nuclear Crisis* (Washington, DC: Brookings, 2004); and Mike Chinoy, *Meltdown: The Inside Story of the North Korean Nuclear Crisis* (New York: St. Martin's Press, 2010).
3. President Barack Obama, "Inaugural Address," White House, January 21, 2009, https://www.whitehouse.gov/blog/2009/01/21/president-barack-obamas-inaugural-address.
4. White House, "Readout of the President's Call with Japanese Prime Minister Taro Aso," May 25, 2009, http://www.presidency.ucsb.edu/ws/index.php?pid=109440; and "Readout of the President's Call with Republic of Korea President Lee Myung-bak," May 25, 2009, https://www.whitehouse.gov/the-press-office/readout-presidents-call-with-republic-korea-president-lee-myung-bak.
5. Japanese Ministry of Defense, "2015 Defense White Paper: China," http://www.mod.go.jp/e/publ/w_paper/pdf/2015/DOJ2015_1-1-3_web.pdf, 33.

6. White House, "Remarks by President Barack Obama in Prague as Delivered," April 5, 2009, https://www.whitehouse.gov/the-press-office/remarks-president-barack-obama-prague-delivered.
7. U.S. Department of Defense, *Nuclear Posture Review Report*, April 2010, http://www.defense.gov/Portals/1/features/defenseReviews/NPR/2010_Nuclear_Posture_Review_Report.pdf. Hereafter the NPR 2010.
8. Ibid., 16.
9. Ibid.
10. U.S. Department of State, "New START," July 23, 2016, http://www.state.gov/t/avc/newstart/index.htm.
11. For example, Andrew O'Neil, *Asia, the U.S., and Extended Deterrence: Atomic Umbrellas in the Twenty-First Century* (New York: Routledge, 2013); Richard C. Bush, "The U.S. Policy of Extended Deterrence in East Asia: History, Current Views, and Implications," *Brookings*, February 2011, https://www.brookings.edu/wp-content/uploads/2016/06/02_arms_control_bush.pdf; Michael H. Keifer, Kurt Guthe, and Thomas Scheber, "Assuring South Korea and Japan as the Role and Number of U.S. Nuclear Weapons Are Reduced," *Defense Threat Reduction Agency*, January 2011, https://www.hsdl.org/?view&did=716179; Rory Medcalf, ed., "Weathering Change: The Future of Extended Nuclear Deterrence," *Lowy Institute*, 2011, https://www.lowyinstitute.org/sites/default/files/pubfiles/Medcalf,_Weathering_change_1.pdf; and Robert A. Manning, "The Future of U.S. Extended Deterrence in Asia to 2025," *Atlantic Council*, 2014, https://www.files.ethz.ch/isn/184441/Future_US_Ext_Det_in_Asia.pdf.
12. "Transcript: Donald Trump Expounds on His Foreign Policy Views," *New York Times*, March 26, 2016, http://www.nytimes.com/2016/03/27/us/politics/donald-trump-transcript.html?_r=0.
13. Oh Young-jin, "Are We Still Allies?" *Korea Times*, June 1, 2016. http://koreatimes.co.kr/www/news/opinon/2016/06/137_206042.html.
14. Julie Makinen, "President Trump? Among U.S. Allies, Japan May Be One of the Most Anxious About That Idea," *Los Angeles Times*, June 26, 2016, http://www.latimes.com/world/asia/la-fg-japan-trump-president-20160625-snap-story.html.
15. Jeffrey Lewis, "No, the U.S. Doesn't Have Plans to Nuke North Korea," *Foreign Policy*, October 17, 2014, http://foreignpolicy.com/2014/10/17/no-the-u-s-doesnt-have-plans-to-nuke-north-korea; and Stephan Haggard, "Nuclear Talk: Leon Panetta's Worthy Fights: A Memoir of Leadership in War and Peace," *North Korea: Witness to Transformation Blog*, November 20, 2014, https://piie.com/blogs/north-korea-witness-transformation/nuclear-talk-leon-panettas-worthy-fights-memoir-leadership.

1. EXTENDED DETERRENCE AND THE NUCLEAR UMBRELLA

1. Bernard Brodie, ed., *The Absolute Weapons: Atomic Power and World Order* (New York: Harcourt Brace, 1946). See also Thomas C. Schelling, *The Strategy of Conflict* (London: Oxford University Press, 1960), 260; and "The Role of Nuclear Weapons," in *Turning Point: The Gulf War and U.S. Military Strategy*, ed. L. Benjamin Ederington and Michael J. Mazarr (Boulder, CO: Westview Press, 1994), 105–115.
2. George W. Bush, *The National Security Strategy of the United States*, September 2002, https://www.state.gov/documents/organization/63562.pdf, 15.
3. For example, T. V. Paul, Patrick M. Morgan, and James J. Wirtz, eds., *Complex Deterrence: Strategy in the Global Age* (Chicago: University of Chicago Press, 2009); Andrew O'Neil, *Asia, the U.S., and Extended Deterrence: Atomic Umbrellas in the Twenty-First Century* (London: Routledge, 2013); Muthiah Alagappa, ed., *The Long Shadow: Nuclear Weapons and Security in 21st Century Asia* (Stanford, CA: Stanford University Press, 2008); and Brad Roberts, *The Case for Nuclear Weapons in the Twenty-First Century* (Stanford, CA: Stanford University Press, 2015).
4. Paul Bracken, *The Second Nuclear Age: Strategy, Danger, and the New Power Politics* (New York: St. Martin's Press, 2012), 3–7.
5. See Toshi Yoshihara and James Holmes, eds., *Strategy in the Second Nuclear Age: Power, Ambition, and the Ultimate Weapon* (Washington, DC: Georgetown University Press, 2012); and Vipin Narang, *Nuclear Strategy in the Modern Era: Regional Power and International Conflict* (Princeton, NJ: Princeton University Press, 2014).
6. Thomas C. Schelling, *Arms and Influence* (New Haven, CT: Yale University Press, 1966), 74.
7. Glenn Snyder, *Deterrence and Defense* (Princeton, NJ: Princeton University Press, 1961), 9–16; and Robert H. Dorff and Joseph R. Cerami, "Deterrence and Competitive Strategies: A New Look at an Old Concept," in Max G. Manwaring, ed., *Deterrence in the 21st Century* (London: Frank Cass, 2001), 109–123.
8. John J. Mearsheimer, *Conventional Deterrence* (Ithaca, NY: Cornell University Press, 1983).
9. George H. Quester, *Deterrence Before Hiroshima: The Airpower Background of Modern Strategy* (New York: Wiley, 1966).
10. Patrick M. Morgan, *Deterrence Now* (Cambridge: Cambridge University Press, 2003), 13–14.
11. Robert Jervis, "The Political Effects of Nuclear Weapons: A Comment," *International Security* 13, no. 2 (Fall 1988): 83.

12. Kenneth N. Waltz, "Nuclear Myths and Political Realities," *American Political Science Review* 84, no. 3 (September 1990): 734.
13. Robert Jervis, *The Meaning of the Nuclear Revolution: Statecraft and the Prospect of Armageddon* (Ithaca, NY: Cornell University Press, 1989).
14. Michael S. Gerson, "Conventional Deterrence in the Second Nuclear Age," *Parameters*, Autumn 2009, 32–48.
15. See Bush, *National Security Strategy*; and Department of Defense, *2006 Quadrennial Defense Review*, February 6, 2006, http://archive.defense.gov/pubs/pdfs/QDR20060203.pdf.
16. John Stone, "Conventional Deterrence and the Challenge of Credibility," *Contemporary Security Policy* 33, no. 1 (April 2012): 108–123.
17. Patrick M. Morgan, *Deterrence: A Conceptual Analysis*, 2d ed. (Beverly Hills: Sage, 1983), 27–47.
18. Rosemary Foot, *The Wrong War: American Policy and Dimensions of the Korean Conflict, 1950–1953* (Ithaca, NY: Cornell University Press, 1985).
19. Thom Shanker and Norimitsu Onishi, "Japan Assures Rice That It Has No Nuclear Intentions," *New York Times*, October 19, 2006, http://www.nytimes.com/2006/10/19/world/asia/19rice.html.
20. Jim Garamone, "Rumsfeld Reaffirms U.S. Promise to Republic of Korea," *U.S. Department of Defense*, October 20, 2006, http://archive.defense.gov/news/newsarticle.aspx?id=1739.
21. For examples, see Ivan Arreguin-Toft, "Unconventional Deterrence: How the Weak Deter the Strong," in *Complex Deterrence*, ed. Paul, Morgan, and Wirtz, 204–221; Terence Roehrig, "Restraining the Hegemon: North Korea, the United States, and Asymmetrical Deterrence," *Pacific Focus* 20, no. 2 (Fall 2005): 7–51; and Derek Smith, *Deterring America: Rogue States and the Proliferation of WMD* (Cambridge: Cambridge University Press, 2006).
22. Scott D. Sagan and Kenneth N. Waltz, *The Spread of Nuclear Weapons: A Debate Renewed* (New York: W. W. Norton, 2003), 9.
23. For assessments of the rationality assumption see Morgan, *Deterrence: A Conceptual Analysis*; Alexander L. George and Richard Smoke, *Deterrence in American Foreign Policy: Theory and Practice* (New York: Columbia University Press, 1974); Robert Jervis, Richard Ned Lebow, and Janice Gross Stein, *Psychology and Deterrence* (Baltimore: Johns Hopkins University Press, 1985); and Richard Ned Lebow and Janice Gross Stein, "Rational Deterrence Theory: I Think, Therefore I Deter," *World Politics* 41, no. 2 (January 1989): 208–224.
24. Morgan, *Deterrence: A Conceptual Analysis*, 104–105; and George and Smoke, *Deterrence in American Foreign Policy*, 75.
25. George and Smoke, *Deterrence in American Foreign Policy*, 75.

26. U.S. Department of Defense, *Annual Report, FY 1977* (Washington, DC: GPO, 1976), III-11.
27. General John H. Tilelli, Jr. "Statement Before the Senate Armed Services Committee," 106th Cong., 1st sess., March 4, 1999.
28. *The Economist*, June 17–23, 2000.
29. Paul D. Shinkman, "Top U.S. Officer: Kim Jong-un Irrational, Unpredictable," *U.S. News & World Report*, January 23, 2014, http://www.usnews.com/news/articles/2014/01/23/top-us-officer-kim-jong-un-irrational-unpredictable.
30. Andrei Lankov, "Why the United States Will Have to Accept a Nuclear North Korea," *Korean Journal of Defense Analysis* 21, no. 3 (September 2009): 252.
31. Roehrig, "Restraining the Hegemon," 16–18.
32. Denny Roy, "North Korea and the 'Madman' Theory," *Security Dialogue* 25, no. 3 (September 1994): 311.
33. Choi Yonghwan, "North Korea's Asymmetric Strategy Toward the United States," *Korea Focus* 12, no. 5 (September/October 2004): 74.
34. William W. Kaufmann, *The Requirements of Deterrence* (Princeton, NJ: Center for International Studies, 1954), 19.
35. "The North Atlantic Treaty," *NATO*, April 4, 1949, http://www.nato.int/cps/en/natolive/official_texts_17120.htm.
36. "The ROK-U.S. Mutual Defense Treaty," signed October 1, 1953, http://avalon.law.yale.edu/20th_century/kor001.asp.
37. "Treaty of Mutual Cooperation and Security Between Japan and the United States," signed January 19, 1960, *Ministry of Foreign Affairs of Japan*, http://www.mofa.go.jp/region/n-america/us/q&a/ref/1.html.
38. Bruce Russett, "The Calculus of Deterrence," *Journal of Conflict Resolution* 11, no. 2 (June 1963): 103–109.
39. Schelling, *Arms and Influence*, 35–91, at 35.
40. Schelling, *The Strategy of Conflict*, 36; and David Garnham, "Extending Deterrence with German Nuclear Weapons," *International Security* 10, no. 1 (Summer 1985): 96–110.
41. Jervis, Lebow, and Stein, *Psychology and Deterrence*.
42. Schelling, *Arms and Influence*, 97–98.
43. Henry Kissinger, *For the Record: Selected Statements, 1977–1980* (Boston: Little, Brown, 1981), 240.
44. Paul Huth and Bruce Russett, "What Makes Deterrence Work?" *World Politics* 36, no. 4 (July 1984): 502.
45. Jervis, *The Meaning of the Nuclear Revolution*, 30.
46. George and Smoke, *Deterrence in American Foreign Policy*, 561.
47. Russett, "The Calculus of Deterrence," 105.
48. George and Smoke, *Deterrence in American Foreign Policy*, 558–561.

49. See Jonathan Mercer, *Reputation in International Politics* (Ithaca, NY: Cornell University Press, 1996); Christopher J. Fettweis, "Credibility and the War on Terror," *Political Science Quarterly* 112, no. 4 (Winter 2007–08): 607–663; and "On the Consequences of Failure in Iraq," *Survival* 49, no. 4 (December 2007): 83–98.
50. Paul Huth, "Extended Deterrence and the Outbreak of War," *American Political Science Review* 82, no. 2 (June 1988): 436–437.
51. Daryl G. Press, *Calculating Credibility: How Leaders Assess Military Threats* (Ithaca, NY: Cornell University Press, 2005), 1.
52. Van Jackson, *Rival Reputations: Coercion and Credibility in U.S.–North Korean Relations* (Cambridge: Cambridge University Press, 2016), 191.
53. Nina Tannenwald, *The Nuclear Taboo: The United States and the Non-Use of Nuclear Weapons Since 1945* (Cambridge: Cambridge University Press, 2007); T. V. Paul, *The Tradition of Non-Use of Nuclear Weapons* (Stanford, CA: Stanford University Press, 2009); and Schelling, *The Strategy of Conflict*, 260.
54. Tannenwald, *The Nuclear Taboo*, 2–3.
55. Paul, *The Tradition of Non-Use of Nuclear Weapons*, 2.
56. Stephen J. Cimbala, *Nuclear Strategizing: Deterrence and Reality* (New York: Praeger, 1988), 7.
57. Paul, *The Tradition of Non-Use of Nuclear Weapons*, 2–3.
58. T. V. Paul, "Self-Deterrence: Nuclear Weapons and the Enduring Credibility Challenge," *International Journal* 7, no. 1 (March 2016): 24.
59. Schelling, "The Role of Nuclear Weapons," 106.
60. Ibid., 110.
61. Scott D. Sagan, "Realist Perspectives on Ethical Norms and Weapons of Mass Destruction," in *Ethics and Weapons of Mass Destruction: Religious and Secular Perspectives*, ed. Sohail H. Hashmi and Steven P. Lee (Cambridge: Cambridge University Press, 2004), 91.
62. Tannenwald, *The Nuclear Taboo*, 6. In *Nuclear First Strike: Consequences of a Broken Taboo* (Baltimore: Johns Hopkins University Press, 2006), George H. Quester examines the results should nuclear weapons ever be used again and the likelihood of rebuilding the norm for nonuse.
63. Morgan, *Deterrence Now*, 270–272.
64. Paul, *The Tradition of Non-Use of Nuclear Weapons*, 12.
65. George P. Shultz, William J. Perry, Henry A. Kissinger, and Sam Nunn, "Kissinger, Shultz, Perry, & Nunn Call for a World Free of Nuclear Weapons," *Wall Street Journal*, January 4, 2007. See also "Toward a Nuclear-Free World," *Wall Street Journal*, January 15, 2008.
66. Keir A. Lieber and Daryl G. Press, "The Nukes We Need: Preserving the American Deterrent," *Foreign Affairs* 88, no. 6 (November/December 2009): 49.

67. Clark Murdoch, Samuel J. Brannen, Thomas Kavako, and Angela Weaver, "Project Atom: A Competitive Strategic Approach to Defining U.S. Nuclear Strategy and Posture for 2025–2050," *Center for Strategic and International Studies*, May 2015, https://csis-prod.s3.amazonaws.com/s3fs-public/legacy_files/files/publication/150716_Murdock_ProjectAtom_Web_Rev2.pdf.
68. Elaine M. Grossman, "Senior U.S. General Sees High Nuclear Threshold," *Global Security Newswire*, October 22, 2007, http://www.nti.org/gsn/article/senior-us-general-sees-high-nuclear-threshold.
69. See Terence Roehrig, *From Deterrence to Engagement: The U.S. Defense Commitment to South Korea* (Lanham, MD: Lexington Books, 2006), 246–250; and Kent E. Calder, *Pacific Alliance: Reviving U.S.-Japan Relations* (New Haven, CT: Yale University Press, 2009).
70. For example, see Uk Heo and Terence Roehrig, *South Korea's Rise: Economic Development, Power, and Foreign Relations* (Cambridge: Cambridge University Press, 2014), 50–66.
71. Timothy W. Crawford, "Endurance of Extended Deterrence," in *Complex Deterrence*, ed. Paul, Morgan, and Wirtz, 291–294. For a discussion of U.S. restraint of South Korea, see Roehrig, *From Deterrence to Engagement*, 148–150.

2. THE NUCLEAR UMBRELLA AND EXTENDED DETERRENCE DURING THE COLD WAR

1. Kurt M. Campbell and Tsuyoshi Sunohara, "Japan: Thinking the Unthinkable," in *The Tipping Point: Why States Reconsider Their Nuclear Choices*, ed. Kurt M. Campbell, Robert J. Einhorn, and Mitchell B. Reiss (Washington, DC: Brookings, 2004), 219–220.
2. Nathan Donohue, "Understanding the Decision to Drop the Bomb on Hiroshima and Nagasaki," *Center for Strategic and International Studies*, August 10, 2012.
3. Cameron Lindsley, "Hiroshima, Nagasaki, and the World Sixty Years Later," *Virginia Quarterly Review* 81, no. 4 (Fall 2005): 26–47.
4. "The Constitution of Japan," http://japan.kantei.go.jp/constitution_and_government_of_japan/constitution_e.html.
5. "Security Treaty Between the United States and Japan, September 8, 1951," http://avalon.law.yale.edu/20th_century/japan001.asp#1.
6. Yukinori Komine, "Okinawa Confidential, 1969: Exploring the Linkage Between the Nuclear Issue and the Base Issue," *Diplomatic History* 37, no. 4 (September 2013): 807–840; and Robert S. Norris, William M. Arkin, and William Burr, "Where They Were," *Bulletin of the Atomic Scientists* 55, no. 6 (November/December 1999): 26–35.

7. Hans M. Kristensen, "Japan Under the Nuclear Umbrella: U.S. Nuclear Umbrella: U.S. Nuclear Weapons and Nuclear War Planning in Japan During the Cold War," *Nautilus Institute*, July 1999, 9–10.
8. "Atomic Energy Basic Act," Act No. 186, December 19, 1955, *Japanese Law Translation*, http://www.japaneselawtranslation.go.jp/law/detail/?printID=&id=2233&re=02&vm=02.
9. Kusunoki Ayako, "The Satō Cabinet and the Making of Japan's Non-Nuclear Policy," *Journal of American–East Asian Relations* 15 (2008): 28.
10. Campbell and Sunohara, "Japan: Thinking the Unthinkable," 221.
11. Michael J. Green and Katsuhisa Furukawa, "Japan: New Nuclear Realism," in *The Long Shadow: Nuclear Weapons and Security in 21st Century Asia*, ed. Muthiah Alagappa (Stanford: Stanford University Press, 2008), 349.
12. "China's Rapid Rise as Nuke Power Surprised Japan," *Kyodo News*, February 25, 2005.
13. "Telegram from the Embassy in Japan to the Department of State," December 29, 1964, *Foreign Relations of the United States* [hereafter *FRUS*] 29 (1964–1968): 55–56.
14. "Memorandum of Conversation," January 12, 1965, *FRUS* 29 (1964–1968): 77.
15. Ibid., 70. Citing newly declassified Japanese diplomatic documents, a Japanese press report indicates that President Johnson replied "you have my assurance" when Prime Minister Satō asked about U.S. protection of Japan under its nuclear umbrella. "Stick to Nonnuclear Policy," *Japan Times*, December 27, 2008, http://search.japantimes.co.jp/cgi-bin/ed20081227a2.html.
16. "Joint Statement Following Meetings with the Prime Minister of Japan," January 13, 1965, in *Public Papers of the Presidents of the United States: Lyndon B. Johnson, 1965*, vol. 1 (Washington, DC: GPO, 1966), 41.
17. Fintan Hoey, "Japan and Extended Nuclear Deterrence: Security and Non-proliferation," *Journal of Strategic Studies* 39, no. 4 (June 2016): 491.
18. Kusunoki, "The Satō Cabinet and the Making of Japan's Non-Nuclear Policy," 31; and Richard J. Samuels and James L. Schoff, "Japan's Nuclear Hedge: Beyond 'Allergy' and Breakout," in *Strategic Asia 2013–14: Asia in the Second Nuclear Age*, ed. Ashley J. Tellis, Abraham M. Denmark, and Travis Tanner (National Bureau of Asian Research, October 2013), 240.
19. "Memorandum of Conversation," November 15, 1967, *FRUS* 29 (1964–1968): 238.
20. "U.S.-Japan Joint Statement Following Discussions with Prime Minister Sato of Japan," November 15, 1967, in *Public Papers of the Presidents of the United States: Lyndon Johnson, 1967*, vol. 2 (Washington, DC: GPO, 1968), 1033–1034.
21. Kusunoki, "The Satō Cabinet and the Making of Japan's Non-Nuclear Policy," 32.
22. "Joint Announcement to the Press Following Discussions with Prime Minister Miki of Japan," August 6, 1975, in *Public Papers of the Presidents of the United States: Gerald R. Ford, 1975*, vol. 2 (Washington DC: GPO, 1976), 1115.

23. Hoey, "Japan and Extended Nuclear Deterrence," 492.
24. "Telegram 267 from Tokyo," January 14, 1969, as cited in fn. 2 in "Telegram from the Embassy in Japan to Department of State," *FRUS* 29 (1964–1968): 314.
25. Kenneth B. Pyle, *Japan Rising: The Resurgence of Japanese Power and Purpose* (New York: Public Affairs, 2007), 251.
26. See "Nuclear Armament Possible but Unrealistic: Secret Reports," *Asahi Shimbun*, November 13, 1994; Selig S. Harrison, "Japan and Nuclear Weapons," in *Japan's Nuclear Future: The Plutonium Debate and East Asian Security*, ed. Selig S. Harrison (Washington, DC: Carnegie Endowment, 1996), 8; and Kusunoki, "The Satō Cabinet and the Making of Japan's Non-Nuclear Policy," 36.
27. Green and Furukawa, "Japan: New Nuclear Realism," 351–325.
28. See Samuels and Schoff, "Japan's Nuclear Hedge."
29. "Gist of White Paper on Defense," *Japan Times*, October 21, 1970.
30. Ibid.
31. Green and Furukawa, "Japan: New Nuclear Realism," 352. Japan published a revised version of this document in 1995 but, beginning in 2004, published these directives under the title "National Defense Program Guidelines."
32. Government of Japan, "National Defense Program Guidelines for FY 2014 and Beyond" Provisional Translation, December 17, 2013, http://www.mod.go.jp/j/approach/agenda/guideline/2014/pdf/20131217_e.pdf.
33. United Nations Office of Disarmament Affairs, "Treaty on the Non-Proliferation of Nuclear Weapons," http://www.un.org/disarmament/WMD/Nuclear/NPT.shtml.
34. As quoted in Harrison, *Japan's Nuclear Future*, 7.
35. Mitchell Reiss, *Without the Bomb: The Politics of Nuclear Nonproliferation* (New York: Columbia University Press, 1988), 125–127.
36. Press Conference, February 17, 1966, as quoted in Selig Harrison, *Japan's Nuclear Future*, 7.
37. Sneider Memo of Conversation, December 2, 1966, as quoted in Kusunoki, "The Satō Cabinet and the Making of Japan's Non-Nuclear Policy," 44.
38. Peter Hayes, *Pacific Powderkeg: American Nuclear Dilemmas in Korea* (Lexington, MA: Lexington, 1991), 36.
39. Robert S. Norris, William M. Arkin, and William Burr, "Where They Were: How Much Did Japan Know?" *Bulletin of the Atomic Scientists* 56, no. 1 (January/February 2000): 11–12.
40. "Nuclear Weapons on Okinawa Declassified December 2015, Photos Available Since 1990," *National Security Archive, George Washington University*, February 16, 2016, http://nsarchive.gwu.edu/nukevault/ebb541-Nukes-on-Okinawa-Declassified-2016.
41. Norris, Arkin, and Burr, "Where They Were: How Much Did Japan Know?," 12.

42. "Land return sought in '67," *Japan Times*, February 19, 2011, http://www.japantimes.co.jp/news/2011/02/19/national/land-return-sought-in-67/#.WLWmMW_yvIU.
43. Department of State, "Secretary's Trip to East Asia, July-August 1969: Outstanding Issues on Okinawa," July 30, 1969, *Digital National Security Archive* 5. See also "Washington Refused to Pull Okinawa Nukes Before Reversion," *Japan Times*, July 9, 2010, http://www.japantimes.co.jp/news/2010/07/09/national/washington-refused-to-pull-okinawa-nukes-before-reversion/#.WLWnEG8rLIU.
44. Kusunoki, "The Satō Cabinet and the Making of Japan's Non-Nuclear Policy," 40.
45. "Joint Statement Between President Richard Nixon and His Excellency Prime Minister Sato of Japan," November 21, 1969, *Public Papers of the Presidents: Richard Nixon, 1969* (Washington DC: GPO, 1971), 955.
46. Ibid.
47. Department of State, "Memorandum of Conversation," November 19, 1969, *Digital National Security Archive: Japan and the U.S., 1960–1970*.
48. "Agreed Minute to Joint Communiqué of United States President Nixon and Prime Minister Sato," November19, 1969, http://www.ioc.u-tokyo.ac.jp/~worldjpn/documents/texts/JPUS/19691119.O2E.html. This document remained secret until 1994, when Wakaizumi Kei, who was the prime minister's special envoy for this issue, wrote a book revealing the agreement.
49. As quoted in Harrison, *Japan's Nuclear Future*, 17–18.
50. For detailed discussions of these considerations to use nuclear weapons, see Nina Tannenwald, *The Nuclear Taboo: The United States and the Non-Use of Nuclear Weapons Since 1945* (Cambridge: Cambridge University Press, 2007), 115–154.
51. "Intelligence Estimate Prepared by the Estimates Group, Office of Intelligence Research," June 25, 1950, *FRUS* 7 (1950): 148–154.
52. As quoted in Walter LaFeber, *The American Age: U.S. Foreign Policy at Home and Abroad* (New York: W. W. Norton, 1994), 512.
53. "Intelligence Estimate Prepared by the Estimates Group," 149.
54. "Memorandum by the Planning Adviser, Bureau of Far Eastern Affairs (Emmerson) to the Assistant Secretary of State for Far Eastern Affairs (Rusk)," November 8, 1950, *FRUS* 7 (1950): 1098–1099.
55. Ibid., 1099.
56. Ibid., 1100.
57. William Stueck, *The Korean War: An International History* (Princeton: Princeton University Press, 1995), 131–132.
58. Harry S. Truman, "The President's News Conference," November 30, 1950, in *Public Papers of the Presidents of the United States: Harry S. Truman, 1950* (Washington, DC: GPO, 1965), 726–727.

59. Ibid., 727.
60. John Lewis Gaddis, *We Now Know: Rethinking Cold War History* (Oxford: Oxford University Press, 1997), 110.
61. "Communique," December 8, 1950, p. 3, http://www.gwu.edu/~nsarchiv/NSAEBB/NSAEBB159/usukconsult-1.pdf.
62. Dean Rusk, *As I Saw It* (New York: W. W. Norton, 1990), 126.
63. T. V. Paul, *The Tradition of Non-Use of Nuclear Weapons* (Stanford: Stanford University Press, 2009), 49.
64. Tannenwald, *The Nuclear Taboo*, 139.
65. Sherman Adams, *First-Hand Report: The Inside Story of the Eisenhower Administration* (London: Hutchinson, 1962), 55.
66. Edward C. Keefer, "President Dwight D. Eisenhower and the End of the Korean War," *Diplomatic History* 10, no. 3 (Summer 1986): 280.
67. See Rosemary J. Foot, "Nuclear Coercion and the Ending of the Korean Conflict," *International Security* 13, no. 3 (Winter 1988/89): 92–112; and Roger Dingman, "Atomic Diplomacy During the Korean War," *International Security* 13, no. 3 (Winter 1988/89): 50–91.
68. Terence Roehrig, *From Deterrence to Engagement: The U.S. Defense Commitment to South Korea* (Lanham, MD: Lexington, 2006), 164–186.
69. *Department of State Bulletin* 29, no. 736 (August 3, 1953): 132–139.
70. "Memorandum on the Substance of Discussion at the Department of State–Joint Chiefs of Staff Meeting," April 13, 1956, *FRUS* 23, part 2 (1955–1957): 243–244.
71. "Memorandum to the President's Special Assistant for National Security Affairs," March 29, 1957, *FRUS* 23, part 2 (1955–1957): 415–416.
72. Hans M. Kristensen, "A History of U.S. Nuclear Weapons in South Korea," *Nuclear Information Project*, September 28, 2005, http://www.nukestrat.com/korea/koreahistory.htm.
73. *Department of State Bulletin* 37, no. 941 (July 8, 1957): 58–59.
74. "Memorandum of Discussion at the 318th Meeting of the National Security Council," April 4, 1957, *FRUS* 23, part 2 (1955–1957): 420–427; and "Memorandum of Discussion at the 326th Meeting of the National Security Council," June 13, 1957, *FRUS* 23, part 2 (1955–1957): 443–454.
75. "Memorandum of Discussion at the 334th Meeting of the National Security Council," August 8, 1957, *FRUS* 23, part 2 (1955–1957): 480–489.
76. "Memorandum of Discussion at the 326th Meeting of the National Security Council," June 13, 1957, *FRUS* 23, part 2 (1955–1957): 443–454.
77. "Memorandum from the Secretary of the Army to the Secretary of Defense," June 27, 1957, *FRUS* 23, part 2 (1955–1957): 464–465.
78. "Memorandum from the Deputy Secretary of Defense (Quarles) to the Secretary of the Army (Brucker)," December 24, 1957, *FRUS* 23, part 2 (1955–1957): 533.

79. John Foster Dulles, "The Evolution of Foreign Policy," *Department of State Bulletin* 30, no. 761 (January 25, 1954): 107–110.
80. U.S. Department of Defense Joint Staff, "Memorandum for the Chairman, Joint Chiefs of Staff," May 14, 1968, *National Security Archive, George Washington University*, http://nsarchive.gwu.edu/NSAEBB/NSAEBB453/docs/doc17.pdf.
81. U.S. Secretary of Defense, "Memorandum for Assistant to the President for National Security Affairs," June 25, 1969, *National Security Archives, George Washington University*, http://nsarchive.gwu.edu/NSAEBB/NSAEBB322/Doc12.pdf.
82. Murrey Marder, "Schlesinger Sees Buildup in Soviet Arms," *Washington Post*, June 21, 1975.
83. Hayes, *Pacific Powderkeg*, 102; and Norris, Arkin, and Burr, "Where They Were," 30.
84. Bruce Cumings, "The Conflict on the Korean Peninsula," in *Asia: Militarization and Regional Conflict*, ed. Yoshikazu Sakamoto (London: Zed, 1988), 105.
85. Ibid.; and Ralph Clough, *Deterrence and Defense in Korea: The Role of U.S. Forces* (Washington, DC: Brookings Institution, 1976), 6.
86. U.S. Department of Defense, "FY 1981 RDTE Congressional Descriptive Summary, Nuclear Munitions," Program Element 6.46.03.A, released under U.S. Freedom of Information Act request to William Arkin, quoted in Peter Hayes, *Pacific Powderkeg*, 95.
87. Harold Brown, *Department of Defense: Annual Report, Fiscal Year 1979* (Washington, DC: GPO, 1979), 68.
88. Hayes, *Pacific Powderkeg*, 49.
89. Ibid.
90. Jack Anderson, "Little Weapons with a Big Bang," *Washington Post*, June 3, 1984, B7.
91. Fred Hiatt, "U.S.: No Use of A-Arms Envisioned in S. Korea," *Washington Post*, December 3, 1987, A54.
92. Ibid.
93. J. McBeth, "Withdrawal Symptoms: Americans Ponder the Removal of Nuclear Weapons," *Far Eastern Economic Review*, September 29, 1988, 35.
94. William J. Crowe and Alan D. Romberg, "Rethinking Pacific Security," *Foreign Affairs* 70, no. 2 (Spring 1991): 134; and Tae-hwan Kwak, "The Reduction of U.S. Forces in Korea in the Inter-Korean Peace Process," *The Korean Journal of Defense Analysis* 2, no. (Winter 1990): 192.
95. George H. W. Bush, "The President's News Conference with Foreign Journalists," July 2, 1992, *Public Papers of the Presidents of the United States: George H. W. Bush, 1992–93*, vol. 1 (Washington, DC: GPO, 1993), 1065.

96. Susan J. Koch, "The Presidential Nuclear Initiatives of 1991–1992" (Washington, DC: National Defense University Press, September 2012), http://ndupress.ndu.edu/Portals/68/Documents/casestudies/CSWMD_CaseStudy-5.pdf.
97. James Sterngold, "Seoul Says It Now Has No Nuclear Arms," *New York Times*, December 19, 1991, A3.

3. THE THREATS THAT DRIVE THE NUCLEAR UMBRELLA: CHINA AND NORTH KOREA

1. Government of Japan, "National Security Strategy," December 17, 2013, http://www.cas.go.jp/jp/siryou/131217anzenhoshou/nss-e.pdf, 12–13.
2. Dennis J. Blasko, "Chinese Army Modernization: An Overview," *Military Review* 85, no. 5 (September-October 2005): 68.
3. Andrew S. Erickson and Adam P. Liff, "Understanding China's Defense Budget: What It Means and Why It Matters," PacNet No. 16, *Pacific Forum CSIS*, March 9, 2011.
4. Edward Wong and Chris Buckley, "China's Military Budget Increasing 10 Percent for 2015, Official Says," *New York Times*, March 4, 2015,. https://www.nytimes.com/2015/03/05/world/asia/chinas-military-budget-increasing-10-for-2015-official-says.html?_r=0.
5. Ben Blancard and Michael Martina, "China's 2016 Defence Budget to Slow in Line with Economy," *Reuters*, March 4, 2016, http://www.reuters.com/article/china-parliament-defence-idUSKCN0W60A5; and Harry J. Kazianis, "China's Great Military Spending: Big Deal or Big Nothing?" *National Interest*, March 7, 2016, http://nationalinterest.org/blog/the-buzz/chinas-great-military-spending-slowdown-big-deal-or-big-15431.
6. U.S. Department of Defense, *Annual Report to Congress: Military and Security Developments Involving the People's Republic of China 2016*, http://www.defense.gov/Portals/1/Documents/pubs/2016%20China%20Military%20Power%20Report.pdf, 77.
7. Sam Perlo-Freeman, Aude Fleurant, Pieter D. Wezeman, and Siemon Wezeman, "Trends in World Military Expenditure, 2015," *SIPRI Fact Sheet*, April 2016, http://books.sipri.org/files/FS/SIPRIFS1604.pdf.
8. Japanese Ministry of Defense, "Annual White Paper, 2015," http://www.mod.go.jp/e/publ/w_paper/pdf/2015/DOJ2015_1-1-3_web.pdf, 33.
9. U.S. Senate, "Statement of Admiral Harry B. Harris, Jr., U.S. Navy Commander, U.S. Pacific Command, Before the Senate Armed Services Committee on U.S. Pacific Command Posture," February 23, 2016, http://www.armed-services.senate.gov/imo/media/doc/Harris_02-23-16.pdf, 3.

10. Barack Obama, *National Security Strategy*, February 2015, http://nssarchive.us/wp-content/uploads/2015/02/2015.pdf, 24.
11. International Institute of Strategic Studies, *Military Balance 2016* (Oxford: Routledge, 2016), 240.
12. Edward Wong, Jane Perlez, and Chris Buckley, "China Announces Cuts of 300,000 Troops at Military Parade Showing Its Might," *New York Times*, September 2, 2015, http://www.nytimes.com/2015/09/03/world/asia/beijing-turns-into-ghost-town-as-it-gears-up-for-military-parade.html.
13. "Type 99," *Military Today*, June 24, 2016, http://www.military-today.com/tanks/type_99.htm.
14. International Institute of Strategic Studies, *Military Balance 2016*, 241–242.
15. Roger Cliff, "The Development of China's Air Force Capabilities," *RAND*, May 20, 2010, http://www.rand.org/pubs/testimonies/CT346.html, 2.
16. *IHS Jane's*, "China—Air Force," *World Air Forces*, July 22, 2015.
17. International Institute of Strategic Studies, *Military Balance 2016*, 245.
18. *IHS Jane's*, "China—Air Force," *World Air Forces*, July 22, 2015.
19. Dave Majumdar, "U.S. Pilots Say New Chinese Stealth Fighter Could Become Equal of F-22, F-35," *USNI News*, November 5, 2014, http://news.usni.org/2014/11/05/u-s-pilots-say-new-chinese-stealth-fighter-become-equal-f-22-f-35.
20. Richard D. Fisher, Jr., "Xi Jinping Visit Reveals H-6 Bomber Details," *IHS Jane's 360*, February 21, 2015, http://world-defense.com/threads/xi-jinping-visit-reveals-h-6-bomber-details.1363/.
21. *IHS Jane's*, "China—Air Force," *World Air Forces*, July 22, 2015.
22. Craig Caffrey, "Closing the Gaps: Air Force Modernization in China," *Jane's Defence Weekly*, October 2, 2015.
23. U.S. Department of Defense, *Annual Report to Congress: Military and Security Developments Involving the People's Republic of China 2016*, 30.
24. *IHS Jane's*, "China—Navy," *World Navies*, November 9, 2015.
25. Toshi Yoshihara and James R. Holmes, *Red Star Over the Pacific: China's Rise and the Challenge to U.S. Maritime Strategy* (Annapolis, MD: Naval Institute Press, 2010).
26. *IHS Jane's*, "China—Navy," *World Navies*, November 9, 2015.
27. International Institute of Strategic Studies, *Military Balance 2016*, 241–242.
28. Lyle J. Goldstein, *Five Dragons Stirring Up the Sea: Challenge and Opportunity in China's Improving Maritime Enforcement Capabilities* (Newport, RI: Naval War College Press, 2010).
29. Andrew S. Erickson and Conor M. Kennedy, "China's Maritime Militia: What It Is and How to Deal with It," *Foreign Affairs*, June 23, 2016, https://www.foreignaffairs.com/articles/china/2016-06-23/chinas-maritime-militia.

30. U.S. Department of Defense, *Annual Report to Congress: Military and Security Developments Involving the People's Republic of China 2016*, 28.
31. Ibid.
32. Kathrin Hille and Mure Dickie, "China Reveals Air Craft Carrier Plans," *Financial Times*, December 17, 2010, http://www.ft.com/cms/s/0/fa7f5e6a-09cc-11e0-8b29-00144feabdco.html#axzz1LOEIdJdS.
33. People's Republic of China, "China's National Defense in 2010," March 31, 2011, http://www.china.org.cn/government/whitepaper/node_7114675.htm, 37.
34. U.S. Department of State, "Adherence to and Compliance with Arms Control, Nonproliferation, and Disarmament Agreements and Commitments," July 2010, http://www.state.gov/documents/organization/145181.pdf, 43.
35. U.S. Department of State, "Compliance with the Convention on the Prohibition of the Development, Production, Stockpiling, and Use of Chemical Weapons and on Their Destruction Condition 10(C) Report," April 2016, http://www.state.gov/t/avc/rls/rpt/2016/255563.htm.
36. U.S. Department of State, "Adherence to and Compliance with Arms Control, Nonproliferation, and Disarmament Agreements and Commitments," 12.
37. U.S. Department of State, "2015 Report on Adherence to and Compliance with Arms Control, Nonproliferation, and Disarmament Agreements and Commitments," June 5, 2015, http://www.state.gov/t/avc/rls/rpt/2015/243224.htm#China.
38. *Jane's* Sentinel Security Assessment, "Strategic Weapons Systems, China," August 13, 2015.
39. Hans M. Kristensen and Robert S. Norris, "Chinese Nuclear Forces, 2015," *Bulletin of the Atomic Scientists* 71, no. 4 (July 1, 2015): 78.
40. Hui Zhang, "How U.S. Restraint Can Keep China's Nuclear Arsenal Small," *Bulletin of the Atomic Scientists* 68, no. 4 (July 1, 2012): 74; and Hans M. Kristensen and Robert S. Norris, "Chinese Nuclear Forces, 2016," *Bulletin of the Atomic Scientists* 72, no. 4 (July 3, 2016): 1.
41. Gregory Kulacki, "China's Military Calls for Putting Its Nuclear Forces on Alert," *Union of Concerned Scientists*, January 2016, http://www.ucsusa.org/sites/default/files/attach/2016/02/China-Hair-Trigger-full-report.pdf.
42. Kristensen and Norris, "Chinese Nuclear Forces, 2016," 1.
43. *Jane's* Sentinel Security Assessment, "Strategic Weapons Systems, China," August 13, 2015.
44. U.S. Department of Defense, *Annual Report to Congress: Military and Security Developments Involving the People's Republic of China 2016*, 25.
45. Ibid., 24.
46. *Jane's* Sentinel Security Assessment, "Strategic Weapons Systems, China," January 17, 2011, http://jmsa.janes.com.

47. Kristensen and Norris, "Chinese Nuclear Forces, 2016," 3.
48. U.S. Department of Defense, *Annual Report to Congress: Military and Security Developments Involving the People's Republic of China 2016*, 25.
49. Felix K. Chang, "China's New Missiles and U.S. Alliances in Asia-Pacific: Impact of Weakening Extended Deterrence—Analysis," *Eurasia Review*, April 14, 2016, http://www.fpri.org/2016/04/chinas-new-missiles-u-s-alliances-asia-pacific-impact-weakening-extended-deterrence/.
50. Bill Gertz, "China Successfully Tests Hypersonic Missile," *Washington Free Beacon*, April 27, 2016, http://freebeacon.com/national-security/china-successfully-tests-hypersonic-missile/; and Erika Solem and Karen Montague, "Chinese Hypersonic Weapons Development—Updated," *China Brief* 16, no. 7 (April 21, 2016), https://jamestown.org/program/updated-chinese-hypersonic-weapons-development/.
51. "DongFeng 21 (CSS-5) Medium Range Ballistic Missile," *Sinodefence.com*, June 4, 2010, http://www.sinodefence.com/strategic/missile/df21.asp.
52. *Jane's* Sentinel Security Assessment, "Strategic Weapons Systems, China," August 13, 2015.
53. U.S. Department of Defense, *Annual Report to Congress: Military and Security Developments Involving the People's Republic of China 2015*, http://www.defense.gov/Portals/1/Documents/pubs/2015_China_Military_Power_Report.pdf, 8.
54. Andrew S. Erickson, *Anti-Ship Ballistic Missile Development: Drivers, Trajectories, and Strategic Implications* (Washington, DC: Jamestown Foundation, May 2013).
55. *Jane's* Sentinel Security Assessment, "Strategic Weapons Systems, China," August 13, 2015, 18.
56. U.S. Department of Defense, *Annual Report to Congress: Military and Security Developments Involving the People's Republic of China 2016*, 38.
57. "DongHai 10 (ChangJian 10) Land-Attack Cruise Missile," *SinoDefence*, October 3, 2009, https://archive.li/folcQ.
58. *Jane's* Sentinel Security Assessment, "Strategic Weapons Systems, China," August 13, 2015.
59. Ibid., 17.
60. U.S. Department of Defense, *Annual Report to Congress: Military and Security Developments Involving the People's Republic of China 2016*, 26.
61. Kristensen and Norris, "Chinese Nuclear Forces, 2016," 5.
62. U.S. Department of Defense, *Annual Report to Congress: Military and Security Developments Involving the People's Republic of China 2010*, https://www.defense.gov/Portals/1/Documents/pubs/2010_CMPR_Final.pdf, 29.
63. U.S. Department of Defense, *Annual Report to Congress: Military and Security Developments Involving the People's Republic of China 2015*, 31.
64. Stockholm International Peace Research Institute, "World Nuclear Forces," *SIPRI Yearbook 2015*, http://www.sipri.org/yearbook/2015/11.

65. Information Office of the State Council, "China's Military Strategy," May 26, 2015, http://www.chinadaily.com.cn/china/2015-05/26/content_20820628_4.htm.
66. M. Taylor Fravel and Evan S. Medeiros, "China's Search for Assured Retaliation: The Evolution of Chinese Nuclear Strategy and Force Structure," *International Security* 35, no. 2 (Fall 2010): 51.
67. Chue Shulong and Rong Yu, "China: Dynamic Minimum Deterrence," in *The Long Shadow: Nuclear Weapons and Security in 21st Century Asia*, ed. Muthiah Alagappa (Stanford, CA: Stanford University Press, 2008), 161–187; Christopher T. Yeaw, Andrew S. Erickson, and Michael S. Chase, "The Future of Chinese Nuclear Policy and Strategy," in *Strategy in the Second Nuclear Age: Power, Ambition, and the Ultimate Weapon*, ed. Toshi Yoshihara and James R. Holmes (Washington, DC: Georgetown University Press, 2012), 53–80; and Jeffrey Lewis, "Minimum Deterrence," *Bulletin of the Atomic Scientists* 64, no. 3 (July/August 2008).
68. U.S. Department of Defense, *Annual Report to Congress: Military and Security Developments Involving the People's Republic of China 2015*, 32.
69. Information Office of the State Council, "China's Military Strategy," May 26, 2015.
70. *Jane's* Sentinel Security Assessment, "Strategic Weapons Systems, China," August 13, 2015.
71. U.S. Department of Defense, *Annual Report to Congress: Military and Security Developments Involving the People's Republic of China 2015*, 32.
72. For an argument regarding U.S. efforts to achieve nuclear primacy, see Keir A. Lieber and Daryl G. Press, "The End of MAD?: The Nuclear Dimension of U.S. Primacy," *International Security* 30, no. 3 (Spring 2006): 7–44.
73. Ben Kesling and Paul Sonne, "Donald Trump Calls for Expansion of Nuclear-Weapon Capabilities," *Wall Street Journal*, December 22, 2016, https://www.wsj.com/articles/donald-trump-calls-for-expansion-of-nuclear-weapon-capabilities-1482443444.
74. Fiona S. Cunningham and M. Taylor Fravel, "Assuring Assured Retaliation: China's Nuclear Posture and U.S.-China Strategic Stability," *International Security* 40, no. 2 (Fall 2015): 15–23.
75. Ibid., 10.
76. Lyle Goldstein, *Meeting China Halfway: How to Defuse the Emerging U.S.-China Rivalry* (Washington, DC: Georgetown University Press, 2015).
77. ROK Ministry of National Defense, *2014 Defense White Paper*, 31.
78. U.S. Department of State, "World Military Expenditures and Arms Transfers 2015: Introduction and Overview," December 24, 2015, http://www.state.gov/t/avc/rls/rpt/wmeat/2015/250863.htm.
79. *IHS Jane's*, "World Armies: North Korea," November 23, 2015.
80. Ibid.
81. ROK Ministry of National Defense, *2014 Defense White Paper*, 29.

82. Office of the Secretary of Defense, "Military and Security Developments Involving the Democratic People's Republic of Korea, 2015," http://www.defense.gov/Portals/1/Documents/pubs/Military_and_Security_Developments_Involving_the_Democratic_Peoples_Republic_of_Korea_2015.pdf, 12–13.
83. International Institute of Strategic Studies, *Military Balance 2016*, 262.
84. ROK Ministry of National Defense, *2014 Defense White Paper*, 28.
85. Kim Eun-jung, "N. Korea Rolls Out 900 New Tanks in Last Seven Years: Source," *Yonhap News*, June 19, 2013, http://english.yonhapnews.co.kr/national/2013/06/18/61/0301000000AEN20130618009700315F.HTML.
86. Terence Roehrig, *From Deterrence to Engagement: The U.S. Defense Commitment to South Korea* (Lanham, MD: Lexington, 2006), 55.
87. Michael O'Hanlon, "Stopping a North Korean Invasion," *International Security* 22, no. 4 (Spring 1998): 136.
88. International Institute of Strategic Studies, *Military Balance 2016*, 265.
89. Ibid., 265.
90. Ibid., 266.
91. Office of the Secretary of Defense, "Military and Security Developments Involving the Democratic People's Republic of Korea, 2015," 11–12.
92. Joseph S. Bermudez, Jr., "North Korea Drones On: Redeux," *38 North*, January 19, 2016, http://38north.org/2016/01/jbermudez011916/.
93. International Institute of Strategic Studies, *Military Balance 2016*, 265.
94. *Jane's* Aerospace, Defence, and Security, "World Navies: Korea, North," March 30, 2016.
95. Ibid.
96. ROK Ministry of National Defense, *2014 Defense White Paper*, 29.
97. *Jane's* Aerospace, Defence, and Security, "World Navies: Korea, North," March 30, 2016.
98. ROK Ministry of National Defense, *2014 Defense White Paper*, 32.
99. International Institute of Strategic Studies, "North Korea's Chemical and Biological Weapons (CBW) Programmes," http://www.iiss.org/publications/strategic-dossiers/north-korean-dossier/north-koreas-weapons-programmes-a-net-asses/north-koreas-chemical-and-weapons-cbw-prog/.
100. Joseph Bermudez, Jr., "North Korea's Chemical Warfare Capabilities," *38 North*, October 10, 2013, http://38north.org/2013/10/jbermudez101013/.
101. Nuclear Threat Initiative, "North Korea—Chemical," December 2015, http://www.nti.org/learn/countries/north-korea/chemical/.
102. *Jane's* Sentinel Security Assessment, "Strategic Weapons Systems—North Korea," January 20, 2011.
103. Nuclear Threat Initiative, "North Korea—Biological," December 2015, http://www.nti.org/learn/countries/north-korea/biological/.

104. "DPRK Proves Successful in H-bomb Test," *KCNA*, January 6, 2016.
105. Daryl G. Kimball and Kelsey Davenport, "A Fourth North Korean Nuclear Test: What It Means; What Must Be Done," *Arms Control Association*, January 19, 2016, https://www.armscontrol.org/blog/ArmsControlNow/2016-01-06/A-Fourth-North-Korean-Nuclear-Test-What-It-Means-What-Must-Be-Done.
106. Siegfried S. Hecker, "What to Make of North Korea's Latest Nuclear Test?" *38 North*, September 12, 2016, http://38north.org/2016/09/shecker091216/.
107. "DPRK Succeeds in Nuclear Warhead Explosion Test," *KCNA*, September 9, 2016.
108. Joel S. Wit and Sun Young Ahn, "North Korea's Nuclear Futures: Technology and Strategy," *U.S.-Korea Institute at SAIS*, February 2015, http://38north.org/wp-content/uploads/2015/09/NKNF_NK-Nuclear-Futures.pdf.
109. James R. Clapper, "Worldwide Threat Assessment of the U.S. Intelligence Community," February 9, 2016, http://www.dni.gov/files/documents/SASC_Unclassified_2016_ATA_SFR_FINAL.pdf.
110. Siegfried Hecker, "A Return Trip to North Korea's Yongbyon Nuclear Complex," *Center for International Security and Cooperation, Stanford University*, November 20, 2010, http://iis-db.stanford.edu/pubs/23035/HeckerYongbyon.pdf.
111. Jeremy Page and Jay Solomon, "China Warns North Korean Nuclear Threat Is Rising," *Wall Street Journal*, April 22, 2015.
112. David Albright and Serena Kelleher-Vergantini, "Plutonium, Tritium, and Highly Enriched Uranium Production at the Yongbyon Nuclear Site," *Institute for Science and International Security*, June 14, 2016, http://isis-online.org/uploads/isis-reports/documents/Pu_HEU_and_tritium_production_at_Yongbyon_June_14_2016_FINAL.pdf.
113. David Albright, "Future Directions in the DPRK's Nuclear Weapons Program: Three Scenarios for 2020," *U.S.-Korea Institute at SAIS*, 2015, http://38north.org/wp-content/uploads/2015/02/NKNF-Future-Directions-2020-Albright-0215.pdf.
114. Terence Roehrig, "North Korea's Nuclear Weapons Program: Motivations, Strategy, and Doctrine," in *Strategy in the Second Nuclear Age: Power, Ambition, and the Ultimate Weapon*, ed. Toshi Yoshihara and James Holmes (Washington, DC: Georgetown University Press, 2012).
115. As quoted in Joseph S. Bermudez, Jr., *A History of Ballistic Missile Development*, Occasional Paper No. 2 (Monterey, CA: Monterey Institute of International Studies, 1999), 2.
116. Greg Thielmann, "Sorting Out the Nuclear and Missile Threats from North Korea," *Arms Control Association*, May 21, 2013, http://www.armscontrol.org/files/TAB_Sorting_Out_North_Korea_2013.pdf; and John Schilling, "A Solid but Incremental Improvement in North Korea's Missiles," *38 North*, March 29, 2016, http://38north.org/2016/03/jschilling032916/.

117. David Wright, "Analysis of North Korea's Musudan Missile Test—Part 1," *Union of Concerned Scientists*, June 24, 2016, http://allthingsnuclear.org/dwright/analysis-of-north-koreas-musudan-missile-test-part-1.
118. Wit and Ahn, "North Korea's Nuclear Futures," 9.
119. Roehrig, *From Deterrence to Engagement*, 89.
120. Joseph S. Bermudez, Jr., "North Korea's Ballistic Missile Submarine Program: Full Steam Ahead," *38 North*, January 5, 2016, http://38north.org/2016/01/sinpo010516/.
121. John Schilling, "A New Submarine-Launched Ballistic Missile for North Korea," *38 North*, April 25, 2016, http://38north.org/2016/04/jschilling042516/.
122. Mary Beth Nikitin, "North Korea's Nuclear Weapons: Technical Issues," *Congressional Research Service*, April 3, 2013, http://www.fas.org/sgp/crs/nuke/RL34256.pdf, 5; and Zhang Hui, "Revisiting North Korea's Nuclear Test," *China Security* 3, no. 3 (Summer 2007): 119–130.
123. Admiral Willam E. Gortney, "Statement Before the Senate Armed Services Committee," March 10, 2016, http://www.northcom.mil/Portals/28/Documents/Gortney_Posture%20Statement_SASC_03-10-16.pdf.
124. "Kim Jong-un Guides Work for Mounting Nuclear Warheads on Ballistic Rockets," *KCNA*, March 9, 2016.
125. Dana Struckman and Terence Roehrig, "Not So Fast: Pyongyang's Nuclear Weapons Ambitions," *Georgetown Journal of International Affairs*, February 20, 2013, http://journal.georgetown.edu/not-so-fast-pyongyangs-nuclear-weapons-ambitions-by-dana-struckman-and-terence-roehrig/.
126. See Alexandre Y. Mansourev, "Kim Jong-un's Nuclear Doctrine and Strategy: What Everyone Needs to Know," *Nautilus Institute, NAPSNet Special Reports*, December 16, 2014; Peter Hayes and Roger Cavazos, "North Korea's Nuclear Force Roadmap: Hard Choices," *Nautilus Institute*, March 2, 2015; Shane Smith, "North Korea's Evolving Nuclear Strategy," *U.S.-Korea Institute at SAIS*, August 2015; and Roehrig, "North Korea's Nuclear Weapons Program."
127. Han S. Park, "Military-First Politics (Songun): Understanding Kim Jong-il's North Korea," in *Academic Paper Series: On Korea*, vol. 1 (Seoul: Korea Economic Institute, 2007), 126; and Mike Chinoy, *Meltdown: The Inside Story of the North Korean Nuclear Crisis* (New York: St. Martin's Press, 2008), 166.
128. "DPRK FM on Its Stand to Suspend Its Participation in Six-Party Talks for Indefinite Period," *Korean Central News Agency*, February 10, 2005.
129. "DPRK Will Bolster Up War Deterrence in Every Way: Rodong Sinmun," *KCNA*, August 11, 2014.
130. "DPRK Proves Successful in H-bomb Test," *KCNA*, January 6, 2016.
131. Terence Roehrig, "North Korea, Nuclear Weapons, and the Stability-Instability Paradox," *Korean Journal of Defense Analyses* 28, no. 2 (Summer 2016): 181–198.

132. Mansourev, "Kim Jong-un's Nuclear Doctrine and Strategy," 9; and Hyeongpil Ham and Jaehak Lee, "North Korea's Nuclear Decision-Making and Plausible Scenarios," *Korean Journal of Defense Analyses* 25, no. 3 (September 2013): 399–413.
133. Vipin Narang, "Nuclear Strategies of Emerging Powers: North Korea and Iran," *Washington Quarterly* 38, no. 1 (Spring 2015): 78.
134. James R. Clapper, "Statement for the Record on the Worldwide Threat Assessment of the U.S. Intelligence Community for the Senate Select Committee on Intelligence," February 16, 2011, https://www.dni.gov/files/documents/Newsroom/Testimonies/20110216_testimony_sfr.pdf, 6.

4. JAPAN AND THE U.S. NUCLEAR UMBRELLA

1. James L. Schoff, "Changing Perceptions of Extended Deterrence in Japan," in *Strategy in the Second Nuclear Age: Power, Ambition, and the Ultimate Weapon*, ed. James Holmes and Toshi Yoshihara (Washington, DC: Georgetown University Press, 2012), 104–105; and Andrew O'Neill, *Asia, the U.S., and Extended Nuclear Deterrence: Atomic Umbrellas in the Twenty-First Century* (New York: Routledge, 2013): 70–93.
2. Yukio Satoh, "Japan's Responsibility Sharing for the U.S. Extended Deterrence," *Discuss Japan: Japan Foreign Policy Forum* no. 19 (March 10, 2014), http://www.japanpolicyforum.jp/archives/diplomacy/pt20140310010210.html.
3. Ministry of Foreign Affairs of Japan, "Treaty of Mutual Cooperation and Security Between Japan and the United States of America," January 19, 1960, http://www.mofa.go.jp/region/n-america/us/q&a/ref/1.html.
4. Lyndon B. Johnson, "Remarks at the State Dinner in Parliament House, Kuala Lumpur, Malaysia," October 30, 1966, *Public Papers of the Presidents of the United States: Lyndon B. Johnson, 1966*, vol. 2 (Washington, DC: GPO, 1967), 1282.
5. Kusunoki Ayako, "The Sato Cabinet and the Making of Japan's Non-Nuclear Policy," *Journal of American–East Asian Relations* 15 (2008): 32.
6. Richard J. Samuels and James L. Schoff, "Japan's Nuclear Hedge: Beyond 'Allergy' and Breakout," in *Strategic Asia 2013–14: Asia in the Second Nuclear Age*, ed. Ashley J. Tellis, Abraham M. Denmark, and Travis Tanner (Seattle: National Bureau of Asian Research, 2013).
7. Government of Japan, "National Defense Program Outline, 1976," October 29, 1976, http://www.ioc.u-tokyo.ac.jp/~worldjpn/documents/texts/docs/19761029.O1E.html.
8. Government of Japan, "National Defense Program Outline, 1995," December 1995, http://www.mofa.go.jp/policy/security/defense96/.

9. Japan Ministry of Defense, "National Defense Program Guidelines, FY 2005," December 10, 2004, http://www.mod.go.jp/e/d_act/d_policy/pdf/national_guidelines.pdf.
10. Ibid.
11. Japan Ministry of Defense, "Defense Minister's Statement on the Approval of the 'National Defense Program Guidelines for FY2011 and Beyond' and the 'Mid-Term Defense Program (FY2011–FY2015),'" December 17, 2010, http://www.mod.go.jp/j/approach/agenda/guideline/2011/daijin_e.pdf.
12. The Council on Security and Defense Capabilities in the New Era, "Japan's Vision for Future Security and Defense Capabilities in the New Era: Toward a Peace-Creating Nation," August 27, 2010, http://www.kantei.go.jp/jp/singi/shin-ampobouei2010/houkokusyo_e.pdf.
13. Japan Ministry of Defense, "National Defense Program Guidelines for FY 2011 and Beyond," December 17, 2010, http://www.mod.go.jp/e/d_act/d_policy/pdf/guidelinesFY2011.pdf, 2.
14. Ibid.
15. Government of Japan, "National Defense Program Guidelines for FY 2014 and Beyond" Provisional Translation, December 17, 2013, http://www.mod.go.jp/j/approach/agenda/guideline/2014/pdf/20131217_e.pdf, 4.
16. Ibid., 5.
17. Ibid., 6
18. Ibid., 6–13.
19. Japan Ministry of Defense, "The Guidelines for Japan-U.S. Defense Cooperation," November 27, 1978, http://www.mod.go.jp/e/d_act/anpo/19781127.html; and "The Guidelines for Japan-U.S. Defense Cooperation," September 23, 1997, http://www.mod.go.jp/e/d_act/anpo/19970923.html.
20. U.S. Department of State, "Joint Statement: U.S.-Japan Security Consultative Committee," December 16, 2002, http://www.mofa.go.jp/region/n-america/us/security/scc/pdfs/jointo212.pdf, 3.
21. Security Consultative Committee, "U.S.-Japan Alliance: Transformation and Realignment for the Future," October 29, 2005, http://www.mofa.go.jp/region/n-america/us/security/scc/pdfs/doco510.pdf, 3.
22. Security Consultative Committee, "Alliance Transformation: Advancing United States–Japan Security and Defense Cooperation," May 1, 2007, http://www.mofa.go.jp/region/n-america/us/security/scc/pdfs/jointo705.pdf.
23. Thom Shanker and Norimitsu Onishi, "Japan Assures Rice That It Has No Nuclear Intentions," *New York Times*, October 19, 2006, http://www.nytimes.com/2006/10/19/world/asia/19rice.html?_r=0.
24. U.S. Department of State, "Joint Statement of the Security Consultative Committee: A Stronger Alliance for a Dynamic Security Environment: The New

Guidelines for U.S.-Japan Defense Cooperation," April 27, 2015, http://www.state.gov/r/pa/prs/ps/2015/04/241125.htm.
25. White House, "Readout of the President's Call with Japanese Prime Minister Shinzo Abe," February 13, 2013, http://www.whitehouse.gov/the-press-office/2013/02/13/readout-presidents-call-japanese-prime-minister-shinzo-abe.
26. James L. Schoff, "Changing Perceptions of Deterrence in Japan," 99–100.
27. Author interview, November 11, 2010.
28. Author interview, June 27, 2013.
29. Author interview, June 21, 2012.
30. Narushige Michishita, "Japan's Response to Nuclear North Korea," in *Joint U.S.-Korea Academic Studies*, vol. 23, *Asia at a Tipping Point: Korea, the Rise of China, and the Impact of Leadership Transitions*, ed. Gilbert Rozman (Washington DC: Korea Economic Institute, 2012), 101.
31. See Samuels and Schoff, "Japan's Nuclear Hedge," 250–251.
32. Author interviews, June 22, 2012.
33. Author interview, November 11, 2010.
34. Author interview, November 9, 2010.
35. Author interview, June 22, 2012.
36. Ibid.
37. See O'Neill, *Asia, the U.S., and Extended Nuclear Deterrence*, 92–93.
38. Japan Ministry of Defense, "The Guidelines for Japan-U.S. Defense Cooperation," April 27, 2015, http://www.mod.go.jp/e/d_act/anpo/shishin_20150427e.html.
39. Quoted in James L. Schoff, *Realigning Priorities: The U.S.-Japan Alliance and the Future of Extended Deterrence* (Cambridge, MA: Institute for Foreign Policy Analysis, March 2009), http://www.ifpa.org/pdf/RealignPriorities.pdf, 30.
40. Author interview, June 21, 2012.
41. O'Neill, *Asia, the U.S., and Extended Nuclear Deterrence*, 89.
42. "Japan, U.S. to Launch Talks on 'Nuclear Umbrella,'" *Global Security Newswire*, NTI, July 20, 2009, http://www.nti.org/gsn/article/japan-us-to-launch-talks-on-nuclear-umbrella/.
43. Author interview, June 22, 2012.
44. Ministry of Foreign Affairs of Japan, "Japan, U.S. Extended Deterrence Dialogue," February 16, 2015, http://www.mofa.go.jp/press/release/press4e_000637.html.
45. "U.S.-Japan Extended Deterrence Dialogue," U.S. Department of State, June 9, 2014, https://groups.google.com/forum/#!topic/wanabidii/iDEEnC8MM-I.
46. Author interview, June 28, 2013
47. Author interviews, June 21, 2012, and June 28, 2013.
48. Author interview, June 27, 2013.

49. Erik Slavin, "U.S., Japan Engage in Anti-Nuclear Talks Amid Japan Defense Debate," *Stars and Stripes*, June 10, 2014, http://www.stripes.com/news/pacific/us-japan-engage-in-anti-nuclear-talks-amid-japan-defense-debate-1.288054.
50. U.S. Department of State, "U.S.-Japan Extended Deterrence Dialogue," June 9, 2014, http://www.state.gov/r/pa/prs/ps/2014/06/227303.htm.
51. Author interview, June 27, 2013.
52. Susan J. Koch, *The Presidential Nuclear Initiatives of 1991–1992* (Washington, DC: National Defense University Press, September 2012), http://ndupress.ndu.edu/Portals/68/Documents/casestudies/CSWMD_CaseStudy-5.pdf.
53. Hans M. Kristensen, "U.S. Navy Instruction Confirms Retirement of Nuclear Tomahawk Cruise Missile," *Federation of American Scientists*, March 18, 2013, http://fas.org/blogs/security/2013/03/tomahawk/.
54. "North Korea's Nuclear Threat/Reinforcing Alliance with U.S. Helps Bolster Nuclear Deterrence," *The Daily Yomiuri* (Internet version), March 23, 2007.
55. *America's Strategic Posture: The Final Report of the Congressional Commission on the Strategic Posture of the United States* (Washington, DC: United States Institute of Peace Press, May 2009), 26.
56. Katsuya Okada, Japanese Minister for Foreign Affairs, "Letter to U.S. Secretary of State Hillary Rodham Clinton," December 24, 2009, https://icnndngojapan.files.wordpress.com/2010/01/20091224_okada_letter_en.pdf.
57. Author interview, November 10, 2010.
58. Author interview, June 27, 2013.
59. U.S. Department of Defense, *Nuclear Posture Review Report*, April 2010, http://www.defense.gov/Portals/1/features/defenseReviews/NPR/2010_Nuclear_Posture_Review_Report.pdf., 28. Hereafter the NPR 2010.
60. Author interview, February 20, 2014.
61. Schoff, "Changing Perceptions of Extended Deterrence in Japan," 106.
62. Author interview, June 28, 2013.
63. O'Neill, *Asia, the U.S., and Extended Nuclear Deterrence*, 88–89; and Schoff, "Changing Perceptions of Extended Deterrence in Japan," 108–109.
64. Maria Tsvetkova, "Putin Says Russia Beefing Up Nuclear Arsenal, NATO Denounces 'Saber-Rattling,'" *Reuters*, June 16, 2015, http://www.reuters.com/article/2015/06/16/us-russia-nuclear-putin-idUSKBN0OW17X20150616.
65. Author interviews, November 9, 2010.
66. Author interview, November 11, 2010.
67. Author interview, June 21, 2012.
68. Schoff, "Realigning Priorities," 38.
69. Author interview, November 10, 2010.
70. Shinichi Ogawa, "The 2010 U.S. Nuclear Posture Review and Its Implications for Japan," *Asia Pacific Bulletin*, no. 56, April 16, 2010.

71. Amy Woolf, "U.S. Strategic Nuclear Forces: Background, Developments, and Issues," *Congressional Research Service*, September 27, 2016, https://fas.org/sgp/crs/nuke/RL33640.pdf.
72. Samuels and Schoff, "Japan's Nuclear Hedge," 249.
73. Masa Takubo, "The Role of Nuclear Weapons: Japan, the U. S. and 'Sole Purpose,'" *Arms Control Association*, November 5, 2009, https://www.armscontrol.org/act/2009_11/Takubo.
74. Mira Rapp-Hooper, "Do Chemical Weapons Threaten U.S. Extended Deterrence in Asia?" *The Diplomat*, September 13, 2013, http://thediplomat.com/2013/09/do-chemical-weapons-threaten-us-extended-deterrence-in-asia/.
75. NPR 2010, 16.
76. Ogawa, "The 2010 U.S. Nuclear Posture Review and Its Implications for Japan."
77. Ken Jimbo, "Extended Deterrence in the Japan-U.S. Alliance," *NAPSNet Special Reports*, May 8, 2012, http://nautilus.org/napsnet/napsnet-special-reports/extended-deterrence-in-the-japan-u-s-alliance/.
78. Author interview, November 10, 2010
79. Author interview, November 9, 2010.
80. Author interview, November 11, 2010.
81. Japan Ministry of Defense, "National Defense Program Guidelines for FY 2011 and Beyond."
82. Ibid., 6–7.
83. Ibid., 7.
84. Sheila Smith, "Japan's 'Dynamic Defense Policy' and China," *Council on Foreign Relations*, December 17, 2010, http://www.cfr.org/japan/japans-dynamic-defense-policy-china/p23663.
85. Martin Fackler, "With Its Eye on China, Japan Builds Up Military," *New York Times*, March 1, 2011, http://www.nytimes.com/2011/03/01/world/asia/01japan.html?_r=0.
86. Author interview, June 21, 2012.
87. "Japan to Build Two More Aegis Destroyers to Boost Missile Defense," *Japan Times*, November 5, 2013, http://www.japantimes.co.jp/news/2013/11/05/national/japan-to-build-two-more-aegis-destroyers-to-boost-missile-defense/#.UxyiHT9dXRg.
88. Chester Dawson, "Japan Shows Off Its Missile-Defense System," *Wall Street Journal*, December 9, 2012, http://online.wsj.com/news/articles/SB10001424127887323316804578165023312727616.
89. Thom Shanker and Ian Johnson, "U.S. Accord with Japan Over Missile Defense Draws Criticism in China," *New York Times*, September 17, 2012, http://www.nytimes.com/2012/09/18/world/asia/u-s-and-japan-agree-on-missile-defense-system.html?pagewanted=all&_r=0.

90. As quoted in Sugio Takahashi, "Dealing with the Ballistic Missile Threat: Whether Japan Should Have a Strike Capability Under Its Exclusively Defense-Oriented Policy," *NIDS Security Reports*, no. 7 (December 2006): 81, note 4.
91. See Takahashi, "Dealing with the Ballistic Missile Threat"; and Daniel A. Pinkston and Kazutaka Sakurai, "Japan Debates Preparing for Future Preemptive Strikes Against North Korea," *Korean Journal of Defense Analysis* 18, no. 4 (Winter 2006): 95–121.
92. International Institute of Strategic Studies, *Military Balance 2016* (Oxford: Routledge, 2016), 262.
93. Japan Ministry of Defense, "The Guidelines for Japan-U.S. Defense Cooperation," April 27, 2015.
94. Japan Ministry of Defense, "National Defense Program Guidelines for FY 2014 and Beyond," December 17, 2013, http://www.mod.go.jp/j/approach/agenda/guideline/2014/pdf/20131217_e2.pdf.
95. Yuka Hayashi, "Japan's Military Moves Toward Pre-Emptive Strike Capability," *Wall Street Journal*, May 30, 2013.
96. Author interview, June 28, 2013.
97. Pinkston and Sakurai, "Japan Debates Preparing for Future Preemptive Strikes Against North Korea," 120–21.
98. Michishita, "Japan's Response to Nuclear North Korea," 104–105.
99. See Jacques E. Hymans, "Veto Players, Nuclear Energy, and Nonproliferation: Domestic Institutional Barriers to a Japanese Nuclear Bomb," *International Security* 36, no. 2 (Fall 2011): 154–189; and Toshi Yoshihara and James R. Holmes, "Thinking About the Unthinkable," *Naval War College Review* 62, no. 3 (Summer 2009): 59–78.
100. Fintan Hoey, "Japan and Extended Nuclear Deterrence: Security and Non-Proliferation," *Journal of Strategic Studies* 39, no. 4 (June 2016): 485–486.
101. Kurt M. Campbell and Tsuyoshi Sunohara, "Japan: Thinking the Unthinkable," in *The Tipping Point: Why States Reconsider Their Nuclear Choices*, ed. Kurt M. Campbell, Robert J. Einhorn, and Mitchell B. Reiss (Washington, DC: Brookings, 2004), 218–219.
102. Mark Fitzpatrick, *Asia's Latent Nuclear Powers: Japan, South Korea, and Taiwan* (New York: Routledge, 2016), 97–99; and Samuels and Schoff, "Japan's Nuclear Hedge," 240–243.
103. Chester Dawson, "In Japan, Provocative Case for Staying Nuclear," *Wall Street Journal*, October 28, 2011, http://www.wsj.com/articles/SB10001424052970203658804576638392537430156.
104. Barbara Demick, "More South Koreans Support Developing Nuclear Weapons," *Los Angeles Times*, May 18, 2013, http://articles.latimes.com/2013/may/18/world/la-fg-south-korea-nuclear-20130519.

105. Author interview, November 10, 2010.
106. Former minister of defense Shigeru Ishiba argued that nuclear weapons "would naturally mean Japan withdrawing from the NPT. We would not able to obtain nuclear fuel. . . . With dependency on nuclear power for about 40 percent of [our] electricity, we would experience a major decline in economic activities. Japan going nuclear would automatically mean the collapse of the NPT regime and there would be nuclear countries all around us." Quoted in Takubo, "The Role of Nuclear Weapons: Japan, the U.S., and 'Sole Purpose.'"
107. Hoey, "Japan and Extended Nuclear Deterrence," 485.
108. Samuels and Schoff, "Japan's Nuclear Hedge," 236.
109. In October 2016, Japan voted against a UN General Assembly committee measure that called for the banning of nuclear weapons. Japan voted against it because of U.S. pressure, but Japanese Foreign Minister Fumio Kishada noted that Japan would join the effort to outlaw nuclear weapons: "At present, I hope to proactively join the negotiations and firmly present our stance." "U.S., Japan Oppose and China Abstains As U.N. Votes to Launch Talks on Nuclear Arms Ban," *Japan Times*, October 28, 2016, http://www.japantimes.co.jp/news/2016/10/28/world/politics-diplomacy-world/u-s-japan-oppose-china-abstains-u-n-votes-launch-talks-nuclear-arms-ban/.

5. SOUTH KOREA AND THE U.S. NUCLEAR UMBRELLA

1. Andrew O'Neill, *Asia, the U.S., and Extended Nuclear Deterrence: Atomic Umbrellas in the Twenty-First Century* (New York: Routledge, 2013), 61.
2. Richard Nixon, "American Policy in the Pacific: Informal Remarks of President Nixon with Newsmen at Guam," July 25, 1969, *Public Papers of the Presidents: Richard M. Nixon, 1969* (Washington, DC: GPO, 1971), 545–549.
3. Kang Choi and Joon-sung Park, "South Korea: Fears of Abandonment and Entrapment," in *The Long Shadow: Nuclear Weapons and Security in 21st Century Asia*, ed. Muthiah Alagappa (Stanford, CA: Stanford University Press, 2008), 376.
4. Don Oberdorfer, *The Two Koreas* (New York: Basic Books, 1997), 13.
5. See Choi and Park, "South Korea: Fears of Abandonment and Entrapment," 376–378; and Se Young Jang, "The Evolution of U.S. Extended Deterrence and South Korea's Nuclear Ambitions," *Journal of Strategic Studies* 39, no. 4 (June 2016): 502–520.
6. Don Oberdorfer, "Park: Seoul Target of North," *Washington Post*, June 26, 1975.
7. U.S. Department of Defense, "Joint Communique, the Eleventh ROK-U.S. Security Consultative Meeting," October 1978.
8. U.S. Department of Defense, "Thirty-Eighth Security Consultative Meeting Joint Communique," October 20, 2006.

9. "S Korean Official: U.S. Pledge on 'Nuclear Defence' Significant," *Yonhap News*, October 21, 2006.
10. Choi and Park, "South Korea: Fears of Abandonment and Entrapment," 381.
11. Jim Mannion, "U.S. Rebuffs Talk of More Detailed Nuclear Umbrella for South Korea," *AFP*, October 19, 2009.
12. U.S. Department of Defense, "Joint Communique, Forty-First U.S.-ROK Security Consultative Meeting," October 22, 2009.
13. U.S. Department of Defense, "Joint Communique, the Forty-Eighth U.S.-ROK Security Consultative Meeting," October 20, 2016.
14. Author interview, May 22, 2013.
15. Paula Hancocks, "Kim Jong-un Too 'Young and Impulsive': South Korean Defense Minister," *CNN*, June 6, 2016, http://www.cnn.com/2016/06/06/asia/korea-han-minkoo-kim-jong-un/.
16. Chang Kwoun Park, "ROK-U.S. Cooperation in Preparation for Hostile Actions by North Korea in Possession of Nuclear Weapons," *Korean Journal of Defense Analysis* 22, no. 4 (December 2010): 507.
17. Park Hwee-rhak and Kim Byung-ki, "Time to Balance Deterrence, Offense, and Defense? Rethinking South Korea's Strategy Against the North Korean Threat," *Korean Journal of Defense Analysis* 24, no. 4 (December 2012): 522.
18. Park and Kim, "Time to Balance," 518.
19. Author interview, May 20, 2013.
20. Park, "ROK-U.S. Cooperation in Preparation for Hostile Actions by North Korea," 512.
21. Author interview, May 20, 2013.
22. Author interview, May 20, 2013.
23. Author interview, June 20, 2012.
24. "Ruling Party's Floor Leader Calls for Nuclear Armament," *Yonhap News*, February 15, 2016, http://english.yonhapnews.co.kr/news/2016/02/15/0200000000AEN20160215002500315.html.
25. Author interview, November 4, 2010.
26. Author interview, May 22, 2013.
27. Author interview, November 5, 2010.
28. As quoted in Scott Snyder, "Finding a Balance Between Assurances and Abolition: South Korean Views of the Nuclear Posture Review," *Nonproliferation Review* 18, no. 1 (March 2011): 147–163.
29. U.S. Department of Defense, *Nuclear Posture Review Report*, April 2010, http://www.defense.gov/Portals/1/features/defenseReviews/NPR/2010_Nuclear_Posture_Review_Report.pdf, 17.
30. Author interview, November 4, 2010.
31. Author interview, May 21, 2013.

32. Author interview, May 22, 2013.
33. Author interview, June 21, 2010.
34. Brad Roberts, *The Case for U.S. Nuclear Weapons in the Twenty-First Century* (Stanford, CA: Stanford University Press, 2016), 66–67.
35. Author interviews, May 21, 2013.
36. Ibid.
37. Choe Sang-hyun, "In Show of Alliance, American Forces Fly B-52 Bomber Over South Korea," *New York Times*, January 10, 2016, http://www.nytimes.com/2016/01/11/world/asia/south-korea-us-flies-b-52-bomber.html?_r=0.
38. Chang Jae-soon, "S. Korea, U.S. Agree to Launch High-Level 'Extended Deterrence' Dialogue," *Yonhap News*, October 19, 2016, http://english.yonhapnews.co.kr/news/2016/10/19/0200000000AEN20161019010455315.html.
39. Jun Ji-hye, "U.S. Hesitant to Deploy Strategic Weapons," *Korea Times*, October 21, 2016, http://www.koreatimes.co.kr/www/news/nation/2016/10/116_216533.html.
40. U.S. Department of State, "Joint Statement on the Inaugural Meeting of the Extended Deterrence Strategy and Consultation Group (EDSCG)," December 20, 2016, https://www.defense.gov/Portals/1/Documents/pubs/Joint-Statement-for-the-Inaugural-Meeting-of-the-Extended-Deterrence-Strategy-and-Consultation-Group.pdf.
41. Jun Ji-hye, "Ministry's Wordplay on U.S. Strategic Assets," *Korea Times*, December 22, 2016, http://www.koreatimes.co.kr/www/news/nation/2016/12/116_220672.html.
42. Author interview, June 21, 2010.
43. Author interview, June 20, 2012.
44. Scott Snyder, "Finding a Balance Between Assurances and Abolition: South Korean Views of the Nuclear Posture Review," *The Nonproliferation Review* 18, no. 1: 160.
45. Author interview, May 23, 2013
46. Author interview, May 22, 2013.
47. Author interview, May 20, 2013.
48. Author interview, June 21, 2012.
49. Kwon Hyuk-chul, "S. Korea–U.S. to Organize a Joint Committee for Extending Nuclear Deterrence," *Hankyoreh*, October 9, 2010, http://english.hani.co.kr/arti/english_edition/e_northkorea/443035.html.
50. See Terence Roehrig, "Reinforcing Deterrence: The U.S. Military Response to North Korean Provocations," in *Joint U.S.-Korea Academic Studies: Facing Reality in East Asia: Tough Decisions on Competition and Cooperation*, ed. Gilbert Rozman (Washington, DC: Korea Economic Institute, 2015), 221–238.
51. Kwanwoo Jun, "U.S., South Korea Sign Pact on Deterrence Against North," *Wall Street Journal*, October 2, 2013, http://www.wsj.com/articles/SB10001424052702304906704579110891808197868.

52. Choi Hyun-joon, "U.S. and South Korea Agreed to "Tailored Deterrence Strategy" at Meeting in Seoul," *Hankyoreh*, October 3, 2013, http://english.hani.co.kr/arti/english_edition/e_international/605656.html.
53. Anna Fifield, "In Drills, U.S., South Korea Practice Striking North's Nuclear Plants, Leaders," *Washington Post*, March 7, 2016, https://www.washingtonpost.com/world/in-drills-us-south-korea-practice-striking-norths-nuclear-plants/2016/03/06/46e6019d-5f04-4277-9b41-e02fc1c2e801_story.html.
54. Brian Padden, "U.S., South Korea to Practice Offense During Joint Exercises," *Voice of America*, February 22, 2016, http://www.voanews.com/content/us-south-korea-forces-to-practice-offense-during-joint-exercises/3201231.html.
55. David Sanger and Thom Shanker, "U.S. Designs a Korea Response Proportional to the Provocation," *New York Times*, April 7, 2013, http://www.nytimes.com/2013/04/08/world/asia/us-and-south-korea-devise-plan-to-counter-north.html?_r=0.
56. Lee Tae-hoon, "Defense Chief Tells Troops to Act First, Report Later," *Korea Times*, March 1, 2011, http://koreatimes.co.kr/www/news/nation/2011/03/113_82270.html.
57. Robert M. Gates, *Duty: Memoirs of a Secretary at War* (New York: Knopf, 2014), 497.
58. For example, see David E. Sanger, "Despite Obama's Moves, Asian Nations Skeptical of U.S. Commitment," *New York Times*, May 23, 2016, http://www.nytimes.com/2016/05/24/world/asia/vietnam-arms-embargo-obama.html?_r=0; and Kim Jiyoon, John J. Lee, and Kang Chungku, "Measuring a Giant: South Korean Perceptions of the United States," *Asan Institute for Policy Studies*, April 20, 2015, http://en.asaninst.org/contents/measuring-a-giant-south-korean-perceptions-of-the-united-states/.
59. Author interview, May 3, 2016.
60. For example, see Brad Roberts's discussion of three possible North Korean theories of victory in *The Case for U.S. Nuclear Weapons in the Twenty-First Century*, 60–69.
61. Kim Dae-joong, "Time for S. Korea to Develop Its Own Nuclear Arms," *Chosun Ilbo*, January 11, 2011, http://english.chosun.com/site/data/html_dir/2011/01/11/2011011101486.html.
62. Terence Roehrig, "North Korea's Nuclear Weapons Program: Motivations, Strategy, and Doctrine," in *Strategy in the Second Nuclear Age: Power, Ambition, and the Ultimate Weapon*, ed. Toshi Yoshihara and James Holmes (Washington, DC: Georgetown University Press, 2012), 93.
63. Author interview, May 11, 2015.
64. Patrick M. Morgan, *Deterrence Now* (Cambridge: Cambridge University Press, 2003), 270–272.
65. ROK Ministry of National Defense, *2014 Defense White Paper*, 60–63.
66. Ibid., 62.

67. "S. Korea Unveils Plan to Raze Pyongyang in Case of Signs of Nuclear Attack," *Yonhap News*, September 11, 2016, http://english.yonhapnews.co.kr/national/2016/09/11/65/0301000000AEN20160911000500315F.html.
68. Daniel Pinkston, "The New South Korean Missile Guidelines and Future Prospects for Regional Stability," *International Crisis Group*, October 25, 2012, http://blog.crisisgroup.org/asia/2012/10/25/the-new-south-korean-missile-guidelines-and-future-prospects-for-regional-stability/.
69. Ibid.
70. Choe Sang-hun, "U.S. Agrees to Let South Korea Extend Range of Ballistic Missiles," *New York Times*, October 7, 2012, http://www.nytimes.com/2012/10/08/world/asia/us-agrees-to-let-south-korea-extend-missile-range.html?_r=0.
71. "Defense Chief Calls for Early Deployment of 800-Km Missiles," *Yonhap News*, January 31, 2013, http://english.yonhapnews.co.kr/fullstory/2013/01/31/43/4500000000AEN20130131011100315F.HTML.
72. Jack Kim, "South Korea Extending Ballistic Missile Range to Counter North's Threat," *Reuters*, April 4, 2014, http://www.reuters.com/article/2014/04/04/us-korea-missile-idUSBREA3305H20140404.
73. Bradley Perrett, "South Korea Tests Lengthened Hyunmu 2 Missile," *Aviation Week and Space Technology*, June 12, 2015, http://aviationweek.com/defense/south-korea-tests-lengthened-hyunmu-2-missile-0.
74. Ju-min Park and Kiyoshi Takenaka, "South Korea Says New Cruise Missile Can Strike North As Regional Tensions Rise," *NBC News*, February 14, 2013, http://www.theinfostride.com/forum/index.php?topic=116363.0.
75. "S. Korean Navy's Aegis Destroyers to Get Upgraded Missile Launch Systems," *Yonhap News*, May 29, 2016, http://english.yonhapnews.co.kr/news/2016/05/29/0200000000AEN20160529004000315.html.
76. Gregory Elich, "Threat to China: Pressure on South Korea to Join U.S. Anti-Ballistic Missile Defense System," *Global Research*, July 1, 2014, http://www.globalresearch.ca/threat-to-china-pressure-on-south-korea-to-join-u-s-anti-ballistic-missile-defense-system/5389304.
77. Andrea Shalal, "Lockheed Sees PAC-3 Missile Deal with South Korea in Coming Months," *Reuters*, March 31, 2015, http://www.reuters.com/article/us-usa-lockheed-martin-southkorea-idUSKBN0MR2RC20150331.
78. Yi Whan-woo, "U.S. Approves PAC-3 Sale to Seoul," *Korea Times*, November 7, 2014, http://www.koreatimes.co.kr/www/news/nation/2015/06/205_167757.html.
79. "L-SAM Long-Range Surface-to-Air Missile," *Global Security.org*, February 21, 2016, http://www.globalsecurity.org/military/world/rok/l-sam.htm.
80. "China Criticizes U.S. Missile Defense Radar in Japan," *Reuters*, October 23, 2014, http://www.reuters.com/article/2014/10/23/us-china-japan-usa-idUSKCN0IC16P20141023.

81. "S. Korea, U.S. Hold Off THAAD Talks," *Yonhap News*, February 23, 2016, http://english.yonhapnews.co.kr/news/2016/02/23/0200000000AEN20160223003953315.html?input=www.tweeter.com.
82. Choe Sang-han, "South Korea Tells China Not to Intervene in Missile-Defense System Talks," *New York Times*, February 24, 2016, http://www.nytimes.com/2016/02/25/world/asia/south-north-korea-us-missile-defense-thaad-china.html?_r=0.
83. Ibid.
84. Kim So-hyun, "Calls Mounting for Return of U.S. Tactical Nukes," *Korea Herald*, March 1, 2011, http://www.koreaherald.com/view.php?ud=20110301000208.
85. As quoted in Toby Dalton, Byun Sunggee, and Lee Sang Tae, "South Korea Debates Nuclear Options," *Carnegie Endowment for International Peace*, April 27, 2016, http://carnegieendowment.org/2016/04/27/south-korea-debates-nuclear-options-pub-63455.
86. Cheon Seongwhun, "Changing Dynamics of U.S. Extended Deterrence on the Korean Peninsula," *Pacific Focus* 26, no. 1 (April 2011): 37–64.
87. Julian Borger, "South Korea Considers Return of U.S. Tactical Nuclear Weapons," *The Guardian*, November 22, 2010, http://www.theguardian.com/world/2010/nov/22/south-korea-us-tactical-weapons-nuclear.
88. Ser Myo-ja, "U.S. Arms Control Chief Backs Nuke Redeployment," *Korea Joong Ang Daily*, March 1, 2011, http://koreajoongangdaily.joins.com/news/article/article.aspx?aid=2932857.
89. Hwang Doo-hyong, "U.S. Has No Plans to Redeploy Tactical Nukes to S. Korea: White House," *Yonhap News*, May 1, 2011, http://english.yonhapnews.co.kr/national/2011/03/01/39/0301000000AEN20110301000300315F.HTML.
90. The amendment's language, in section 1046, called for the secretary of defense to submit a report on the "feasibility and strategic value of deploying additional conventional and nuclear forces to the Western Pacific region to ensure the presence of a robust conventional and nuclear capability, including a forward-deployed nuclear capability, of the United States in response to the ballistic missile and nuclear weapons development of North Korea and the other belligerent actions North Korea has made against allies of the United States." *National Defense Authorization Act for Fiscal Year 2013*, 112th Cong., 2d sess., H.R. 4310, https://www.gpo.gov/fdsys/pkg/BILLS-112hr4310enr/pdf/BILLS-112hr4310enr.pdf, 303.
91. Terence Roehrig, *From Deterrence to Engagement: The U.S. Defense Commitment to South Korea* (Lanham, MD: Lexington Books, 2006), 192–193.
92. Ernest W. Lefever, *Nuclear Arms in the Third World* (Washington, DC: Brookings Institution, 1979), 85–86.
93. Robert Gillette, "U.S. Squelched Apparent S. Korea A-Bomb Drive," *Los Angeles Times*, November 4, 1978.

94. Leonard S. Spector, *Nuclear Ambitions* (Boulder, CO: Westview, 1990), 122; Lefever, *Nuclear Arms in the Third World*, 130.
95. Mark Fitzpatrick, *Asia's Latent Nuclear Powers: Japan, South Korea, and Taiwan* (New York: Routledge, 2016).
96. K. J. Kwon, "Under Threat, South Koreans Mull Nuclear Weapons," *CNN*, March 18, 2013, http://www.cnn.com/2013/03/18/world/asia/south-korea-nuclear/.
97. Kim Jiyoon and Karl Friedhoff, "The Fallout: South Korean Public Opinion Following North Korea's Third Nuclear Test," *Asan Institute for Policy Studies*, February 24, 2013, http://en.asaninst.org/contents/issue-brief-no-46-the-fallout-south-korean-public-opinion-following-north-koreas-third-nuclear-test/.
98. Yi Whan-woo, "NK Test Stirs Call for Nuclear Armament," *Korea Times*, January 18, 2016, http://koreatimes.co.kr/www/news/nation/2016/01/113_195722.html.
99. Dalton, Sunggee, and Tae, "South Korea Debates Nuclear Options."
100. Park Geun-hye, "Statement at the Third Nuclear Security Summit," *Korea.Net*, March 25, 2014, http://www.korea.net/Government/Briefing-Room/Presidential-Speeches/view?articleId=118516.
101. Author interview, June 20, 2012.
102. Choi and Park, "South Korea: Fears of Abandonment and Entrapment," 390.
103. Author interview, May 21, 2013.
104. Mark Hibbs, "Will South Korea Go Nuclear?" *Foreign Policy*, March 15, 2013, http://foreignpolicy.com/2013/03/15/will-south-korea-go-nuclear/.
105. "S. Korea's Nuclear Armament Would Make the United States Safer: Expert," *Korea Times*, May 4, 2016.
106. Author interview, May 20, 2013.
107. See Mark Fitzpatrick, "Why South Korea Should Not 'Go Nuclear,'" *Korea Herald*, February 19, 2016, http://www.koreaherald.com/view.php?ud=20160219000241; Terence Roehrig, "The Case for a Nuclear-Free South," *Korea JoongAng Daily*, June 19, 2014, http://koreajoongangdaily.joins.com/news/article/article.aspx?aid=2990820; and Peter Hayes and Chung-in Moon, "Should South Korea Go Nuclear?" *Nautilus Institute*, July 28, 2014, http://nautilus.org/napsnet/napsnet-policy-forum/should-south-korea-go-nuclear/.

6. THE U.S. NUCLEAR UMBRELLA: PLANNING, CAPABILITIES, AND CREDIBILITY

1. Robert M. Gates, "Strengthening Security Partnerships in the Asia-Pacific," Ninth IISS Asian Security Summit, *The Shangri-La Dialogue*, June 5, 2010, http://www.iiss.org/conferences/the-shangri-la-dialogue/shangri-la-dialogue-2010/plenary-session-speeches/first-plenary-session/robert-gates/.

2. White House, "Remarks by President Obama and Prime Minister Abe of Japan at Hiroshima Peace Memorial," May 27, 2016, https://www.whitehouse.gov/the-press-office/2016/05/27/remarks-president-obama-and-prime-minister-abe-japan-hiroshima-peace.
3. William J. Broad, "Reduction of Nuclear Arsenal Has Slowed Under Obama, Report Finds," *New York Times*, May 26, 2016, http://www.nytimes.com/2016/05/27/science/nuclear-weapons-obama-united-states.html.
4. John Foster Dulles, "The Strategy of Massive Retaliation," *Department of State Bulletin*, January 12, 1954.
5. Ibid.
6. Fred Kaplan, *The Wizards of Armageddon* (New York: Simon & Schuster, 1983), 185–200.
7. Herman Kahn, *On Thermonuclear War* (Piscataway, NJ: Transaction Publishers, 2007).
8. Henry Kissinger, *The Necessity for Choice* (New York: Doubleday, 1962), 518.
9. "Statement of Secretary of Defense Melvin R. Laird Before the Senate Armed Services Committee on the FY 1973 Defense Budget and FY 1973–1977 Program," February 15, 1972 (Washington DC: GPO, 1972), 79.
10. Terence Roehrig, *From Deterrence to Engagement : The U.S. Defense Commitment to South Korea* (Lanham, MD: Lexington, 2006), 188–193.
11. George W. Bush, *The National Security Strategy of the United States*, September 2002, https://www.state.gov/documents/organization/63562.pdf, 13.
12. M. Elaine Bunn, "Can Deterrence Be Tailored?" *Strategic Forum*, no. 225 (National Defense University, January 2007).
13. U.S. Department of Defense, *Quadrennial Defense Review Report*, February 6, 2006, http://archive.defense.gov/pubs/pdfs/QDR20060203.pdf, 49. Hereafter 2006 QDR.
14. U.S. Department of Defense, *2001 Nuclear Posture Review*, http://archive.defense.gov/news/Jan2002/d20020109npr.pdf.
15. 2006 QDR, 49.
16. U.S. Department of Defense, "Joint Communique, Fortieth U.S.-ROK Security Consultative Meeting," October 17, 2008, http://www.globalsecurity.org/military//library/news/2008/10/40thscm-jointcommunique.pdf.
17. U.S. Department of Defense, "Joint Communique, Forty-First U.S.-ROK Security Consultative Meeting," October 22, 2009.
18. U.S. Department of Defense, *Nuclear Posture Review Report*, April 2010, https://www.defense.gov/Portals/1/features/defenseReviews/NPR/2010_Nuclear_Posture_Review_Report.pdf, 31.
19. Ibid., 17.
20. Ibid., 16.

21. "A Conversation with General C. Robert Kehler," *Council on Foreign Relations*, May 30, 2012, http://www.cfr.org/united-states/conversation-general-c-robert-kehler/p35267.
22. Michael Chernin and Sabin Ray, "On the Frontline of U.S. Nuclear Policy with Under Secretary Rose Gottemoeller," *Brown Journal of World Affairs* 21, no. 1 (Fall 2014): 255–256.
23. Author interview, May 23, 2013.
24. For a discussion of these definitional distinctions, see Amy Woolf, "Nonstrategic Nuclear Weapons," *Congressional Research Service*, RL32572, February 23, 2015, 6–8.
25. In the past, each missile wing consisted of 150 missiles, but the Air Force is in the process of reducing the force to 400 to meet New START limits. See Amy F. Woolf, "U.S. Strategic Nuclear Forces: Background, Developments, and Issues," *Congressional Research Service*, March 10, 2016.
26. U.S. Department of State, Bureau of Arms Control, Verification and Compliance, "New START Treaty Aggregate Numbers of Strategic Offensive Arms," January 1, 2015.
27. U.S. Department of State, "New START," http://www.state.gov/t/avc/newstart/index.htm.
28. Hans M. Kristensen, "W80-1 Warhead Selected for New Nuclear Cruise Missile," *Federation of American Scientists*, October 10, 2014, https://fas.org/blogs/security/2014/10/w80-1_lrso/.
29. U.S. Department of Defense, *Nuclear Posture Review Report*, April 2010, 28.
30. Hans M. Kristensen, "Non-Strategic Nuclear Weapons," Special Report No. 3, *Federation of American Scientists*, May 2012. https://fas.org/blogs/security/2012/05/nonstrategicnukes/.
31. See Woolf, "Nonstrategic Nuclear Weapons"; and Tom Nichols, Douglas Stuart, and Jeffrey D. McCausland, eds., *Tactical Nuclear Weapons and NATO* (Carlisle, PA: Strategic Studies Institute, U.S. Army War College, April 2012), http://www.strategicstudiesinstitute.army.mil/pdffiles/PUB1103.pdf.
32. Kristensen, "Non-Strategic Nuclear Weapons," 14.
33. U.S. Air Force, "AGM-86B/C/D Missiles," May 24, 2010, http://www.af.mil/AboutUs/FactSheets/Display/tabid/224/Article/104612/agm-86bcd-missiles.aspx.
34. Mike Martin, "Air Force Reveals B-21 Long Range Strike Bomber," *U.S. Air Force*, February 26, 2016, http://www.af.mil/News/ArticleDisplay/tabid/223/Article/673784/air-force-reveals-b-21-long-range-strike-bomber.aspx.
35. Hans M. Kristensen, "W80-1 Warhead Selected for New Nuclear Cruise Missile," *Federation of American Scientists*, October 10, 2014, http://fas.org/blogs/security/2014/10/w80-1_lrso/.

36. Greg Thielmann, "Nuclear Cruise Missiles: Asset or Liability?" *Arms Control Association*, March 5, 2015, http://www.armscontrol.org/system/files/Threat_Assessment_Brief_Nuclear_Cruise_Missiles_Asset_or_Liability.pdf.
37. "U.S. B-2 Bombers Conduct Extended Deterrence Mission to the Republic of Korea," *USFK*, March 28, 2013, http://www.afgsc.af.mil/News/ArticleDisplay/tabid/2612/Article/454647/us-b-2-bombers-conduct-extended-deterrence-mission-to-the-republic-of-korea.aspx.
38. Author interview, June 21, 2012.
39. George H. Quester, *Nuclear First Strike: Consequences of a Broken Taboo* (Baltimore: Johns Hopkins University Press, 2006), 112.
40. "Oral History: Charles Horner," *Frontline, PBS*, http://www.pbs.org/wgbh/pages/frontline/gulf/oral/horner/1.html.
41. Colin L. Powell, *My American Journey* (New York: Random House, 1995), 486.
42. Nina Tannenwald, *The Nuclear Taboo: The United States and the Non-Use of Nuclear Weapons Since 1945* (Cambridge: Cambridge University Press, 2007), 361–362.
43. T. V. Paul, *The Tradition of Non-Use of Nuclear Weapons* (Stanford, CA: Stanford University Press, 2009), 197.
44. T. V. Paul, "Self-Deterrence: Nuclear Weapons and the Enduring Credibility Challenge," *International Journal* 7, no. 1 (March 2016): 24.
45. Robert S. McNamara, "The Military Role of Nuclear Weapons: Perceptions and Misperceptions," *Foreign Affairs* 62, no. 1 (Fall 1983): 79.
46. Daryl G. Press, Scott D. Sagan, and Benjamin A. Valentino, "Atomic Aversion: Experimental Evidence on Taboos, Traditions, and the Non-Use of Nuclear Weapons," *American Political Science Review* 107, no. 1 (February 2013): 189.
47. George Bush and Brent Scowcroft, *A World Transformed* (New York: Knopf, 1998), 463.
48. Quester, *Nuclear First Strike*, 115.
49. Scott D. Sagan, "Realist Perspectives on Ethical Norms and Weapons of Mass Destruction," in *Ethics and Weapons of Mass Destruction: Religious and Secular Perspectives*, ed. Sohail H. Hashmi and Steven P. Lee (Cambridge: Cambridge University Press, 2004), 91.
50. Paul, *The Tradition of Non-Use of Nuclear Weapons*, 212.
51. Ibid.
52. Thomas M. Nichols, *No Use: Nuclear Weapons and U.S. National Security* (Philadelphia: University of Pennsylvania Press, 2013), 161–162.
53. Author interview, June 21, 2010.
54. Alison A. Kaufman and Daniel M. Hartnett, "Managing Conflict: Examining Recent PLA Writings on Escalation Control," *CNA*, February 2016, https://www.cna.org/cna_files/pdf/DRM-2015-U-009963-Final3.pdf.

55. Justin McCurry and Tania Branigan, "Obama says U.S. Will Defend Japan in Island Dispute with China," *The Guardian*, April 24, 2014, http://www.theguardian.com/world/2014/apr/24/obama-in-japan-backs-status-quo-in-island-dispute-with-china.
56. U.S. Department of Defense, "Air-Sea Battle: Service Collaboration to Address Anti-Access and Area Denial Challenges," May 2013, http://archive.defense.gov/pubs/ASB-ConceptImplementation-Summary-May-2013.pdf.
57. Raoul Heinrichs, "AirSea Battle: Dangerous, Costly and Excessive," *PNYX*, August 17, 2011.
58. Joshua Rovner, "AirSea Battle and Escalation Risks," Changing Military Dynamics in East Asia Policy Brief 12, January 2012, *eScholarship*, http://escholarship.org/uc/item/08m367zt.
59. David C. Gompert, Astrid Stuth Cevallos, and Cristina L. Garafola, "War with China: Thinking Through the Unthinkable," *RAND Corporation*, 2016, http://www.rand.org/pubs/research_reports/RR1140.html, ix.
60. Author interview, February 20, 2014.
61. Patrick M. Morgan, *Deterrence: A Conceptual Analysis*, 2d ed. (Beverly Hills, CA: Sage, 1983), 27–47.
62. Richard Wyn Jones, *Security, Strategy, and Critical Theory* (Boulder, CO: Lynne Rienner, 1999), 137.
63. "Report to the President by the Committee on Nuclear Proliferation," *Foreign Relations of the United States, 1964–1968*, vol. 11, document 64 (January 21, 1965): 173.
64. Ibid., 174.
65. Ibid., 177.
66. Jacques Hymans, *The Psychology of Nuclear Proliferation: Identity, Emotions and Foreign Policy* (Cambridge: Cambridge University Press, 2006); John E. Mueller, *Atomic Obsession: Nuclear Alarmism from Hiroshima to Al-Qaeda* (Oxford: Oxford University Press, 2009); and Phillip Bleek, "Does Proliferation Beget Proliferation? Why Nuclear Dominoes Rarely Fall" (Ph.D. dissertation, Georgetown University, 2010).
67. Nicholas L. Miller, "Nuclear Dominoes: A Self-Defeating Prophecy," *Security Studies* 23, no. 1 (2014): 33–73; and Gene Gerzhoy, "Alliance Coercion and Nuclear Restraint: How the United States Thwarted West Germany's Nuclear Ambitions," *International Security* 39, no. 4 (Spring 2015): 91–129.
68. Miller, "Nuclear Dominoes," 72.
69. Gerzhoy, "Alliance Coercion and Nuclear Restraint"; and Francis J. Gavin, "Blasts from the Past: Proliferation Lessons from the 1960s," *International Security* 29, no. 3 (Winter 2004/05): 100–135.
70. Roehrig, *From Deterrence to Engagement*, 149.

71. Ronald Reagan, *The National Security Strategy of the United States*, January 1987, http://nssarchive.us/NSSR/1987.pdf.
72. Barack Obama, *National Security Strategy*, February 2015, http://nssarchive.us/wp-content/uploads/2015/02/2015.pdf.
73. Author interview, May 20, 2013.
74. Author interview, November 3, 2010.
75. U.S. Department of Defense, *Nuclear Posture Review*, April 2010, 31.
76. Van Jackson, "The U.S. Doesn't Need Tactical Nuclear Weapons in Asia," *The Diplomat*, July 2, 2015, http://thediplomat.com/2015/07/the-us-doesnt-need-tactical-nuclear-weapons-in-asia/.
77. Jonathan Reshon and Jennifer S. Lerner, "Decision-Making, the Role of Emotions in Foreign Policy," in *The Encyclopedia of Peace Psychology*, ed. Daniel J. Christie (Indianapolis: Blackwell, 2012); Rose McDermott, "Emotions in Foreign Policy Decision Making," in *Oxford Research Encyclopedia: Politics*, ed. William R. Thompson (Oxford: Oxford University Press, 2016); and Hymans, *The Psychology of Nuclear Proliferation*.
78. Author interview, May 20, 2014.
79. Author interview, July 9, 2014.
80. Author interview, May 23, 2013.

7. IMPLICATIONS FOR SECURITY AND EXTENDED DETERRENCE IN NORTHEAST ASIA

1. U.S. Department of Defense, *Nuclear Posture Review Report*, April 2010, http://www.defense.gov/Portals/1/features/defenseReviews/NPR/2010_Nuclear_Posture_Review_Report.pdf, 16. Hereafter the NPR 2010.
2. Van Jackson, "Raindrops Keep Falling on My Nuclear Umbrella," *Foreign Policy*, May 18, 2015, http://foreignpolicy.com/2015/05/18/raindrops-keep-falling-on-my-nuclear-umbrella-us-japan-south-north-korea/.
3. David Santoro and John K. Warden, "Assuring Japan and South Korea in the Second Nuclear Age," *Washington Quarterly* 38, no. 1 (Spring 2015): 147–165.
4. Paul J. Saunders, "Extended Deterrence and Security in East Asia: A U.S.-Japan-South Korea Dialogue," Fourth Meeting of the Contemporary American Studies project, *The Tokyo Foundation*, January 23, 2013, http://www.tokyofoundation.org/en/articles/2013/extended-deterrence-and-security-in-east-asia.
5. Patrick M. Morgan, *Deterrence Now* (Cambridge: Cambridge University Press, 2003), 270–272.
6. Kier Lieber and Daryl Press, "The Nukes We Need," *Foreign Affairs* 88, no. 6 (November/December 2009): 39–51; and Clark Murdock, Samuel J. Brannon, Thomas Karako, and Angela Weaver, *Project Atom: A Competitive Strategies*

Approach to Defining U.S. Nuclear Strategy and Posture for 2025–2050 (Washington, DC: Center for Strategic and International Studies, May 2015), https://csis-prod.s3.amazonaws.com/s3fs-public/legacy_files/files/publication/150716_Murdock_ProjectAtom_Web_Rev2.pdf.
7. Murdock et al., *Project Atom*.
8. Richard J. Samuels and James L. Schoff, "Japan's Nuclear Hedge: Beyond 'Allergy' and Breakout," in *Strategic Asia 2013–14: Asia in the Second Nuclear Age*, ed. Ashley J. Tellis, Abraham M. Denmark, and Travis Tanner (Seattle: National Bureau of Asian Research, 2013), 245–246.
9. Patrick M. Morgan, "Considerations Bearing on a Possible Retraction of the American Nuclear Umbrella Over the ROK," National Committee on North Korea, 2009, http://www.ncnk.org/resources/publications/Morgan%20Considerations%20Bearing_on_a_Possible_Retraction_of_the_American_Nuclear_Umbrella.pdf.
10. 2010 NPR, 32–33.
11. Robert Jervis, *The Illogic of American Nuclear Strategy* (Ithaca, NY: Cornell University Press, 1984), 156.
12. Denis Healey, *The Time of My Life* (New York: W. W. Norton, 1989), 243.
13. Paul C. Avey, "Who's Afraid of the Bomb? The Role of Nuclear Non-Use Norms in Confrontations Between Nuclear and Non-Nuclear Opponents," *Security Studies* 24, no. 4 (June 2016): 563.
14. Morgan, "Considerations Bearing on a Possible Retraction of the American Nuclear Umbrella Over the ROK," 5–6.
15. Healey, *The Time of My Life*, 243.
16. 2010 NPR, 31.
17. Chester Dawson, "In Japan, Provocative Case for Staying Nuclear," *Wall Street Journal*, October 28, 2011, http://www.wsj.com/articles/SB10001424052970203658804576638392537430156.
18. "Transcript: Donald Trump Expounds on His Foreign Policy Views," *New York Times*, March 26, 2016, http://www.nytimes.com/2016/03/27/us/politics/donald-trump-transcript.html?_r=0.
19. "Milwaukee Republican Presidential Town Hall," *CNN*, March 29, 2016, http://cnnpressroom.blogs.cnn.com/2016/03/29/full-rush-transcript-donald-trump-cnn-milwaukee-republican-presidential-town-hall/.
20. David Nakamura, "White House Denounces Trump's Asian Nuclear Idea as 'Catastrophic,'" *Washington Post*, March 31, 2016, https://www.washingtonpost.com/politics/white-house-denounces-trumps-asian-nuclear-idea-as-catastrophic/2016/03/31/c80226d4-f760-11e5-a3ce-f06b5ba21f33_story.html.

Selected Bibliography

DETERRENCE AND NUCLEAR WEAPONS

Alagappa, Muthiah, ed. *The Long Shadow: Nuclear Weapons and Security in 21st Century Asia*. Stanford: Stanford University Press, 2008.

Arreguin-Toft, Ivan. "Unconventional Deterrence: How the Weak Deter the Strong." In *Complex Deterrence: Strategy in the Global Age*, ed. T. V. Paul, Patrick M. Morgan, and James J. Wirtz. Chicago: University of Chicago Press, 2009.

Avey, Paul C. "Who's Afraid of the Bomb? The Role of Nuclear Non-Use Norms in Confrontations Between Nuclear and Non-Nuclear Opponents." *Security Studies* 24, no. 4 (June 2016): 563–596.

Bleek, Phillip. "Does Proliferation Beget Proliferation? Why Nuclear Dominoes Rarely Fall." Ph.D. diss., Georgetown University, 2010.

Bracken, Paul. *The Second Nuclear Age: Strategy, Danger, and the New Power Politics*. New York: St. Martin's, 2012.

Brodie, Bernard, ed. *The Absolute Weapons: Atomic Power and World Order*. New York: Harcourt Brace, 1946.

Bush, Richard. "The U.S. Policy of Extended Deterrence in East Asia: History, Current Views, and Implications." *Brookings*. February 2011. https://www.brookings.edu/wp-content/uploads/2016/06/02_arms_control_bush.pdf.

Cimbala, Stephen J. *Nuclear Strategizing: Deterrence and Reality*. New York: Praeger, 1988.

Crawford, Timothy W. "Endurance of Extended Deterrence." In *Complex Deterrence: Strategy in the Global Age*, ed. T. V. Paul, Patrick M. Morgan, and James Wirtz. Chicago: University of Chicago Press, 2009.

Dorff, Robert H., and Joseph R. Cerami. "Deterrence and Competitive Strategies: A New Look at an Old Concept." In *Deterrence in the 21st Century*, ed. Max G. Manwaring. London: Frank Cass, 2001.

Fettweis, Christopher J. "Credibility and the War on Terror." *Political Science Quarterly* 112, no. 4 (Winter 2007–08): 607–663.

———. "On the Consequences of Failure in Iraq." *Survival* 49, no. 4 (December 2007): 83–98.

Fitzpatrick, Mark. *Asia's Latent Nuclear Powers: Japan, South Korea, and Taiwan*. New York: Routledge, 2016.

Garnham, David. "Extending Deterrence with German Nuclear Weapons." *International Security* 10, no. 1 (Summer 1985): 96–110.

Gavin, Francis J. "Blasts from the Past: Proliferation Lessons from the 1960s." *International Security* 29, no. 3 (Winter 2004–05): 100–135.

George, Alexander L., and Richard Smoke. *Deterrence in American Foreign Policy: Theory and Practice*. New York: Columbia University Press, 1974.

Gerson, Michael S. "Conventional Deterrence in the Second Nuclear Age." *Parameters*, Autumn 2009, 32–48.

Gerzhoy, Gene. "Alliance Coercion and Nuclear Restraint: How the United States Thwarted West Germany's Nuclear Ambitions." *International Security* 39, no. 4 (Spring 2015): 91–129.

Haggard, Stephan. "Nuclear Talk: Leon Panetta's Worthy Fights: A Memoir of Leadership in War and Peace." *North Korea: Witness to Transformation Blog*. November 20, 2014. https://piie.com/blogs/north-korea-witness-transformation/nuclear-talk-leon-panettas-worthy-fights-memoir-leadership.

Healey, Denis. *The Time of My Life*. New York: Norton, 1989.

Huth, Paul. "Extended Deterrence and the Outbreak of War." *American Political Science Review* 82, no. 2 (June 1988): 436–437.

Huth, Paul, and Bruce Russett. "What Makes Deterrence Work?" *World Politics* 36, no. 4 (July 1984): 496–526.

Hymans, Jacques. *The Psychology of Nuclear Proliferation: Identity, Emotions, and Foreign Policy*. Cambridge: Cambridge University Press, 2006.

International Institute of Strategic Studies. *Military Balance 2016*. Oxford: Routledge, 2016.

Jervis, Robert. *The Illogic of American Nuclear Strategy*. Ithaca, NY: Cornell University Press, 1984.

———. *The Meaning of the Nuclear Revolution: Statecraft and the Prospect of Armageddon*. Ithaca, NY: Cornell University Press, 1989.

———. "The Political Effects of Nuclear Weapons: A Comment." *International Security* 13, no. 2 (fall 1988): 80–90.

Jervis, Robert, Richard Ned Lebow, and Janice Gross Stein. *Psychology and Deterrence*. Baltimore: Johns Hopkins University Press, 1985.
Kaufmann, William W. *The Requirements of Deterrence*. Princeton, NJ: Center for International Studies, 1954.
Keifer, Michael H., Kurt Guthe, and Thomas Scheber, "Assuring South Korea and Japan As the Role and Number of U.S. Nuclear Weapons Are Reduced." *Defense Threat Reduction Agency*. January 2011. https://www.hsdl.org/?view&did=716179.
Kissinger, Henry. *For the Record: Selected Statements, 1977–1980*. Boston: Little, Brown, 1981.
Lebow, Richard Ned, and Janice Gross Stein. "Rational Deterrence Theory: I Think, Therefore I Deter." *World Politics* 41, no. 2 (January 1989): 208–224.
Lewis, Jeffrey. "No, the U.S. Doesn't Have Plans to Nuke North Korea." *Foreign Policy*. October 17, 2014. http://foreignpolicy.com/2014/10/17/no-the-u-s-doesnt-have-plans-to-nuke-north-korea/.
Liddell Hart, B. H. *Deterrent or Defense: A Fresh Look at the West's Military Position*. New York: Praeger, 1960.
Lieber, Keir A., and Daryl G. Press. "The Nukes We Need: Preserving the American Deterrent." *Foreign Affairs* 88, no. 6 (November–December 2009): 39–51.
Manning, Robert A. *The Future of U.S. Extended Deterrence in Asia to 2025*. Washington, DC: Atlantic Council, 2014. https://www.files.ethz.ch/isn/184441/Future_US_Ext_Det_in_Asia.pdf.
Mearsheimer, John J. *Conventional Deterrence*. Ithaca, NY: Cornell University Press, 1983.
Medcalf, Rory, ed. "Weathering Change: The Future of Extended Nuclear Deterrence." *Lowy Institute*. 2011. https://www.lowyinstitute.org/sites/default/files/pubfiles/Medcalf,_Weathering_change_1.pdf.
Mercer, Jonathan. *Reputation in International Politics*. Ithaca, NY: Cornell University Press, 1996.
Miller, Nicholas L. "Nuclear Dominoes: A Self-Defeating Prophecy." *Security Studies* 23, no. 1 (2014): 33–73.
Morgan, Patrick M. *Deterrence: A Conceptual Analysis*, 2d ed. Beverly Hills, CA: Sage, 1983.
——. *Deterrence Now*. Cambridge: Cambridge University Press, 2003.
Mueller, John E. *Atomic Obsession: Nuclear Alarmism from Hiroshima to Al-Qaeda*. Oxford University Press, 2009.
Murdoch, Clark, Samuel J. Brannen, Thomas Karako, and Angela Weaver. "Project Atom: A Competitive Strategic Approach to Defining U.S. Nuclear Strategy and Posture for 2025–2050." *Center for Strategic and International Studies*. May 2015. https://csis-prod.s3.amazonaws.com/s3fs-public/legacy_files/files/publication/150601_Murdock_ProjectAtom_Web.pdf.

Narang, Vipin. *Nuclear Strategy in the Modern Era: Regional Power and International Conflict.* Princeton, NJ: Princeton University Press, 2014.

O'Neil, Andrew. *Asia, the U.S. and Extended Deterrence: Atomic Umbrellas in the Twenty-First Century.* London: Routledge, 2013.

Paul, T. V. "Self-Deterrence: Nuclear Weapons and the Enduring Credibility Challenge." *International Journal* 7, no. 1 (March 2016): 20–40.

———. *The Tradition of Non-Use of Nuclear Weapons.* Stanford, CA: Stanford University Press, 2009.

Paul, T. V., Patrick M. Morgan, and James J. Wirtz, eds. *Complex Deterrence: Strategy in the Global Age.* Chicago: University of Chicago Press, 2009.

Press, Daryl G. *Calculating Credibility: How Leaders Assess Military Threats.* Ithaca, NY: Cornell University Press, 2005.

Quester, George H. *Deterrence Before Hiroshima: The Airpower Background of Modern Strategy.* New York: Wiley, 1966.

———. *Nuclear First Strike: Consequences of a Broken Taboo.* Baltimore: Johns Hopkins University Press, 2006.

Reiss, Mitchell. *Without the Bomb: The Politics of Nuclear Nonproliferation.* New York: Columbia University Press, 1988.

Roberts, Brad. *The Case for Nuclear Weapons in the Twenty-First Century.* Stanford, CA: Stanford University Press, 2015.

Roehrig, Terence. "Restraining the Hegemon: North Korea, the United States, and Asymmetrical Deterrence." *Pacific Focus* 20, no. 2 (Fall 2005): 7–51.

Russset, Bruce. "The Calculus of Deterrence." *Journal of Conflict Resolution* 11, no. 2 (June 1963): 97–109.

Sagan, Scott D. "Realist Perspectives on Ethical Norms and Weapons of Mass Destruction." In *Ethics and Weapons of Mass Destruction: Religious and Secular Perspectives,* ed. Sohail H. Hashmi and Steven P. Lee. Cambridge: Cambridge University Press, 2004.

Sagan, Scott D., and Kenneth N. Waltz. *The Spread of Nuclear Weapons: A Debate Renewed.* New York: Norton, 2003.

Schelling, Thomas C. *Arms and Influence.* New Haven, CT: Yale University Press, 1966.

———. "The Role of Nuclear Weapons." In *Turning Point: The Gulf War and U.S. Military Strategy,* ed. L. Benjamin Ederington and Michael J. Mazarr. Boulder, CO: Westview, 1994.

———. *The Strategy of Conflict.* London: Oxford University Press, 1960.

Shultz, George P., William J. Perry, Henry A. Kissinger, and Sam Nunn. "Kissinger, Shultz, Perry, & Nunn Call for a World Free of Nuclear Weapons." *Wall Street Journal,* January 4, 2007.

Smith, Derek. *Deterring America: Rogue States and the Proliferation of WMD.* Cambridge: Cambridge University Press, 2006.

Snyder, Glenn. *Deterrence and Defense: Toward a Theory of National Security*. Princeton, NJ: Princeton University Press, 1961.
Stone, John. "Conventional Deterrence and the Challenge of Credibility." *Contemporary Security Policy* 33, no. 1 (April 2012): 108–123.
Tannenwald, Nina. *The Nuclear Taboo: The United States and the Non-Use of Nuclear Weapons Since 1945*. Cambridge: Cambridge University Press, 2007.
Waltz, Kenneth N. "Nuclear Myths and Political Realities." *American Political Science Review* 84, no. 3 (September 1990): 731–745.
Yoshihara, Toshi, and James Holmes, eds. *Strategy in the Second Nuclear Age: Power, Ambition, and the Ultimate Weapon*. Washington, DC: Georgetown University Press, 2012.

CHINA

Blasko, Dennis J. "Chinese Army Modernization: An Overview." *Military Review* 85, no. 5 (September–October 2005). https://www.questia.com/library/journal/1P3-942160941/chinese-army-modernization-an-overview.
Chang, Felix K. "China's New Missiles and U.S. Alliances in Asia-Pacific: The Impact of Weakening Extended Deterrence." *Foreign Policy Research Institute*. April 14, 2016. http://www.fpri.org/2016/04/chinas-new-missiles-u-s-alliances-asia-pacific-impact-weakening-extended-deterrence/.
Chu Shulong and Rong Yu. "China: Dynamic Minimum Deterrence." In *The Long Shadow: Nuclear Weapons and Security in 21st Century Asia*, ed. Muthiah Alagappa. Stanford, CA: Stanford University Press, 2008.
Cliff, Roger. "The Development of China's Air Force Capabilities." *RAND Corporation*. May 20, 2010. http://www.rand.org/pubs/testimonies/CT346.html.
Cunningham, Fiona S., and M. Taylor Fravel. "Assuring Assured Retaliation: China's Nuclear Posture and U.S.-China Strategic Stability." *International Security* 40, no. 2 (Fall 2015): 15–23.
Erickson, Andrew S. *Chinese Anti-Ship Ballistic Missile (ASBM) Development: Drivers, Trajectories, and Strategic Implications*. Washington, DC: Jamestown Foundation, May 2013.
Erickson, Andrew S., and Conor M. Kennedy. "China's Maritime Militia: What It Is and How to Deal with It." *Foreign Affairs*. June 23, 2016. https://www.foreignaffairs.com/articles/china/2016-06-23/chinas-maritime-militia.
Erickson, Andrew S., and Adam P. Liff. "Understanding China's Defense Budget: What It Means and Why It Matters." PacNet No. 16, *Pacific Forum CSIS*, March 9, 2011.
Fravel, M. Taylor, and Evan S. Medeiros. "China's Search for Assured Retaliation: The Evolution of Chinese Nuclear Strategy and Force Structure." *International Security* 35, no. 2 (Fall 2010): 48–87.

Goldstein, Lyle J. *Five Dragons Stirring Up the Sea: Challenge and Opportunity in China's Improving Maritime Enforcement Capabilities.* Newport, RI: Naval War College Press, 2010.

———. *Meeting China Halfway: How to Defuse the Emerging U.S.-China Rivalry.* Washington, DC: Georgetown University Press, 2015.

Information Office of the State Council. "China's Military Strategy." *China Daily.* May 26, 2015. http://www.chinadaily.com.cn/china/2015-05/26/content_20820628_4.htm.

Kazianis, Harry J. "China's Great Military Spending Slowdown: Big Deal or Big Nothing?" *National Interest.* March 7, 2016. http://nationalinterest.org/blog/the-buzz/chinas-great-military-spending-slowdown-big-deal-or-big-15431.

Kulacki, Gregory. "China's Military Calls for Putting Its Nuclear Forces on Alert." *Union of Concerned Scientists.* January 2016. http://www.ucsusa.org/sites/default/files/attach/2016/02/China-Hair-Trigger-full-report.pdf.

Kristensen, Hans M., and Robert S. Norris. "Chinese Nuclear Forces, 2015." *Bulletin of the Atomic Scientists* 71, no. 4 (July 1, 2015).

Lieber, Keir A., and Daryl G. Press. "The End of MAD? The Nuclear Dimension of U.S. Primacy." *International Security* 30, no. 3 (Spring 2006): 7–44.

Lewis, Jeffrey. "Minimum Deterrence." *Bulletin of Atomic Scientists* 64, no. 3 (July–August 2008): 38–41.

People's Republic of China. "China's National Defense in 2010." March 31, 2011. http://www.china.org.cn/government/whitepaper/node_7114675.htm.

———. "2015 Defense White Paper: China," http://www.mod.go.jp/e/publ/w_paper/pdf/2015/DOJ2015_1-1-3_web.pdf.

Perlo-Freeman, Sam, Aude Fleurant, Pieter D. Wezeman, and Siemon Wezeman. "Trends in World Military Expenditure, 2015." *Stockholm International Peace and Research Institute.* April 2016. http://books.sipri.org/files/FS/SIPRIFS1604.pdf.

Solem, Erika, and Karen Montague. "Updated—Chinese Hypersonic Weapons Development." *China Brief* 16, no. 7. *Jamestown Foundation.* April 21, 2016. https://jamestown.org/program/updated-chinese-hypersonic-weapons-development/.

U.S. Department of Defense. "Annual Report to Congress: Military and Security Developments Involving the People's Republic of China, 2015." http://www.defense.gov/Portals/1/Documents/pubs/2015_China_Military_Power_Report.pdf.

Yeaw, Christopher T., Andrew S. Erickson, and Michael S. Chase. "The Future of Chinese Nuclear Policy and Strategy." In *Strategy in the Second Nuclear Age: Power, Ambition, and the Ultimate Weapon,* ed. Toshi Yoshihara and James R. Holmes. Washington DC: Georgetown University Press, 2012.

Yoshihara, Toshi, and James R. Holmes. *Red Star Over the Pacific: China's Rise and the Challenge to U.S. Maritime Strategy.* Annapolis, MD: Naval Institute Press, 2010.

Zhang, Hui. "How U.S. Restraint Can Keep China's Nuclear Arsenal Small." *Bulletin of the Atomic Scientists* 68, no. 4 (July 1, 2012).

JAPAN

Ayako, Kusunoki. "The Satō Cabinet and the Making of Japan's Non-Nuclear Policy." *Journal of American-East Asian Relations* 15 (2008): 25–50.

Calder, Kent E. *Pacific Alliance: Reviving U.S.-Japan Relations*. New Haven, CT: Yale University Press, 2009.

Campbell, Kurt M., and Tsuyoshi Sunohara. "Japan: Thinking the Unthinkable." In *The Tipping Point: Why States Reconsider Their Nuclear Choices*, ed. Kurt M. Campbell, Robert J. Einhorn, and Mitchell B. Reiss. Washington, DC: Brookings, 2004.

Donohue, Nathan. "Understanding the Decision to Drop the Bomb on Hiroshima and Nagasaki." *Center for Strategic and International Studies*. August 10, 2012. www.apwsman.com/uploads/3/1/2/2/31225077/apush_drop_the_bomb_2016.docx.

Green, Michael J., and Katsuhisa Furukawa. "Japan: New Nuclear Realism." In *The Long Shadow: Nuclear Weapons and Security in 21st Century Asia*, ed. Muthiah Alagappa. Stanford, CA: Stanford University Press, 2008.

Harrison, Selig S. "Japan and Nuclear Weapons." In *Japan's Nuclear Future: The Plutonium Debate and East Asian Security*, ed. Selig S. Harrison. Washington DC: Carnegie Endowment, 1996.

Hayes, Peter. *Pacific Powderkeg: American Nuclear Dilemmas in Korea*. Lexington, MA: Lexington, 1991.

Hoey, Fintan. "Japan and Extended Nuclear Deterrence: Security and Non-proliferation." *Journal of Strategic Studies* 39, no. 4 (June 2016): 484–501.

Hymans, Jacques E. C. "Veto Players, Nuclear Energy, and Nonproliferation: Domestic Institutional Barriers to a Japanese Nuclear Bomb." *International Security* 36, no. 2 (Fall 2011): 154–189.

Jimbo, Ken. "Extended Deterrence in the Japan-U.S. Alliance." *NAPSNet Special Reports*, May 8, 2012. http://nautilus.org/napsnet/napsnet-special-reports/extended-deterrence-in-the-japan-u-s-alliance/.

Komine, Yukinori. "Okinawa Confidential, 1969: Exploring the Linkage Between the Nuclear Issue and the Base Issue." *Diplomatic History* 37, no. 4 (September 2013): 807–840.

Kristensen, Hans M. "Japan Under the Nuclear Umbrella: U.S. Nuclear Umbrella: U.S. Nuclear Weapons and Nuclear War Planning in Japan During the Cold War." *Nautilus Institute*. July 1999. http://oldsite.nautilus.org/archives/nukepolicy/Nuclear-Umbrella/index.html.

Lindsley, Cameron. "Hiroshima, Nagasaki, and the World Sixty Years Later." *Virginia Quarterly Review* 81, no. 4 (Fall 2005): 26–47.

Michishita, Narushige. "Japan's Response to Nuclear North Korea." In *Joint U.S.-Korea Academic Studies: Asia at a Tipping Point: Korea, the Rise of China, and the Impact of Leadership Transitions*, vol. 23, ed. Gilbert Rozman. Washington, DC: Korea Economic Institute, 2012.

Norris, Robert S., William M. Arkin, and William Burr. "Where They Were." *Bulletin of the Atomic Scientists* 55, no. 6 (November–December 1999): 26–35.

———. "Where They Were: How Much Did Japan Know?" *Bulletin of the Atomic Scientists* 56, no. 1 (January–February 2000). https://www.archives.gov/files/declassification/pidb/meetings/norris-arkin-burr.pdf.

Ogawa, Shinichi. "The 2010 U.S. Nuclear Posture Review and Its Implications for Japan." *Asia Pacific Bulletin*, no. 56 (April 16, 2010).

Pinkston, Daniel A., and Kazutaka Sakurai. "Japan Debates Preparing for Future Preemptive Strikes Against North Korea." *Korean Journal of Defense Analysis* 18, no. 4 (Winter 2006): 95–121.

Pyle, Kenneth B. *Japan Rising: The Resurgence of Japanese Power and Purpose*. New York: Public Affairs, 2007.

Rapp-Hooper, Mira. "Do Chemical Weapons Threaten U.S. Extended Deterrence in Asia?" *The Diplomat*. September 13, 2013. http://thediplomat.com/2013/09/do-chemical-weapons-threaten-us-extended-deterrence-in-asia/.

Samuels, Richard J., and James L. Schoff. "Japan's Nuclear Hedge: Beyond 'Allergy' and Breakout." In *Strategic Asia 2013–14: Asia in the Second Nuclear Age*, ed. Ashley J. Tellis, Abraham M. Denmark, and Travis Tanner, 233–264. Seattle: National Bureau of Asian Research, 2013.

Satoh, Yukio. "Japan's Responsibility Sharing for the U.S. Extended Deterrence." *Discuss Japan: Japan Foreign Policy Forum*, no. 19, March 10, 2014. http://www.japanpolicyforum.jp/archives/diplomacy/pt20140310010210.html.

Schoff, James. "Changing Perceptions of Deterrence in Japan." In *Strategy in the Second Nuclear Age: Power, Ambition, and the Ultimate Weapon*, ed. James Holmes and Toshi Yoshihara. Washington DC: Georgetown University Press, 2012.

———. "Changing Perceptions of Extended Deterrence in Japan." *Carnegie Endowment for International Peace*. November 20, 2012. http://carnegieendowment.org/2012/11/20/changing-perceptions-of-extended-deterrence-in-japan-pub-50076.

———. *Realigning Priorities: The U.S.-Japan Alliance and the Future of Extended Deterrence*. Cambridge, MA: Institute for Foreign Policy Analysis, March 2009. http://www.ifpa.org/pdf/RealignPriorities.pdf.

Smith, Sheila. "Japan's 'Dynamic Defense Policy' and China." *Council on Foreign Relations*. December 17, 2010. http://www.cfr.org/japan/japans-dynamic-defense-policy china/p23663.

Takahashi, Sugio. "Dealing with the Ballistic Missile Threat: Whether Japan Should Have a Strike Capability Under Its Exclusively Defense-Oriented Policy." *NIDS Security Reports*, no. 7, December 2006.

Takubo, Masa. "Role of Nuclear Weapons: Japan, the U. S. and 'Sole Purpose.'" *Arms Control Association*. November 5, 2009. https://www.armscontrol.org/act/2009_11/Takubo.

Yoshihara, Toshi, and James R. Holmes. "Thinking About the Unthinkable: Tokyo's Nuclear Option." *Naval War College Review* 62, no. 3 (Summer 2009): 59–78.

NORTH KOREA

Albright, David. "Future Directions in the DPRK's Nuclear Weapons Program: Three Scenarios for 2020." U.S.-Korea Institute at SAIS, 2015. http://38north.org/wp-content/uploads/2015/02/NKNF-Future-Directions-2020-Albright-0215.pdf.

Albright, David, and Serena Kelleher-Vergantini. "Plutonium, Tritium, and Highly Enriched Uranium Production at the Yongbyon Nuclear Site." *Institute for Science and International Security*. June 14, 2016. http://isis-online.org/uploads/isis-reports/documents/Pu_HEU_and_tritium_production_at_Yongbyon_June_14_2016_FINAL.pdf.

Bermudez, Joseph S., Jr. *A History of Ballistic Missile Development*. Occasional Paper No. 2. Monterey, CA: Monterey Institute of International Studies, 1999.

———. "North Korea Drones On: Redeux." *38 North*. January 19, 2016. http://38north.org/2016/01/jbermudez011916/.

———. "North Korea's Ballistic Missile Submarine Program: Full Steam Ahead," *38 North*. January 5, 2016. http://38north.org/2016/01/sinpo010516/.

———. "North Korea's Chemical Warfare Capabilities." *38 North*. October 10, 2013. http://38north.org/2013/10/jbermudez101013/.

Chinoy, Mike. *Meltdown: The Inside Story of the North Korean Nuclear Crisis*. New York: St. Martin's, 2010.

Clapper, James R. "Worldwide Threat Assessment of the U.S. Intelligence Community." February 9, 2016. http://www.dni.gov/files/documents/SASC_Unclassified_2016_ATA_SFR_FINAL.pdf.

Ham, Hyeongpil, and Jaehak Lee. "North Korea's Nuclear Decision-Making and Plausible Scenarios." *Korean Journal of Defense Analyses* 25, no. 3 (September 2013): 399–413.

Hayes, Peter, and Roger Cavazos. "North Korea's Nuclear Force Roadmap: Hard Choices." *NAPSNet Special Reports*, March 2, 2015. http://nautilus.org/napsnet/napsnet-special-reports/north-koreas-nuclear-force-roadmap-hard-choices/.

Hecker, Siegfried S. "A Return Trip to North Korea's Yongbyon Nuclear Complex." *NAPSNet Special Reports*, November 20, 2010. http://nautilus.org/napsnet

/napsnet-special-reports/a-return-trip-to-north-koreas-yongbyon-nuclear-complex/.

———. "What to Make of North Korea's Latest Nuclear Test?" *38 North*. September 12, 2016. http://38north.org/2016/09/shecker091216/#_ftn1.

Kimball, Daryl G., and Kelsey Davenport. "A Fourth North Korean Nuclear Test: What It Means; What Must Be Done." *Arms Control Association*. January 19, 2016. https://www.armscontrol.org/blog/ArmsControlNow/2016-01-06/A-Fourth-North-Korean-Nuclear-Test-What-It-Means-What-Must-Be-Done.

Mansourev, Alexandre Y. "Kim Jong-un's Nuclear Doctrine and Strategy: What Everyone Needs to Know." *NAPSNet Special Reports*, December 16, 2014. http://nautilus.org/napsnet/napsnet-special-reports/kim-jong-uns-nuclear-doctrine-and-strategy-what-everyone-needs-to-know/.

Mazarr, Michael J. *North Korea and the Bomb*. New York: St. Martin's, 1995.

Narang, Vipin. "Nuclear Strategies of Emerging Powers: North Korea and Iran." *Washington Quarterly* 38, no. 1 (Spring 2015): 73–91.

Nikitin, Mary Beth. "North Korea's Nuclear Weapons: Technical Issues." *CRS Report for Congress*, RL 34256, January 20, 2011. http://www.fas.org/sgp/crs/nuke/RL34256.pdf.

Office of the Secretary of Defense, "Military and Security Developments Involving the Democratic People's Republic of Korea 2015." http://www.defense.gov/Portals/1/Documents/pubs/Military_and_Security_Developments_Involving_the_Democratic_Peoples_Republic_of_Korea_2015.PDF.

O' Hanlon, Michael. "Stopping a North Korean Invasion." *International Security* 22, no. 4 (Spring 1998): 135–170

Park, Han S. "Military-First Politics (Songun): Understanding Kim Jong-il's North Korea." In *Academic Paper Series, On Korea*, vol. 1 (Seoul: Korea Economic Institute, 2007).

Roehrig, Terence. "North Korea, Nuclear Weapons, and the Stability-Instability Paradox." *Korean Journal of Defense Analyses* 28, no. 2 (Summer 2016): 181–198.

———. "North Korea's Nuclear Weapons Program: Motivations, Strategy, and Doctrine." In *Strategy in the Second Nuclear Age: Power, Ambition, and the Ultimate Weapon*, ed. Toshi Yoshihara and James Holmes. Washington, DC: Georgetown University Press, 2012.

Schilling, John. "A New Submarine-Launched Ballistic Missile for North Korea," *38 North*. April 25, 2016. http://38north.org/2016/04/jschilling042516/.

———. "A Solid but Incremental Improvement in North Korea's Missiles." *38 North*. March 29, 2016. http://38north.org/2016/03/jschilling032916/.

Smith, Shane. "North Korea's Evolving Nuclear Strategy." *U.S.-Korea Institute at SAIS*. August 2015. http://38north.org/wp-content/uploads/2015/09/NKNF_Evolving-Nuclear-Strategy_Smith.pdf.

Struckman, Dana, and Terence Roehrig. "Not So Fast: Pyongyang's Nuclear Weapons Ambitions." *Georgetown Journal of International Affairs*, February 20, 2013. http://journal.georgetown.edu/not-so-fast-pyongyangs-nuclear-weapons-ambitions-by-dana-struckman-and-terence-roehrig/.

Thielmann, Greg. "Sorting Out the Nuclear and Missile Threats from North Korea." *Arms Control Association*. May 21, 2013. http://www.armscontrol.org/files/TAB_Sorting_Out_North_Korea_2013.pdf.

Wit, Joel S., and Sun Young Ahn. "North Korea's Nuclear Futures: Technology and Strategy." *U.S.-Korea Institute at SAIS*. February 2015. http://38north.org/wp-content/uploads/2015/09/NKNF_NK-Nuclear-Futures.pdf.

Wit, Joel S., Daniel B. Poneman, and Robert L. Gallucci. *Going Critical: The First North Korean Nuclear Crisis*. Washington, DC: Brookings, 2004.

Wright, David. "Analysis of North Korea's Musudan Missile Test—Part 1." *Union of Concerned Scientists*. June 24, 2016. http://allthingsnuclear.org/dwright/analysis-of-north-koreas-musudan-missile-test-part-1.

Zhang Hui. "Revisiting North Korea's Nuclear Test." *China Security* 3, no. 3 (Summer 2007): 119–130.

SOUTH KOREA

Adams, Sherman. *First-Hand Report: The Inside Story of the Eisenhower Administration*. London: Hutchinson, 1962.

Cheon, Seongwhun. "Changing Dynamics of U.S. Extended Deterrence on the Korean Peninsula." *Pacific Focus* 26, no. 1 (April 2011): 37–64.

Choi, Kang, and Joon-sung Park. "South Korea: Fears of Abandonment and Entrapment." In *The Long Shadow: Nuclear Weapons and Security in 21st Century Asia*, ed. Muthiah Alagappa. Stanford, CA: Stanford University Press, 2008.

Choi, Yonghwan, "North Korea's Asymmetric Strategy Toward the United States." *Korea Focus* 12, no. 5 (September–October 2004). http://www.koreafocus.or.kr/design1/layout/content_print.asp?group_id=65.

Clough, Ralph. *Deterrence and Defense in Korea: The Role of U.S. Forces*. Washington, DC: Brookings Institution, 1976.

Crowe, William J., and Alan D. Romberg. "Rethinking Pacific Security." *Foreign Affairs* 70, no. 2 (Spring 1991): 123–140.

Cumings, Bruce. "The Conflict on the Korean Peninsula." In *Asia: Militarization and Regional Conflict*, ed. Yoshikazu Sakamoto. London: Zed, 1988.

Dalton, Toby, Byun Sunggee, Lee Sang Tae. "South Korea Debates Nuclear Options." *Carnegie Endowment for International Peace*. April 27, 2016. http://carnegieendowment.org/2016/04/27/south-korea-debates-nuclear-options-pub-63455.

Dingman, Roger. "Atomic Diplomacy During the Korean War." *International Security* 13, no. 3 (Winter 1988–89): 50–91.
Fitzpatrick, Mark. "Why South Korea Should Not 'Go Nuclear.'" *Korea Herald*. February 19, 2016. http://www.koreaherald.com/view.php?ud=20160219000241.
Foot, Rosemary. "Nuclear Coercion and the Ending of the Korean Conflict," *International Security* 13, no. 3 (Winter 1988–89): 92–112.
——. *The Wrong War: American Policy and Dimensions of the Korean Conflict, 1950–1953*. Ithaca, NY: Cornell University Press, 1985.
Gaddis, John Lewis. *We Now Know: Rethinking Cold War History*. Oxford: Oxford University Press, 1997.
Hayes, Peter, and Chung-in Moon. "Should South Korea Go Nuclear?" *NAPSNet Policy Forum*, July 28, 2014. http://nautilus.org/napsnet/napsnet-policy-forum/should-south-korea-go-nuclear/.
Heo, Uk, and Terence Roehrig. *South Korea's Rise: Economic Development, Power, and Foreign Relations*. Cambridge: Cambridge University Press, 2014.
Hibbs, Mark. "Will South Korea Go Nuclear?" *Foreign Policy*, March 15, 2013. http://foreignpolicy.com/2013/03/15/will-south-korea-go-nuclear/.
Jackson, Van. *Rival Reputations: Coercion and Credibility in U.S.-North Korean Relations*. Cambridge: Cambridge University Press, 2016.
Jang, Se Young. "The Evolution of U.S. Extended Deterrence and South Korea's Nuclear Ambitions." *Journal of Strategic Studies* 39, no. 4 (June 2016): 502–520.
Keefer, Edward C. "President Dwight D. Eisenhower and the End of the Korean War." *Diplomatic History* 10, no. 3 (Summer 1986): 267–289.
Kim, Jiyoon, and Karl Friedhoff. "The Fallout: South Korean Public Opinion Following North Korea's Third Nuclear Test." *Asan Institute for Policy Studies*. February 24, 2013. http://en.asaninst.org/contents/issue-brief-no-46-the-fallout-south-korean-public-opinion-following-north-koreas-third-nuclear-test/.
Kim, Jiyoon, John J. Lee, and Kang Chungku. "Measuring A Giant: South Korean Perceptions of the United States." *Asan Institute for Policy Studies*. April 20, 2015. http://en.asaninst.org/contents/measuring-a-giant-south-korean-perceptions-of-the-united-states/.
Koch, Susan J. *The Presidential Nuclear Initiatives of 1991–1992*. Washington, DC: National Defense University Press, September 2012. http://ndupress.ndu.edu/Portals/68/Documents/casestudies/CSWMD_CaseStudy-5.pdf.
Kristensen, Hans M. "A History of U.S. Nuclear Weapons in South Korea." *Nuclear Information Project*. September 28, 2005. http://www.nukestrat.com/korea/koreahistory.htm.
Kwak, Tae-hwan. "The Reduction of U.S. Forces in Korea in the Inter-Korean Peace Process," *The Korean Journal of Defense Analysis* 2, no. 2 (Winter 1990): 171–194.

LaFeber, Walter. *The American Age: U.S. Foreign Policy at Home and Abroad*. New York: Norton, 1994.

Lankow, Andrei. "Why the United States Will Have to Accept a Nuclear North Korea." *Korean Journal of Defense Analysis* 21, no. 3 (September 2009): 251–264.

Lefever, Ernest W. *Nuclear Arms in the Third World*. Washington, DC: Brookings, 1979.

Norris, Robert S., William M. Arkin, and William Burr. "Where They Were." *Bulletin of the Atomic Scientists* 55, no. 6 (November–December 1999): 26–35.

Oberdorfer, Don. *The Two Koreas*. New York: Basic Books, 1997.

Park, Chang Kwoun. "ROK-U.S. Cooperation in Preparation for Hostile Actions by North Korea in Possession of Nuclear Weapons." *Korean Journal of Defense Analysis* 22, no. 4 (December 2010): 499–513.

Park, Hwee-rhak, and Kim Byung-ki. "Time to Balance Deterrence, Offense, and Defense? Rethinking South Korea's Strategy Against the North Korean Threat." *Korean Journal of Defense Analysis* 24, no. 4 (December 2012): 515–532.

Pinkston, Daniel. "The New South Korean Missile Guidelines and Future Prospects for Regional Stability." *International Crisis Group*. October 25, 2012. http://blog.crisisgroup.org/asia/2012/10/25/the-new-south-korean-missile-guidelines-and-future-prospects-for-regional-stability/.

ROK Ministry of National Defense, *2014 Defense White Paper*.

Roehrig, Terence. "The Case for a Nuclear-Free South," *JoongAng Daily*, June 19, 2014. http://koreajoongangdaily.joins.com/news/article/article.aspx?aid=2990820.

——. *From Deterrence to Engagement: The U.S. Defense Commitment to South Korea*. Lanham, MD: Lexington Books, 2006.

——. "Reinforcing Deterrence: The U.S. Military Response to North Korean Provocations," 221–238. *Joint U.S.-Korea Academic Studies: Facing Reality in East Asia: Tough Decisions on Competition and Cooperation*, vol. 26, ed. Gilbert Rozman. Washington, DC: Korea Economic Institute of America, 2015.

Roy, Denny. "North Korea and the 'Madman' Theory." *Security Dialogue* 25, no. 3 (September 1994): 307–316.

Spector, Leonard S. *Nuclear Ambitions*. Boulder, CO: Westview, 1990.

Snyder, Scott. "Finding a Balance Between Assurances and Abolition: South Korean Views of the Nuclear Posture Review." *Nonproliferation Review* 18, no. 1 (March 2011): 147–163.

Stueck, William. *The Korean War: An International History*. Princeton, NJ: Princeton University Press, 1995.

UNITED STATES AND THE NUCLEAR UMBRELLA

Brown, Harold. *Department of Defense: Annual Report, Fiscal Year 1979*. Washington, DC: GPO, 1979.

Bunn, M. Elaine. "Can Deterrence Be Tailored?" *Strategic Forum*, no. 225. National Defense University, January 2007.

Bush, George H. W., and Brent Scowcroft. *A World Transformed*. New York: Knopf, 1998.

Chermin, Michael, and Sabin Ray. "On the Frontline of U.S. Nuclear Policy with Under Secretary Rose Gottemoeller." *Brown Journal of World Affairs* 21, no. 1 (Fall–Winter 2014): 253–260.

Council on Foreign Relations. "A Conversation with General C. Robert Kehler." *Council on Foreign Relations*. May 30, 2012. http://www.cfr.org/united-states/conversation-general-c-robert-kehler/p35267.

Dulles, John Foster. "The Evolution of Foreign Policy." *Department of State Bulletin* 30, no. 761 (January 25, 1954): 107–110.

——. "The Strategy of Massive Retaliation." *Department of State Bulletin*, January 12, 1954.

Gates, Robert M. *Duty: Memoirs of a Secretary at War*. New York: Knopf, 2014.

Gompert, David C., Astrid Stuth Cevallos, and Cristina L. Garafola. "War with China: Thinking Through the Unthinkable." *RAND Corporation*. 2016. http://www.rand.org/pubs/research_reports/RR1140.html.

Jackson, Van. "Raindrops Keep Falling on My Nuclear Umbrella." *Foreign Policy*, May 18, 2015. http://foreignpolicy.com/2015/05/18/raindrops-keep-falling-on-my-nuclear-umbrella-us-japan-south-north-korea/.

——. "The U.S. Doesn't Need Tactical Nuclear Weapons in Asia." *The Diplomat*, July 2, 2015. http://thediplomat.com/2015/07/the-us-doesnt-need-tactical-nuclear-weapons-in-asia/.

Kahn, Herman. *On Thermonuclear War*. New Brunswick, NJ: Transaction, 2007.

Kaplan, Fred. *The Wizards of Armageddon*. New York: Simon & Schuster, 1983.

Kaufman, Alison A., and Daniel M. Hartnett. "Managing Conflict: Examining Recent PLA Writings on Escalation Control." *CNA*. February 2016. https://www.cna.org/cna_files/pdf/DRM-2015-U-009963-Final3.pdf.

Kissinger, Henry. *The Necessity of Choice*. New York: Doubleday, 1962.

Kristensen, Hans M. "Non-Strategic Nuclear Weapons," Special Report No. 3. *Federation of American Scientists*. May 2012. https://fas.org/blogs/security/2012/05/nonstrategicnukes/.

——. "U.S. Navy Instruction Confirms Retirement of Nuclear Tomahawk Cruise Missile." *Federation of American Scientists*. March 18, 2013. http://fas.org/blogs/security/2013/03/tomahawk/.

——. "W80-1 Warhead Selected for New Nuclear Cruise Missile." *Federation of American Scientists*. October 10, 2014. https://fas.org/blogs/security/2014/10/w80-1_lrso/.

McDermott, Rose. "Emotions in Foreign Policy Decision Making." In *Oxford Research Encyclopedia: Politics*, ed. William R. Thompson. Oxford: Oxford University Press, 2016.

McNamara, Robert S. "The Military Role of Nuclear Weapons: Perceptions and Misperceptions." *Foreign Affairs* 62, no. 1 (Fall 1983): 59–80.

Morgan, Patrick M. "Considerations Bearing on a Possible Retraction of the American Nuclear Umbrella Over the ROK." National Committee on North Korea, 2009. http://www.ncnk.org/resources/publications/Morgan%20Considerations%20Bearing_on_a_Possible_Retraction_of_the_American_Nuclear_Umbrella.pdf.

Nichols, Thomas M. *No Use: Nuclear Weapons and U.S. National Security.* Philadelphia: University of Pennsylvania Press, 2013.

Nichols, Tom, Douglas Stuart, and Jeffrey D. McCausland, eds. *Tactical Nuclear Weapons and NATO.* Carlisle, PA: Strategic Studies Institute, U.S. Army War College, April 2012. http://www.strategicstudiesinstitute.army.mil/pdffiles/PUB1103.pdf.

Perry, William J., and James R. Schlesinger. *America's Strategic Posture: The Final Report of the Congressional Commission on the Strategic Posture of the United States.* Washington, DC: United States Institute of Peace Press, May 2009.

Powell, Colin L. *My American Journey.* New York: Random House, 1995.

Press, Daryl G., Scott D. Sagan, and Benjamin A. Valentino. "Atomic Aversion: Experimental Evidence on Taboos, Traditions, and the Non-Use of Nuclear Weapons." *American Political Science Review* 107, no 1 (February 2013): 188–206.

Public Papers of the Presidents of the United States. Washington, DC: GPO.

Renshon, Jonathan, and Jennifer S. Lerner. "Decision Making, the Role of Emotions in Foreign Policy." In *The Encyclopedia of Peace Psychology,* ed. Daniel J. Christie. Indianapolis: Blackwell, 2012.

Rovner, Joshua. "AirSea Battle and Escalation Risks." Changing Military Dynamics in East Asia Policy Brief 12, January 2012. http://escholarship.org/uc/item/08m367zt.

Rusk, Dean. *As I Saw It.* New York: Norton, 1990.

Sagan, Scott D. "Realist Perspectives on Ethical Norms and Weapons of Mass Destruction." In *Ethics and Weapons of Mass Destruction: Religious and Secular Perspectives,* ed. Sohail H. Hashmi and Steven P. Lee. Cambridge: Cambridge University Press, 2004.

Santoro, David, and John K. Warden. "Assuring Japan and South Korea in the Second Nuclear Age." *Washington Quarterly* 38, no. 1 (Spring 2015): 147–165.

Saunders, Paul J. "Extended Deterrence and Security in East Asia: A U.S.–Japan–South Korea Dialogue." Fourth Meeting of the Contemporary American Studies project. *Tokyo Foundation.* January 23, 2013. http://www.tokyofoundation.org/en/articles/2013/extended-deterrence-and-security-in-east-asia.

Thielmann, Greg. "Nuclear Cruise Missiles: Asset or Liability?" *Arms Control Association.* March 5, 2015. http://www.armscontrol.org/system/files/Threat_Assessment_Brief_Nuclear_Cruise_Missiles_Asset_or_Liability.pdf.

U.S. Department of Defense. "Air-Sea Battle: Service Collaboration to Address Anti-Access and Area Denial Challenges." May 2013. http://archive.defense.gov/pubs/ASB-ConceptImplementation-Summary-May-2013.pdf.

———. *Nuclear Posture Review 2001.* http://archive.defense.gov/news/Jan2002/d20020109npr.pdf.

———. *Nuclear Posture Review Report.* April 2010. http://www.defense.gov/Portals/1/features/defenseReviews/NPR/2010_Nuclear_Posture_Review_Report.pdf.

———. *Quadrennial Defense Review.* February 6, 2006. http://archive.defense.gov/pubs/pdfs/QDR20060203.pdf.

U.S. Department of State. *The Foreign Relations of the United States.* Washington, DC: GPO.

U.S. Office of the President. *National Security Strategy*: Ronald Reagan, 1987; George W. Bush, 2002; Barack Obama, 2015.

Woolf, Amy. "Nonstrategic Nuclear Weapons." *Congressional Research Service.* March 23, 2016. https://www.fas.org/sgp/crs/nuke/RL32572.pdf.

———. "U.S. Strategic Nuclear Forces: Background, Developments, and Issues." *Congressional Research Service.* September 27, 2016. https://www.fas.org/sgp/crs/nuke/RL33640.pdf.

Wyn Jones, Richard. *Security, Strategy, and Critical Theory.* Boulder, CO: Lynne Rienner, 1999.

Index

Abe, Shinzo, 102–03, 122
Agnew, Spiro, 126
Agreed Framework (1994), 3, 100, 114
Ahn, Sun Young, 90
Air-Sea Battle, 174
Albright, David, 88
Anti-Access/Area Denial (A2/AD), 71, 174, 191
Aso, Taro, 4
Avey, Paul, 193
Australia, 156

Bracken, Paul, 14
Bush, George H. W., 62, 109, 171
Bush, George W., 30, 110, 154

Cartwright, James, 34
Campbell, Kurt, 101, 108, 121
Carter, Jimmy, 148
Cheonan, 85, 93, 124, 142, 151, 186
China: ballistic missiles, 73–76; chemical and biological weapons, 72–73; conventional forces, 68–72; cruise missiles, 76; defense spending, 66–68; "no first use," 78–79, 195; nuclear strategy and doctrine, 77–80; nuclear weapons, 73–74, 77; SLBMs, 76–77; unmanned aerial vehicles, 70
Choi, Kang, 149
Chung, Mong-joon, 145, 149
Cimbala, Stephen, 30
Clapper, James, 87
Clinton, Hillary, 110
Congressional Strategic Posture Commission (2009), 110
Cunningham, Fiona S., 80

decoupling, 2, 112, 120, 131, 138, 145
Deng Xiaoping, 65
deterrence theory: asymmetric, 9, 17, 19–20, 27, 31, 34, 82, 94, 152, 191; by denial, 14–16; by punishment 14–16, 128, 141, 172, 185; conventional deterrence 15–17, 21, 24, 32, 34; credibility, 2–3, 8–11, 23–35, 36–37, 49, 55–56, 62, 98, 101–02, 104–09, 111, 113, 115–16, 123–24, 131–34, 140,

deterrence theory (*continued*)
    145, 148, 150–52, 156–57, 167, 169, 172, 175, 180–81, 188–89, 192–95, 197; extended 16–17, 19–20, 23, 26–28, 31–32, 35–37; general, 17–20, 26, 35, 79, 103, 106, 173, 175, 184; immediate 17–20, 26, 28, 35, 80, 94, 103, 175; primary 16–17, 31, 140; rationality 20–23; symmetric 19–20; tailored deterrence 16, 116, 158–59, 182, 183
Deterrence Strategy Committee 134
Diaoyu islands, 64, 118, 173
Dulles, John Foster, 55, 57, 58, 156

electromagnetic pulse, 139
Eisenhower, Dwight, 55, 57–58
Erickson, Andrew, 71
Extended Deterrence Dialogue (EDD), 107–109, 115, 134
Extended Deterrence Policy Committee (EDPC), 134–136

France, 53, 67, 73, 77, 148
Fravel, M. Taylor, 78, 80
Fukuda, Takeo, 47
Fukushima-Daiichi, 121, 196

Gates, Robert, 136, 154, 159
Gavin, Frances, 176
George, Alexander, 28
Gerzhoy, Gene, 176
Gilpatric Committee, 176
Goldwater-Nichols Act, 162
Gorbachev, Mikhail, 62
Gortney, William, 91
Gottemoeller, Rose, 161
gray zones, 64, 102, 187

Han, Min-koo, 128
Harris, Harry, Jr., 67

Hatoyama, Ichiro, 40, 118
Healey, Denis, 194–95
Hecker, Siegfried, 87
Hibakusha, 39
Hiroshima, 39, 51, 155
Horner, Charles, 169
Huth, Paul, 27, 28

Ikeda, Hayato, 41
India, 52, 55, 67, 73–74, 77, 81, 88, 148, 176
International Atomic Energy Agency (IAEA), 45, 62
Iran, 13, 16, 20, 37, 83, 86, 151, 158, 178
Ishibashi, Tanzan, 40
Israel, 23, 141

Jackson, Van, 29, 178, 186
JAM-GC, 174
Japan: Article 9, 39, 41, 118; ballistic missile defense, 117–118; civil defense, 102, 120; four pillars, 44, 99; exclusive defense-oriented policy, 119, 122; National Defense Program Guidelines (2013), 102, 119, (2010), 100–01, 116, (2004), 100, (1995), 100, (1976), 100; nuclear allergy, 39, 45, 47, 50, 63, 97, 120, 122; nuclear ambitions, 40–3, 45–6; three non-nuclear principles, 44; U.S.-Japan Mutual Security Treaty, 1, 19, 24, 39–41, 43–44, 49, 62, 98, 173, 187
Jervis, Robert, 193
Johnson, Alexis, 45, 48
Johnson, Lyndon B., 42–43, 59, 63, 99, 170, 176, 206n15

Kehler, Robert, 161
Kelleher-Vergantini, Serena, 88

Kennedy, Conor, 71
Kennedy, John F., 170
Kerry, John, 114
Kim Il-sung, 21, 51, 88
Kim Jong-il, 21
Kim Jong-un, 5, 21–22, 85, 90–91, 105, 128, 185, 194
Kim Kwan-jin, 136, 142
Kim Tae-young, 146
Kishi, Nobusuke, 41
Kissinger, Henry, 27, 32, 59, 126
Korean Airline 858, 186
Korean War, 18, 35, 51, 54, 56, 58, 65, 85, 151, 157

Laird, Melvin, 157
Lankov, Andrei, 22
Lee, Myung-bak, 4, 146
Lee Teng-hui, 65–66
Lieber, Kier, 33
Lucky Dragon, 40

MacArthur, Douglas, 51–53
Mao Zedong, 23, 78, 176
McNamara, Robert, 170
Medeiros, Evan, 78
Miller, Nicholas, 176
Missile Technology Control Regime (MTCR), 141–42
Miyazawa, Kiichi, 50
Moon, Chung-in, 150
Morgan, Patrick, 17, 31, 140, 193
Murdoch, Clark, 33

Nagasaki, 39, 51
Nakasone, Yasuhiro, 45
Narang, Vipin, 94
Narushige, Michishita, 121
New START, 7–8, 33, 80, 163, 233n25
Nichols, Thomas, 172

Nixon, Richard: 48–50, 55, 59, 125; Nixon doctrine, 50, 125, 148, 177
"no first use," 7, 25, 78–79, 94, 114–15, 160, 194–95
North Atlantic Treaty Organization: 2, 24, 27, 165; Nuclear Planning Group, 107, 134
North Korea: ballistic missiles, 86–92; conventional forces, 81–85, chem/bio weapons, 85–86; defense spending, 81; "no first use," 94, 195; nuclear weapons, 86–92; SLBMs, 90–91; strategy and doctrine, 92–95; unmanned aerial vehicles, 83–4
Nuclear Nonproliferation Treaty (NPT), 7, 45–47, 49, 51, 114, 122, 148, 150–51, 160, 176–78
Nuclear Posture Review (2010): 7, 33, 110, 130–31, 159–60, 183, 196; negative security assurance, 7, 114–15, 160, 194; "sole purpose," 7, 33, 114–15, 160, 183
Nuclear Security Summit (2012), 151, (2014), 149
nuclear taboo, 30, 32, 34, 108, 170, 172, 175
Nunn, Sam, 32

Obama, Barack, 4, 6–8, 33, 68, 80, 103, 106, 111, 113–14, 131, 136, 146–47, 154–55, 159–60, 177, 187, 194
Okada, Katsuya, 110–11, 115
Okinawa, 1, 25, 39–40, 43, 46–50, 89, 98, 154

Park, Chang Kwoun, 128
Park, Chung-hee, 126
Park, Geun-hye, 5, 65
Paul, T. V., 30–31, 54–55, 170–172, 194
People's Liberation Army, 4, 65, 68–79

Perry, William J., 32
Pinkston, Daniel, 120
Press, Daryl, 28, 33, 170
Pueblo, 59, 186
Putin, Vladimir, 5–6, 64, 112, 154

Quester, George, 168, 171

Reagan, Ronald, 160, 177
Reischauer, Edwin, 41,
Rice, Condoleezza, 4, 19, 103
Roy, Denny, 22
Rumsfeld, Donald, 19, 127
Rusk, Dean, 42, 54
Russett, Bruce, 24, 27–28
Russia/Soviet Union, 2, 3, 5–7, 54, 64, 66, 67, 69, 73–4, 78, 84–5, 90, 100, 105, 112, 113–14, 146–47, 151, 155, 163–64, 169–70, 175, 188, 194
Sagan, Scott, 171
Sakurai, Kazutaka, 120
Samore, Gary, ix, 146
Samuels, Richard, 116, 122
Satō, Eisaku, 41–7, 49–50, 63, 99, 176, 206n15
Saudi Arabia, 67, 151, 178, 180
Scaparrotti, Curtis, 44
Schelling, Thomas, 24, 26, 31, 156, 183
Schlesinger, James, 59, 125, 148
Schoff, James, 122
Scowcroft, Brent, 171
Senkaku islands, 64, 67, 101, 105, 107, 113
Shultz, George, 32
Six Party Talks, 3, 151
Smoke, Richard, 28
"sole purpose" declaration, 7, 33, 114–15, 160, 183
South China Sea, 23, 113, 173–74, 187

South Korea: ballistic missiles, 141–42; cruise missiles, 142–43; "kill chain," 141; Korea Air and Missile Defense (KAMD), 143–44; nuclear ambitions, 59, 126, 148–52; unmanned aerial vehicles, 141–42,
U.S.-Japan Mutual Security Treaty, 1, 19, 24, 56, 62, 127
stability-instability paradox, 3, 93, 186
Strategic Offensive Reductions Treaty, 154

Taiwan, 23, 65–66, 70–71, 76, 79
Tannenwald, Nina, 30, 31, 55, 170, 194
TLAM/N, 109–11, 165, 172, 191
Trans-Pacific Partnership, 136–37
Truman, Harry, 51–55
Trump, Donald, 8, 9, 80, 112, 137, 148, 155, 177, 196, 197

United Nations Command (UNC), 51, 57
United States: QDR (2006), 158, 159, 183, national command authority, 162, 196–98; New Triad, 16, 159, 183; "no first use," 7, 25, 114–115, 160, 194; non-proliferation goals, 176–79, 196–98; rebalance to Asia, 103, 123, 136; strategic nuclear weapons, 163–64; tactical nuclear weapons, 2–3, 30–31, 38, 53–55, 58–63, 69–70, 79, 94, 110, 125–27, 131, 135, 141, 145–47, 154–56, 158, 163–65, 169, 186, 190; THAAD, 144–45
U.S. Forces Korea (USFK), 21, 126, 144, 162, 166
U.S.-Japan Alliance: Security Consultative Committee, 103, 115; Guidelines for Defense Cooperation, 102, 107, 115, 119

U.S. National Security Strategy (1987), 177; (2002), 13, 158; (2015), 177

U.S.-ROK alliance: 123 Nuclear Cooperation Agreement, 150; Combined counter-Provocation Plan, 93, 135, 152, 186; OPLAN 5015, 135; Security Consultative Meeting (SCM), 62, 126–27, 132, 134–5, 159; Tailored Deterrence Strategy, 135, 152, 162

Valentino, Benjamin, 171

Waltz, Kenneth, 16, 21
Wit, Joel, 90

Xi Jinping, 5, 23, 65, 68, 144

Yeonpyeong island, 93, 124, 135–36, 138–9, 142, 151, 186

GPSR Authorized Representative: Easy Access System Europe, Mustamäe tee 50, 10621 Tallinn, Estonia, gpsr.requests@easproject.com

www.ingramcontent.com/pod-product-compliance
Lightning Source LLC
Chambersburg PA
CBHW021939290426
44108CB00012B/897